12.95

P9-CAN-701

THE NEW
DOBERMAN PINSCHER

A majestic array of Canadian Dobermans. Left to right: Ch. Pyrmont Cyrus von Alarich CD, Ch. Pyrmont Rank's Anna v Palos CDX, Indian Ch. Pyrmont Cyrus Favorite Farina, Pyrmont Flaming Favila v Cyrus, Pyrmont Embla v Cyrus CD, and Dutch imp. Ch. Graaf Marnix von Neerlandstam CDX (at 9 months).

The NEW
DOBERMAN
PINSCHER

by JOANNA WALKER

*with special chapters by
other noted authorities*

Sixth Printing—1980

Howell Book House Inc.
230 Park Avenue
New York, N.Y. 10169

Copyright © 1977 by Howell Book House Inc.
All rights reserved.

Library of Congress Catalog Card No. 76-51090
ISBN 0-87605-111-5

Three chapters in this book — Origin of the Breed,
Illena and the Seven Sires, and A Pictorial Study
of Doberman Gait — are reprinted from *The Complete
Doberman Pinscher,* copyright © 1969, 1953 by
Howell Book House Inc.

No part of this book may be used or reproduced in any manner
whatsoever without written permission from the publisher,
except in the case of brief excerpts quoted in reviews.

Printed in U.S.A.

Ch. Marks-Tey Shawn CD, 1967–1975.

To Shawn
The only sorrow he ever brought me
was the day he left me.

Ch. Galaxy's Corry Missile Belle, America's top winning dog of all breeds for 1973, a Quaker Oats Award winner for that year, and Best Working at Westminster in 1974. Owned by Elaine M. Herndon and Mr. and Mrs. N. J. Reese, and handled by Corky Vroom. (Here winning at Del Monte under Mrs. Irene K. Schlintz.) Missile Belle, a lovely black, is by Ch. Tarrado's Corry ex Ch. Leemac's Coco Puff Morgansonne, and was bred by Claire McCage and Barbara Flores. She started her show career with a bang, going Winners Bitch at the Doberman Pinscher Club of America Specialty under Peggy Adamson, owner-handled. Her tremendous record includes 30 all-breed Bests in Show, 6 Specialties, 69 Group Firsts and 113 Bests of Breed. She has proved that she can produce as well as win, and won the Brood Bitch class at the 1975 National and was the dam of the Futurity winner. This puppy, Herndon's Born Free Uganda is now a champion, and several littermates are very near to title.

In its Christmas 1976 issue, the all-breed magazine *Kennel Review* listed the top winning American showdogs for the period from 1956 through 1976, as based on the Phillips and Kennel Review rating systems, both of which award dogs points in accordance with the number of dogs they have won over at each show. Ch. Galaxy's Corry Missile Belle's total of 56,309 points in 1973 was considerably higher than that scored by any other Working dog through the twenty years.

It is interesting to observe that of the Top Twenty Working Dogs for the period, six (more than any other breed) were Dobermans. Along with Missile Belle, they included (with their place on the all-time list shown in parentheses): (4) Ch. Dolph von Tannenwald, 1971-36,250 pts.; (8) Ch. Galaxy's Corry Carina, 1974-34,291; (10) Ch. Weichardt's A-Go-Go, 1971-32,663; (12) Ch. Sultana v Marienburg, 1967-31,856; and (19) Ch. Rancho Dobe's Maestro, 1970-25,891. All are pictured in this book.

Contents

The Authors   10

Foreword—*by Herman L. Fellton*   13
        President, Doberman Pinscher Club of America

Acknowledgments   15

1. The Doberman Pinscher—*by Frank Grover*   17

      The Character of a Doberman, 18

      The Utility of the Doberman, 21

      The Beauty of the Doberman, 22

2. Origin of the Breed   27

3. The Early Doberman in America   33

4. Illena and the Seven Sires—*by Peggy Adamson*   39

5. The Modern Doberman in America   51

6. Current Doberman Kennels   111
   of the United States

7. Official AKC Standard   127
   for the Doberman Pinscher

8. An In-Depth Look at the Standard   131
   —*by Ruth McCourt*

      The Head, 134

      Body, 136

      What the Judges Look For, 140

      Ring Procedures in Judging the Doberman, 142

9. Characteristic Movement in Dobermans   146
   —*by Frank Grover*

10. A Pictorial Study of Doberman Gait   150
    —*by Curtice W. Sloan*

    Doberman Trotting, 150

    Doberman Galloping, 161

11. Doberman Color—*by Anita and Robert W. Silman*   171

    Coat Color and the Standard, 171

    Coat Color Inheritance, 174

12. Doberman Temperament—*by Vic Monteleon*   179

    Doberman Temperament—The Past, 181

    Doberman Temperament—The Present, 182

    Temperament Testing and Observation, 185

    The Group Puppy Tests (at 5 weeks), 188

    Individual Puppy Tests (7-8 weeks), 188

    Maturity Tests, 193

13. The Obedience Doberman—*by Bernie Brown*   195

    Highest Scoring Dogs in
    DPCA Trials (1937–1975), 206

14. The Doberman in Canada—*by Pat Blenkey*   209

15. The Doberman in Europe—*by Ingrid Hallberg*   225

    Germany, 225

    Holland, 232

    Belgium, 237

    Switzerland, 237

    Italy, 238

    France, 238

    Training the Guard Dog in France, 243

    The Show Doberman in France, 245

16. The Doberman in England—*by Mike Bradshaw*   255

    American Imports, 259

    Stud Book Entries of First Generation Produced
    from Dobermans Imported from America, 262

    Kennel Club Registrations for Dobermans
    (1951–1974), 264

17. The Doberman in Scandinavia   267

       Norway—*by Maida Jonnson,* 267

       Sweden—*by Lilith Edstrom,* 276

       Finland—*by Keijo Alen,* 286

18. The Doberman in Australia—*by H. Peter Luyten*   290

19. The Doberman in Southeast Asia—*by Roberto A. DeSantos*   305

       Malaysia and Singapore—*by Jackie Perry,* 307

20. Buying and Owning a Doberman   313

       The Joy of Owning a Doberman, 318

21. Selection of a Stud   323

22. Grooming Your Doberman   329

       Grooming for Show, 332

23. Coat and Skin Problems—*by Anita and Robert W. Silman*   335

24. Tail Docking and Ear Taping   339

25. The Doberman Pinscher Club of America   347

Ch. Weichardt's A-Go-Go with two of her puppies.

JOANNA WALKER was born and raised in Purley, Surrey, England. She has always had a keen interest in all animals, dogs and horses in particular, and during World War II was active in an organization that rescued lost and bombed out dogs and cats. Joanna came to America in 1947 to be married to Keith Walker, and he gave her a Doberman puppy as a wedding gift. They named the dog Jet of Marks-Tey, for Marks-Tey had been the prefix under which Joanna had raised and shown rabbits in earlier years.

The Walkers got their first show bitch in 1955, purchasing Ch. Damsyn the Waltzing Brook CD from Peggy Adamson as a nine-weeks-old puppy, and finishing her to championship themselves. Keith subsequently became an all-breeds handler, and has finished many of the over 40 champions that carry the Marks-Tey prefix.

Marks-Tey, located at Centralia, Illinois, is a small hobby kennel, and the Walkers keep no more than six Dobermans at a time, as they are all house dogs. Joanna has twice won leading breeder awards from the Doberman Pinscher Club of America, and is active in Obedience and in the Egyptian Kennel Club. She is on the Educational Committee for the DPCA, and writes a monthly column on dogs for the local newspaper. She still owns a horse, and rides a great deal.

The Walkers have one daughter, Sheila, now married and the mother of two, and her family also owns Dobermans.

FRANK GROVER and his wife Kathleen have owned Dobermans since 1942. Their first show dog was Ch. Abbenoir UDT, the first of her breed to win all the titles. Mr. and Mrs. Grover began activity with dogs in the Chicago area where they bred under the name of Barrierdobes. Frank was president of the Doberman Pinscher Club of Chicago for four years, and during this time the club's specialty shows were the largest in the country, exceeding even the National Specialties in entry. In 1959, the Grovers moved to Carmel Valley, California, where they became active in the Cabrillo Doberman Club. Frank also served as president of the Del Monte Kennel Club, and was for two years president of the Doberman Pinscher Club of America. An active judge, licensed to do most of the Working Group and Obedience, he was one of the judges of the 1976 DPCA Specialty. He and his wife now live in Texas, where he is president of a company that makes educational motion pictures.

PEGGY ADAMSON is one of the most respected names in dogs A past president of the Doberman Pinscher Club of America, she owns the Damasyn Kennels and is a Working Group judge. She has judged at the National Specialty six times, and has also judged in England, Australia, New Zealand, Brazil, Mexico, Trinidad and Canada. In the past, Mrs. Adamson used to handle her own dogs, but has given this up.

RUTH McCOURT purchased her first Doberman back in 1938. Her first champion was Ch. Brenda v Trail, out of Dictator. At first, she and husband Ben used the kennel name of Rancho Chino, but this was later changed to El Dorado. During the 1940-50s, the McCourts were not only active in showing Dobermans but also Arabian horses, Berkshire pigs and even turkeys, as well as raising a family. Mrs. McCourt has been an active member of the Orange Empire Dog Club since 1945, and is a past president. She has also been president of the California-Sierra Doberman Pinscher Club, and has been active with the DPCA (including several terms as Vice-President) since 1959. She is licensed to judge most of the Working Group.

ROBERT and ANITA SILMAN make their home near Peoria, Illinois, with their four children, several cats and their Dobermans. Their foundation bitch was Dobereich's Duress, and they use the kennel name of Housecarl. Robert, who is a chemist with the USDA, is from New York, while Anita hails from Texas. It was after their well-known "H" litter produced the blue Heather that Anita became very interested in the dilution colors and started to study them in earnest.

VIC MONTELEON is Chairman of the Temperament Testing Program for the Doberman Pinscher Club of America. Mr. Monteleon and his wife use the kennel name of Montwood, and are not only actively showing in conformation, but are also active in all types of training — Obedience, protction and tracking. He has been an Obedience instructor in the San Diego area.

BERNIE BROWN is a writer by profession. He and his wife Elaine are very active in Obedience, not only with Dobermans but with other breeds as well. Bernie has a top scoring Golden Retriever and Elaine has a Sheltie who is a constant High Dog in Trial winner, and they share place in the Browns' hearts with a champion U.D. Doberman.

PAT BLENKEY and her husband, John, moved from England to Canada in 1963. They purchased their first Doberman from Tavey Kennels, and so admired the lovely bitch Ch. Tavey's Stormy Wrath, owned by Julia Curnow, they named their kennel Wrath in her honor. Pat and John are members of the Doberman Pinscher Club of Canada, and are particularly active in Obedience work, she as a trainer, and he as a judge.

INGRID HALLBERG was born in Chicago, daughter of a Swedish father and Austrian mother. Following musical training in Chicago and New York, she pursued an operatic and concert career in Rome, Milan, Venice, Paris, Munich and German theatres. Ingrid was given her first Doberman by her husband in 1968, and has been active in the breed ever since, both in Europe and the United States. She has written for several magazines and is particularly interested in seeing the Doberman retain its true working abilities.

MIKE BRADSHAW is a school teacher, and with his wife Meg and daughter Jinny resides in Sutton Colfield near Birmingham, England. A Doberman judge, he and his wife have a small kennel (Zeitgeist) principally based on American bloodlines.

MAIDA JONSSON was born in France and came to America at an early age. Her background included periods as a ballet dancer, riding instructor, costume designer and secretary. In 1965, she and her then husband moved to Norway, and she has been there since. She is active in the Norwegian Doberman Club, and writes for several publications.

LILITH EDSTROM was born just north of Stockholm, Sweden. A life long lover of all animals, she acquired her first Doberman at age of twenty. In 1968, she and her husband went to Germany and purchased Bryan von Forell. Lilith is also very interested in photography.

KEIJO ALEN is a marketing manager in Helsinki, Finland. A Doberman judge, he and his wife breed under the kennel name of Timitra. Their first Doberman was a German import, Danja von Eichenhain. Mr. Alen has been Vice-President of the Finnish Doberman Club.

H. PETER LUYTEN, a breeder, handler and Championship show judge, was a founding member of the Doverman Club of New South Wales, and is a past president of the Doberman Club of Victoria (Australia).

ROBERTO A. DeSANTOS, working in Asia for IBM, recently accepted a scholarship from the Asian Institute of Technology in Thailand toward getting a Masters degree in agricultural systems engineering and management. Always interested in genetics, he hopes to apply this knowledge to a good breeding program in Dobermans, and has imported several bitches in whelp along with studs. Mr. and Mrs. DeSantos plan to return to the United States upon completing his degree.

Happy Dobermans at play.

Foreword

W HILE still in my teens in the 1920s, I saw my first Doberman Pinscher at the Westminster Kennel Club show in Madison Square Garden (the old Garden) in New York City—and it was love at first sight! There were the several other breeds I had encountered in person, in books (Albert Payson Terhune's Collies and Richard Harding Davis' White Bull Terriers, for example) and in the movies (the German Shepherd, Rin Tin Tin), which had great appeal and interest for me — and still have now. But the smooth, sleek, powerful, beautiful Doberman represented the embodiment, the very epitome, of purebred Dogdom. So began, over 50 years ago, a loving association which has intensified rather than diminished with the years.

In 1935, Judith, my wife of one year (who equally shared my love for dogs) and I finally acquired our first Doberman. His name was Mephisto of Westphalia and he was purchased from our neighbors in New Jersey, the Westphalia Kennels owned by Francis F. H. Fleitmann and managed by Mrs. Ellie Buckley. From that time on our interest and association with the breed deepened almost into an obsession. We spent much time at dog shows exhibiting and observing the dogs and the judging. Shows were benched in those days and the dogs had to remain in their assigned spaces for most of the day and, of course, their owners remained on the grounds also, so that there was ample opportunity for the exchange of comments, opinions and purebred dog lore in general and Doberman experience and information in particular.

In addition we studied all available literature on the Doberman. We read and reread Schmidt and Gruenig's books on the breed. It is this recollection of how valuable an authoritative, well-written and comprehensive book can be to newcomers to the breed, as well as to more experienced fanciers, that makes me especially happy to be writing this Foreword to *The New Doberman Pinscher* by Joanna Walker, with special added chapters by other noted authorities.

In recent years the Doberman population in this country has increased alarmingly; so much so that one has to be extremely concerned about the welfare of the breed. It is flattering in one sense that so many people have taken a liking to the Doberman, but frightening that so many individuals with little or no knowledge about the origins, function, physical structure and temperament of the breed, about its strengths and potential weaknesses, will be owning, exhibiting and, particularly, breeding the Doberman. These novices must be educated, as thoroughly and as quickly as possible. Membership in the Doberman Pinscher Club of America and in one of its regional Chapter Clubs would be helpful in this regard.

This book does a remarkably complete job of covering all aspects of the breed: its origins and history, its physical structure, its gait and its current status in this country and abroad. Equally as important, it discusses Doberman temperament and the Doberman in Obedience trials.

At the 1976 National Convention and Specialty Show, the DPCA Board of Directors, recognizing that temperament needs to be given comparable emphasis with conformation, that the function of the breed must not be disregarded, voted to establish a Registry of Merit for Doberman Pinschers. Dobermans that are AKC Champions holding at least one AKC Obedience or Tracking title, and who have also passed a temperament test, will receive a Register of Merit (ROM) award from the DPCA. Temperament tests will be conducted under the auspices of the ROM committee, and dogs which have been certified in such a manner will receive a Working Aptitude Certificate. This action signifies the beginning of a new era in which conscious focus and dedication will be on the Total Doberman; sound in mind and body; dogs which act as well as look like Dobermans.

The ready availability of this new and timely book on the Doberman Pinscher will be of inestimable value in protecting our breed. It is a comprehensive, well written, objective and authoritative breed book. One may not agree with every statement made in it, but, then, one would never find unanimity of opinion and belief in any gathering of so-called experts on this or any breed of purebred dog. It should be read and studied by all novice and veteran Doberman owners, exhibitors, handlers, breeders and judges. I am delighted to recommend this book most highly to all those interested in our breed.

HERMAN L. FELLTON
President
Doberman Pinscher Club of America

Marietta, Georgia
February 1977

I AM DEEPLY GRATEFUL to the many who have helped in compiling this book, and for the many kind words of encouragement they have expressed. I especially appreciate the cooperation of those who, on such short notice, have sent me treasured pictures of their wonderful Dobermans.

Special thanks are due those whose written contributions are so important a part of this book:

To *Frank Grover* for his chapter on Gait.

To *Ruth McCourt* for so clear an interpretation of the Standard.

To *Robert* and *Anita Silman* for the excellent chapter on Color.

To *Vic Monteleon* for the chapter on Temperament Testing.

To *Bernie Brown* for his interesting chapter on Obedience.

To *Ingrid Hallberg* for all the help she has given me with the chapter on Europe. She had many contacts to make in such a short space of time, and came through 100%.

To *Maida Jonsson, Lilith Edstrom* and *Keijo Alen,* for their wonderful contribution on Scandinavian Dobermans. I hope I will be forgiven for any mistakes in the spelling of names in the captions, for many of these were written by hand and hard to read, and of course were not familiar to me.

To *Mike Bradshaw* for his thorough chapter on England, and its emphasis on the American aspect.

To *Pat Blenkey* for the chapter on Canada—a chapter she cooperatively rewrote after the Post Office lost the first copy.

To *Roberto DeSantos* and *Jackie Perry* for their fine contribution on Asiatic Dobermans.

To *Peter Luyten* for his chapter on Australian Dobermans, and the many wonderful pictures of dogs from "Down-Under."

We are happy to include, with permission of the publisher, three memorable chapters from *The Complete Doberman Pinscher:*

The authoritative chapter on Origin of the Breed.

The chapter by *Peggy Adamson* on "Illena and the Seven Sires," which simply could not be improved upon, and is an invaluable record of bloodlines in America.

The incomparable pictures and text on gait by the late *Curt Sloan,* a classic treatment of the subject.

I am especially grateful to Herman Fellton, president of the Doberman Pinscher Club of America for his fine Foreword, and to *Nancy Hogans,* Chairman of the Archives Committee, for allowing me full use of her records, and for her encouragement.

My only regret is that I could not include more pictures and information on this wonderful breed, but this would have run into two books.

JOANNA WALKER

Tess Henseler's famous Doberman Drill Team at the 1959 Westminster Kennel Club show at Madison Square Garden, New York City.—*Shafer*

1

The Doberman Pinscher

by Frank Grover

W E HAD NEIGHBORS once who watched our Dobermans and then announced, "We have decided that a Doberman is a Cadillac of dogs." Most persons who have owned Dobermans will agree. There are other fine dogs; then there are Dobermans—the dog of dogs.

Talking about Doberman ownership is a little like trying to explain a family relationship, for a Doberman demands and takes a full place in your life. A Doberman either trains you, or is trained by you; for most of us, it is a little of both. You can't put a Doberman away, forget about him, and take him out when you want to show him off. A Doberman isn't that way; he wants to be with you, to help you, torment you, love you and guard you. And, he will work out ways to get what he wants.

A Doberman is an affectionate animal; but his affection is noble. You can't bribe a Doberman with a pat on the head—he doesn't enjoy "just being patted" the way many other breeds do. He wants to be close to you, to have your hand on his head, to rest his head on your knee, or to sit on your shoe with his back to you. He won't leave you for a stranger who offers to scratch his ear. Scratching an ear may be nice, but it isn't as nice as resting his rump on your shoe. Seldom do you find a "licking" Doberman. A single kiss, a touch of the tongue, a touch of his nose to your ear, that is his way, a special greeting. To lick (unless you have a wound that needs healing) would be too undignified for most Dobermans. Yet, with his black eyes, short tail, and graceful body he can tell you more plainly how special you are than could all the licking and rubbing or petting in the world.

A Doberman is an energetic dog with lots of strength, speed, and agility. He can run with a horse, maneuver quickly enough to catch a rabbit, track faster than a Bloodhound, tree mountain lions, and beat you to the davenport every time if you let him!

17

A Doberman is a gentle dog with the firmness of the strong. He will let a baby teethe on his ears and nod with pleasure. He will take his six year old mistress walking to show her off and guide her with the mature judgment that knows it is well to let a six year old have her own way—unless it is dangerous.

A Doberman is a sensitive dog, keenly alert to your feelings and wishes. If someone visits you whom you don't like, watch the dog, for he will be watching your visitor. After he has been with you a few years, you will find often you don't need to speak a wish. He will know and respond. You become a part of him, and he becomes a part of you; and the only tragic part of owning a Doberman is that a part of you is buried with him when he dies.

The Doberman in pose is a noble and lovely thing. But the most thrilling part of a Doberman's beauty is in action. When you take your dog out into a field and let him run and you see him lay out in a smooth flowing gallop, this is the Doberman that is without peer—a dog of dogs. An animal so natural you think that all evolution has been aimed at him; and yet the precise control of selected breedings of little more than seventy years is what has crystalized this form and motion.

The Character of a Doberman

Each Doberman is different; yet each exhibits "Doberman characteristics of mind and disposition." We have never owned one that was not a "character." Some are more so than others.

Called the dog with the human mind, the Doberman will do just about anything but talk; and often a Doberman will hold quite a lengthy conversation with you about something that is very important to him at the moment.

Probably the most distinguishing thing about a Doberman is the speed of reaction. Where another dog is doing one thing, a Doberman will do ten. They learn through watching; they learn through trial and error; and often they seem to reason things out.

It isn't unusual to have a Doberman that opens doors. One of ours has been known to move a chair over to the stove so as to climb up to steal a roast from the top of the stove. Another was known to methodically lift out petunia plants from a newly planted bed, and then get concerned because the bed did not look right and spend ten minutes trying to put the plants back again.

Though deeply loyal, they are clowns with minds of their own. We have heard of one great Obedience worker who would become peeved with his owner. When the dog was in one of his "peeves" the owner knew something would be done at the next show. Just what, only time would tell. The dog was known to go out on his scent work and bury the articles. He was known to do his directed jumping in reverse. His prize performance came one day when he worked beautifully until he was left on the sits and downs. Just as his owner

18

The Doberman is a gentle dog with the firmness of the strong. *Above:* Jack, a two year old Doberman donated for war service by his owner, Mrs. Carrie Pace of Johnston City, Tennessee. Jack was commended by the Commandant of the Marine Corps for "Outstanding performance of duty against the enemy on Bouganville Island." Many such dogs were used by the Marine Corps during World War II. *Below:* Walkaways Wildfire, bred by Mary Jane Ladd of St. Louis and exported to England, shown soon after he was out of quarantine and in his new home. Wildfire had never been raised with children, but quickly took over as protector of little Jinny Louise, held here by her mother Meg Bradshaw.

19

Marks-Tey Heather with her litter sired by Ch. Derek of Marks-Tey, and Siamese friend Kim. Kim, who lived to be 14½, always took a great interest in all the puppies and would lay close to them, or even among them, and let them climb all over him.

left the ring, the dog left his position, scampered over, swatted his owner on the seat of the pants and then returned to the place he had been left and sat as if nothing had happened!

Another great Obedience Doberman performed beautifully one hot day. On the long down, the owner was out of sight and the Dobe inched forward until she was in the shade. Just before the time was up for the handlers to return to the ring, she inched back to her original position.

The Utility of the Doberman

Dobermans were first bred as a watch and guard dog. No breed excels them at this task. In Chicago, in 1955, one large university started using trained Dobermans to try to reduce vandalism. Not only was it reduced, it was eliminated. Last year our city newspapers had three accounts of Dobermans that saved the lives of their owners protecting them from attack or armed robbery.

One of our club members credits his Doberman of only three weeks ownership with having saved his life when an armed robber invaded his home.

It is staggering to think of how much our city and industries could benefit financially and in providing safety for watchmen and employees through the use of trained Dobermans.

One of our club members owns a tavern and has kept Dobermans for years. The dogs mingle with the customers as long as the customers are in front of the bar; but if one tries to step behind the bar, he is met with a big black dog "on guard."

We have often wondered why insurance companies have not been aware enough to offer special rates where trained Dobermans are used. The facts are there. Perhaps it only requires prompting to get action.

On the gentler side, the Doberman guides the blind. A few trainers of guide dogs have stated that the Doberman is not suited to this work, but these are comments of the uninformed. Blind persons all over the country are using Dobermans. One of the largest foundations specializing in guide dog work kept records on various breeds in training, and they found that the Doberman had the best training record, the best record for "rejects" and the best record for continued devotion. Naturally, not all Dobermans are suited to guide dog training, but those that are make wonderful eyes for their masters.

Did you ever think of a Doberman as a field dog? He has been successfully trained for retrieving and hunting. Many Dobes "point" naturally and work a scent as retrievers. They have been trained for big game, where their speed and stamina make them highly successful in tracking and treeing mountain lions and other big dangerous predators.

Where police departments have been wise enough to see the many advantages of trained dogs, the Doberman has found a role in keeping order in human society.

Dobermans have been used to teach safety to children. Probably the most famous performer in safety education in the nation is a Doberman known as "Safety Girl." A Detroit policeman trained her to show primary grade children how to cross streets and he and "Safety Girl" have traveled all over the nation. In Fort Wayne, Charles Dunifun, also a policeman, uses his Doberman in the same way.

Dobermans have a unique spot in Obedience trials in dog shows. The whole training movement in America came through Dobermans. Dobermans were taken from show to show, giving demonstrations. Many of the founders of training clubs were Doberman people; and when it came to War Dog work these Doberman folk became the leaders. Today, those of us who want a great performing dog in Obedience work usually turn to Dobermans. As one top professional trainer and exhibitor says, "In obedience a top working Doberman can be topped only by another Doberman. No other breed can compete for cleanliness, speed and performance."

These, then, are some of the uses of a Doberman—guard, guide, field, police, stunt, and Obedience. In all the Doberman excels and has a unique place.

The Beauty of the Doberman

An all-rounder judge once said, "Even a poor specimen of a Doberman is a truly beautiful dog. One lives near us and seldom do I drive home and see him running with the other dogs of the neighborhood but what I think, look at that gorgeous animal. I know he isn't a very good specimen, but a Doberman stands out from all other breeds."

This quality is not an accident. Though the Doberman was originally bred for its character, the breed was taken over by a group of men who sought a geometrically and esthetically perfect dog. They bred to a design. Their design was based on mathematical equation and functional principles. They began with what they wanted the dog to do—to be a short-backed galloper, to be agile, to be fast, to be powerful, to be sturdy—and they worked out the proportions and principles of movement that would be necessary.

A square dog, a dog with ample body, a dog with a long muzzle, etc. His legs were to be just so long and angled a certain way to let him move true and to let him move with speed and quick changes of direction. They applied this ideal form to a breeding program, and in less than twenty years had evolved just about our present breed type. To this mathematical outline, they added features for beauty—a sleek dry coat, with precise, clean markings; a long arched neck for balance and nobility, a dark eye, almond shape and set fairly deep, for appearance only. This is the Doberman you see today. A dog with the "beauty built in." There is no such thing as an ugly Doberman, today. There are some that are closer to perfection than others, that is all.

The loyalty of Dobermans is beyond the understanding of most of us. It extends not only to their owners but to their companions. Males in particular be-

A sight not often seen in the United States. Swedish show and working dog Ch. Juliette-ville's Ippon, sired by Ch. Bryan v Forell ex Ch. Alle, with owner Karsten Jeppessu.

Blind students being taught the use of Dobermans as guide dogs at the Pathfinder School established by Glenn Staines in the 1930s.

come deeply attached to females with whom they are raised. It is not unusual to hear of Dobes that mourn to death for a lost mate. Nor is it unusual to hear of Dobermans that recognize a friend after years of separation.

Doberman lore is so filled with stories it would take books to tell them all. There was the Doberman who loved ice cream and would charge up to neighbor children and bark in their faces until they dropped their cones; then she would grab the cone and eat it. "I used to have to buy more ice cream for my neighbor's children," her owner used to say. Then there was the Doberman who grew jealous of his mistress talking on the phone and would go to the closet, bring out a pair of shoes, plop them down in front of her and threaten to chew them if she didn't hang up. Or the Doberman who tiptoed around the house whenever her mistress had a headache. Or the Doberman who sang for food. Or the Doberman who was not allowed to guard because his mate was the guard dog—but when she had puppies, he took over guard duty until she weaned the puppies; then he retired again and raised the puppies himself. Sometime we hope to write a book filled with stories of what Doberman "characters" have done, and when we do, perhaps we will be including accounts of what your Doberman has done. For each is different, each is a character—but a beloved character.

24

Dudek's Maximilian CDX, owned by Stanley Dudek of Miami, Fla., is pictured winning High in Trial (with a 195½—37 dogs in competition) at the Doberman Pinscher Club of Florida Specialty, March, 1976, under judge Samuel A. Gardner. Max has been completely trained and handled by his owner who is confined to a wheel chair.

Karl Friedrich Louis Dobermann (at left) and friends. A rare photograph, taken in Germany in 1870.

2

Origin of the Breed

THE ORIGIN of most breeds of dogs is veiled in obscurity and we can only conjecture as to their beginning. Before the days of dog shows, pedigree records were not kept. Breeding was haphazard and based on working qualities rather than refinement of type.

Transportation was difficult and breeders of a local community were forced to use the local studs. It was natural for the farmer who kept dogs for herding cattle to breed his bitches to a neighbor's dog that excelled in herding qualities. Likewise the hunter selected as a suitable mate for his bitch, a stud that was famous for pointing game.

While these early breeders knew nothing of the Mendelian theory, they believed that ''like begets like,'' and through many generations of inbreeding a type was established in the local community which in time reproduced itself.

Not so in the case of the Doberman Pinscher! We know definitely where and when it originated. Although there are vague stories of dogs similar to the Doberman previous to the time that Herr Karl Friedrich Louis Dobermann owned a black and tan Pinscher who accompanied him on his rounds as night watchman in the town of Apolda, we do not give credence to these stories.

Herr Dobermann was born on February 2, 1823, and while a young man, worked as an official of the court of aldermen. He was later given the position of dogcatcher and administrator of the chamber of accounts at Niederrossla—Apolda, as well as flayer and official of the tax office. He was also employed as the night police officer and selected a likely specimen from the dog pound to accompany him on his rounds, not only as a guard but to scent out an intruder.

This dog he called Schnupp, and he undoubtedly did not consider him fit for breeding purposes because records show that Schnupp was castrated at nine months of age.

Herr Dobermann was interested in breeding dogs that were not only good guard dogs themselves, but would also produce progeny with the same qualities.

Among his friends were a night watchman, Herr Räbel, and a watchman on the tower Böttger, who were also interested in dog breeding, and they collaborated with a shepherd in a neighboring village.

Early in the year 1870, Herr Dobermann owned a black male with red markings and a lot of gray undercoat. This type was more common in later years. His son, Louis Dobermann, master of woven goods at Apolda, has described this male, Schnupp, as ''a dog of such great intelligence as is seldom found. He was clever and fearless and knew how to bite. My father could not have chosen a better one.''

When Herr Dobermann first acquired Schnupp, he lived in an apartment where he was unable to breed dogs; but in 1874 he moved to a larger apartment, and in 1880 purchased a house situated so that he could breed a few dogs and train them. He acquired a female of the same color as Schnupp but with less gray undercoat. He named her ''Bismarck,'' but a superior officer warned him that it was unlawful to give a female dog the name of a great statesman, so he changed her name to ''Bisart.'' It is said that Bisart was very keen and her master had to be careful with her. When she was in season and accompanied Herr Dobermann on his rounds, no other protection was needed than to allow Schnupp to accompany him. Should the local ''gallants'' approach her, it was only necessary for Herr Dobermann to say to Schnupp, ''Let's get rid of the other dogs.'' Schnupp would immediately chase them off.

Louis Dobermann tells us that his father bred some very good puppies from Bisart. They were almost all black with red markings, but in each of the first three or four litters there were one or two puppies that were black with red and white markings. Because of their sturdy bodies, they were very popular with the public and Herr Dobermann did not destroy them.

One of Bisart's daughters, named Pinko, had a natural bobtail, and he kept her for breeding purposes. He used a bobtailed stud with Pinko as he believed that from these he would get puppies with short tails, thus eliminating the necessity of docking; but the result was only one bobtailed dog in a litter. Among Pinko's get there were a few blues.

A review of the prices Herr Dobermann obtained for his puppies is very interesting in comparison with what is being asked today. A male puppy five to six weeks old sold for two Deutschmarks, fifty pfennig. (At that time, four marks and twenty pfennig were valued at one dollar.) A female of the same age would bring one Deutschmark, fifty pfennig. It is said that the dogs were of the best quality, with their tails and ears cropped.

The town of Apolda in which Herr Dobermann resided is located in the state of Thuringia. Beginning in 1860, a dog market or dog show was held there each year on the first Sunday after Whitsuntide, sponsored by a club organized for the promotion of breeding purebred dogs. The government of Apolda surrendered the entrance fees to this show, which were fifty pfennig for each dog, to the club to be used as prize money, for buying certificates, and to pay the necessary bills. The market was situated in the old part of Apolda and the dogs were arranged in six groups and classified as luxury dogs, hounds, house dogs, butcher dogs, etc. It is said that nearly one hundred dogs were exhibited, and they were accommodated on two benches forming a right angle. The show began at eight o'clock in the morning and remained open until one in the afternoon. There was music by a band. We quote from an interesting report on the dogs benched in the market place in one of these shows: "In the first part, which was designated 'dogs of luxury,' there were, among others, four big Pinschers, two of very good quality. In the next there was a very good smooth-haired, brindled white and brown German dog, with brown ears, powerful and well built, and two brown giants, undoubtedly of German parentage, while among the others were four gray colored dogs which seemed to have mixed blood. (This gray color is the same that had been seen in hounds since 1860.) There was a gray Pointer of pure German stock with a tail, however, which was too strong and with red haws in the eyes. There was a two-year-old bitch of nice appearance, with a litter of two beautiful puppies, all belonging to the same kennel. They were the best dogs among the grays. The breeder had known their ancestry for several generations and had owned some of the stock himself. He said it was a pure breed. Another kennel had an exhibit of twelve house dogs, all of poor quality with the exception of a Pinscher."

Herr Dobermann always attended this dog market and was on the lookout for any dog that seemed to have the qualities necessary for training and he was especially interested in types bordering on the Doberman Pinscher as we know him.

Older specialists affirm that the Doberman breed existed before Herr Dobermann helped to popularize it. Nevertheless, after his death on the ninth of June, 1894, the breed was named for him.

Formerly, these dogs were occasionally called "Thuringia Pinscher" or "Police-soldier dogs." The name "Schnupp" was a popular name for dogs at the beginning of the century.

Records show that at a dog show in Apolda, an heirloom photograph showing Herr Dobermann and his friends was given as a prize; and it is doubtful if these early dog breeders would have given such recognition to Herr Dobermann had he not been actually the originator of the breed that we now know as the Doberman Pinscher.

The word "Pinscher" meaning Terrier, after the word "Dobermann" has not been used in Germany since 1949, as it is now recognized that the name is not appropriate for this breed.

The first dog show to be held in Germany was at Hamburg in 1863, but it was not until 1876 that the first "German Dog Stud Book" was founded; and

Training a working dog in the old days.

in the same year there came into being the first dog magazine to be published in Germany. This was a weekly journal, *The Dog, Organ for breeders and fanciers of purebred dogs,* consisting of four pages, commercial size, with pictures.

From an issue printed in 1882 we quote: "In the German dog shows there is some confusion about the English Black and Tan Terrier or Manchester Terrier, and our shorthaired Pinscher. The Pinscher's head is not shaped like that of the Greyhound breeds. The Pinscher seems to be gaining more and more in favor with the public." In a show report of that same year at Hanover, we quote: "There have been no great numbers of the German Pinscher, but some very good specimens."

Undoubtedly breeders used various crosses in these earlier years, and in one magazine there appeared an article in which the author tried to explain the numerous crosses that had been tried out in order to duplicate Herr Dobermann's breeding. These crosses of miscellaneous dogs were made in great number and the results had been useful, clever, elegant, courageous, and alert dogs. It seems that all of the ancestors of the German Doberman gave of their best quality of body and spirit, because the Doberman excels as a runner and as a jumper and is useful for each purpose; both his size and his practical short hair are of great advantage.

There have been many speculations advanced regarding the origin of the Doberman. We will not try to examine them all. It is better to rely on known facts.

An old breeder, Mr. Albert Ammon, wrote:

"My grandfather, in the years 1830–1860, owned an inn with a slaughter house at Grobenbodungen, in Worbis, Saxony, near Thuringia. I always spent my holidays at my grandfather's, and when there, Audi, a great butcher dog, was always with me. Audi was a bitch nearly 65 cm. high, (about 25½ inches) black with much undercoat and red markings, a little white spot at the chest, long ears, and a curled tail. The butchers seldom owned horses and carts. They used to drive the cattle for hours and hours. I remember very well that on one occasion, when my grandfather was driving his cattle from the Harz Mountains, Audi had her puppies en route. Grandfather gave her to a friend and drove his cattle with another dog which he borrowed, arriving home very late at night. He was indeed astonished when the next morning he found Audi in the stable with seven puppies. She had walked the distance seven times in four hours, and each time she brought a puppy with her.

"In later years, when I bred Terriers and Collies, I read of a Mr. Göller who offered for sale the new breed, Dobermannpinscher. In the year 1899 I bought my first dog of this breed from Mr. Göller. At once I noted the resemblance between this new breed and Audi, my grandfather's dog of decades before, with only one difference: Mr. Göller's dogs had no cropped ears and tails.

"Concerning this similarity, Mr. Göller said: 'I am quite convinced that it was principally the German Shepherd dog, the smooth haired Pointer, the blue

Great Dane, and the German smooth haired Pinscher which played a remarkable part in the creation of this breed. Those dogs that I bought in the villages had no undercoat, or very little, but red markings, short, absolutely black hair like hounds, little marked lips, and long toes. Those dogs which came from Apolda were more like German Shepherd Dogs and Pinschers.''

It is very interesting to hear the conclusion of Mr. Richard Strebel, one of the most prominent German dog specialists, who believed that the Doberman does not belong to the Pinscher group; that is to say, the Terriers. He supposed that this breed came from the Shepherds, that it is probably a cross between the Shepherds and the Pinschers. It was his supposition that there had been crosses of the Shepherds of Thuringia and the Black and Tan Terrier of England, and that the Doberman had inherited not only the coat of what we know as the Manchester Terrier but also his disposition, which is keen, alert, quick, and fearless.

Keen, alert and fearless.

3

The Early Doberman in America

RECORDED HISTORY of the Doberman in America begins with 1908, two years after issuance of the first German stud book of the breed. In that year, the American Kennel Club granted use of "Doberman" as a kennel prefix to Theodore F. Jager of Pittsford, N. Y. (the AKC no longer allows use of breed names as kennel prefixes). And at back of the 1908 AKC stud register, listed under "Foreign Dogs," Doberman Intelectus (#122650) became the first of the breed to be registered in this country.

Intelectus, a black and tan whelped June 20, 1908, was identified as having been bred by Doberman Kennels and owned by Carl Schulyheiss. His sire was Doberman Bertel (a German import, originally named Bertel v Hohenstein) and his dam was Doberman Hertha (also a Hohenstein import). Hertha made further history in that she became the first of the breed to win AKC championship—in 1912. The first male (and first American-bred) Doberman to win his championship was Ch. Doberman Dix.

While the dogs of these early years left little impression on the breed (being overwhelmed by the great importations of the 1920s and '30s), they did help popularize the breed. By 1914, there were Doberman breeders in New York, Pennsylvania, New Jersey, throughout New England, in the Midwest and as far west as Washington.

A Doberman Pinscher Club of America is included in the listing of specialty clubs in the *American Kennel Gazette*, the AKC's official magazine, as early as 1913 (and on through 1919). However, the real beginnings of the present DPCA, and strong development of the breed, appear to date from a meeting of breeders and exhibitors that took place at the Westminster show in New York in 1921.

And in 1921 began the wave of imports that were soon to dominate the American scene. By this time, the breed in Germany had recovered from the

33

Ch. Troll vd Engelsburg, two-time German Sieger of the mid-30s, winner of 48 Bests in Show in America and Canada. Sire of Siegers Ch. Ferry and Freya v Rauhfelsen. Owned in America by E. Bornstein.

Ch. Ferry v Rauhfelsen of Giralda, German Sieger import, first Doberman to win Best in Show at Westminster (1939). Owned by Mrs. M. Hartley Dodge.

Ch. Blank vd Domstadt, sire of Dictator.

Ch. Maida v Coldod, dam of Alcor.

effects of World War I, and the cream began finding its way to our shores. Over the next 15 years or so, most of the Siegers and Siegerins, and virtually every top German sire, sooner or later reached America.

We will here only briefly note some of the more notable of these imports. This is not to demean their importance, but the years water away influence of past generations and we must put the emphasis of our limited space on the dogs of more immediate impact.

First of these outstanding dogs to come was Ch. Lord vd Hortsburg, imported in 1921 by George H. Earle III's Red Roof Kennels. Lord was by far the best import to his time, and proved very popular at stud.

Ch. Benno v Burgholz, a 1922 Sieger, was imported in 1923—the first known Sieger in this country.

Ch. Claus vd Spree (who left behind him in Germany a to-be Sieger son) sired 12 American champions in the '20s including the Best in Show winner Ch. Big Boy of White Gate.

An important early-20's import from Holland was Ch. Prinz Carlo vd Koningstad, brought to America by F.F.H. Fleitmann's Westphalia Kennels. Carlo (who also left a Sieger son behind him) was the sire of imports Ch. Prinzessin Elfrieda v Koningstad, Ch. Prinzessin Ilisa v Koningstad, and Ch. Prinz Favoriet vd Koningstad—who between them produced 24 AKC champions. Favoriet's 15 champions included Ch. Carlo of Rhinegold, the first American-bred to win Best in Show. Ilisa was the dam of Princess Ilisa of Westphalia, who became the first American-bred to win a German Siegerin title.

Lux vd Blankenburg, imported in 1927 at age of eight by Glenn S. Staines' Pontchartrain Kennels, stands as one of the all-time sires of the breed. Although he was a slow maturer, and did not become a Sieger until his fifth year, Lux was a sire of such dominance that he sired the winners of six Sieger and Siegerin titles. Nineteen of his get became American champions, and 20 more had champion descendants. A study revealed that of the 245 Dobermans who finished to AKC championship between 1946 and 1950, over half (154) traced directly to Lux.

An example of Lux's progeny was Ch. Claus v Sigalsburg, the 1926 German and Austrian Sieger , who became quite a winner in America, too—scoring 13 Bests in Show during 1928 and 1929.

Sieger Muck v Brunia was brought to America at age of three, but managed to leave behind him two Sieger sons—Troll vd Engelsburg and Blitz vd Domstadt. Muck sired 10 American-bred champions.

Blitz stayed in Germany, but his brother Blank vd Domstadt became an American champion in 1936, and was sire of 13 American-bred champions. Six matings of Blank with Siegerin Ossi v Stahlhelm, a daughter of Troll vd Engelsburg, produced 11 champions including the great American-bred sires Ch. Domossi of Marienland and Ch. Dictator v Glenhugel.

Ch. Favoriet v Franzhof, sire of 13 champions including Ch. Christie's Barrier. Favoriet, whelped in 1941, was half-brother to Alcor.

Ch. Emperor of Marienland, whose outstanding winning included the Group at Westminster in 1948. A top sire, he produced four Best in Show winners among his first eight champions. Owned by Mr. and Mrs. Wilhelm Knauer's Meadowmist Kennels.

Ch. Merak v Millsdod, black, full brother and kennelmate to Alcor. Owned by Dr. and Mrs. A. Ernest Mills.

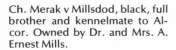

Troll vd Engelsburg became celebrated as both a winner and sire. His German get (bred before his importation to America in 1937) included the winning dog and bitch of the 1938 Sieger show, Ferry and Freya v Rauhfelsen, the 1937 Siegerin Ossi v Stahlhelm, and the World Siegerin Alfa v Hollingen. Thirteen of his get (including five American-breds) finished to American championship. Winner of two German Sieger and one World Sieger titles, Troll became a Canadian as well as an American champion, and scored 48 Bests in Show and 78 Group Firsts.

Troll's son, Ferry v Rauhfelsen, is in the record books himself as the first Doberman to go Best in Show at Westminster Kennel Club show in Madison Square Garden, New York City—a win he scored in 1939 just three weeks after his importation to America by Mrs. M. Hartley Dodge. The judge was George Thomas, who placed Ferry over a group of finalists that included such immortals as the Cocker, My Own Brucie and the Fox Terrier, Nornay Saddler.

Great bitches were being imported in this period, too, and probably the most outstanding was Ferry's dam, Ch. Jessy vd Sonnenhoehe. Jessy, whelped in 1934, had been Best of Breed at two successive Sieger shows and had produced a Sieger and Siegerin (Ferry and Freya) in Germany. In America, she was dam of seven champions out of a mating with Ch. Kurt vd Rheinperle (a sire of 20 champions), and of six champions out of a mating with Kurt's son, Pericles of Westphalia. From the Pericles litter came Ch. Westphalia's Uranus, who in turn was to sire the great American-bred producers Ch. Favoriet v Franzhof and Ch. Alcor v Millsdod.

Which brings us to World War II. Importations, which had already dwindled to a trickle, now ceased entirely. American breeders were thrown upon their own resources, but these were ample. Having had the best of German dogs to work with for close to two decades, as well as guidance from many German authorities that had been invited to judge at American shows, the American breeders had built well.

The story of the successful takeover with American-breds forms the background of a chapter titled "Illena and the Seven Sires" by Peggy Adamson that was written in 1951, and included in the earlier editions of this book. We include it again in this edition as an interesting account, written from an at-the-time perspective, of this important era in American Doberman development.

The immortal Ch. Dictator v Glenhugel, pictured at six years old in August 1947. This great red dog was owned by Peggy Adamson.

```
                              Luz v Roedeltal
                    Ch. Muck v Brunia
                              Hella vd Winterburg
          Ch. Blank v Domstadt
                              Ch. Sg. Hamlet v Herthasee
                    Nora vd Ruppertsburg
                              Ada vd Adelshore
CH. DICTATOR v GLENHUGEL
                              Ch. Muck v Brunia
                    Ch. Troll v Engelsburg
                              Adda v Heek
          Ch. Ossi v Stahlheim
                              Helios v Siegester
                    Kleopatra v Burgund
                              Siegerin Freya v Burgund
```

4

Illena and the Seven Sires*

by Peggy Adamson

IN THE HISTORY of the American Doberman, eight dogs produced more than ten American champions each. These were: Ch. Westphalia's Rameses, Ch. Dow's Illena of Marienland, Ch. Favoriet von Franzhof, Ch. Westphalia's Uranus, Ch. Emperor of Marienland, Ch. Domossi of Marienland, Ch. Alcor von Millsdod, and Ch. Dictator von Glenhugel.

Rameses produced 11 American champions of record; Illena, 12; Favoriet, 13; Uranus, 14; Emperor, 18; Domossi, 20; Alcor, 26, and Dictator, 37.

These figures are recorded in the American Kennel Club as of July, 1951, and can probably be considered final for Domossi, Rameses, and Uranus, who have been dead for a number of years; also for Illena, who is alive but whose last litter was in 1946. Emperor died suddenly in 1949, Alcor and Favoriet in the spring of 1951. Of the Seven Sires, Dictator alone is living today, occasionally siring a litter but no longer at public stud. The number of champions by the latter four could therefore be increased appreciably.

The year 1941 was the golden year of the American Doberman. That year alone gave birth to Illena and the younger four of the Seven Sires: Emperor and Favoriet in the spring, and Alcor and Dictator in the fall, the latter two within a day of each other. All of the five were sired by the older three except Dictator, who was Domossi's younger brother. Rameses, the oldest, was whelped in 1938, Domossi and Uranus in 1939. Three of the Famous Seven

---

*This article, written in 1951, is presented as an "at-the-time" report of one of the most eventful decades in Doberman development. Dictator, the only one of the seven sires living at time of the article, died in 1952. The total of his champion progeny increased to 52.

Ch. Alcor v Millsdod (1941–1951), owned by Dr. and Mrs. A. Ernest Mills.

died as a result of heart attacks: Domossi, at the age of 7; Emperor, at the age of 8; and Alcor shortly before his tenth birthday. Uranus, Rameses and Favoriet lived to the age of ten.

The Seven Sires were responsible for an era in American Dobermans which was as exciting and colorful as the dogs themselves. They towered over the Doberman world like mighty titans and the competition among them was brisk, awesome—and sometimes fierce. The dog magazines fattened on their advertising, the like of which the breed has not seen before or since. Their names were familiar to the veriest novice, and their offspring could be found in the remotest hinterlands. Each had his loyal partisans, and the legends concerning them were inexhaustible. With their passing, passes an era. History will not soon see the time when seven males of such stature live contemporarily again.

All of them lived on the Eastern seaboard, although Domossi and Dictator were bred in the Middle West. Five were kennel dogs, the exceptions being Alcor and Dictator, who were raised from puppyhood by their owners and valued by them primarily for their companionship.

These dogs were descendants of the best of the German imports. Domossi and Dictator were line-bred to Ch. and Sieger Muck v Brunia through his two imported sons, Ch. Blank vd Domstadt, their sire, and Ch. and Sg. Troll vd Engelsburg, their dam's sire. Their dam, the red Ch. and Siegerin Ossi v Stahlhelm, was a granddaughter of Helios v Siegestor through Kleopatra v Burgund. Rameses and Uranus were line-bred to Helios v Siegestor. Both were sons of the imported Ch. and Siegerin Jessy vd Sonnenhoehe, Rameses by the imported Ch. Kurt vd Rheinperle-Rhinegold, and Uranus by Kurt's American son, Pericles of Westphalia. Illena's dam, Ch. Dow's Cora v Kienlesberg, was also by Kurt out of the imported Ch. Gretl v Kienlesberg, a half-sister to Jessy through Cherloc v Rauhfelson.

Domossi and Dictator were full brothers, Dictator being the younger by two years. Emperor was the son of Domossi, Illena was the daughter of Rameses, and Alcor and Favoriet were the sons of Uranus. Uranus and Rameses were half-brothers, as were Alcor and Favoriet. Emperor's dam, Ch. Wesphalia's Rembha, was a litter sister of Rameses. Favoriet's dam, Adele v. Miegel, was a daughter of Rameses' litter brother, Ch. Westphalia's Rajah. Alcor's dam, Ch. Maida v. Coldod, was a daughter of Inka v. Lindenhof, a full sister to the sire of Dictator and Domossi.

Dictator, Domossi and Favoriet were reds. Almost half (17) of the Dictator champions were red; three of the Domossi champions were red; and five of the Favoriet champions were red. Prior to Dictator's time, the only stud producing as many as seven red champions had been Dictator's sire, Blank, who was a black.

Alcor, Rameses and Illena were dominant black and all their champions were therefore black. Emperor and Uranus were black recessive. Two of the Emperor champions were red, and three of the Uranus champions were red.

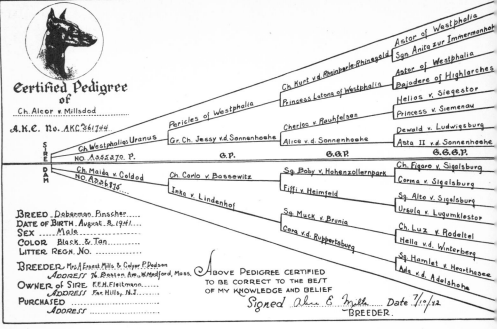

Certified Pedigree
of

Ch. Alcor v. Millsdod

A.K.C. No. AKC 561744

SIRE

Ch. Westphalias Uranus
NO. A355270. P.

Pericles of Westphalia

Ch. Westphalias Uranus

Gr. Ch. Jessy v.d. Sonnenhoehe
G.P.

Ch. Kurt v.d. Rheinperle-Rhinegold

Princess Latona of Westphalia

Cherloc v. Rauhfelsen

Alice v. d. Sonnenhoehe
G.G.P.

Astor of Westphalia

Sgn. Anita zur Immermanhof

Astor of Westphalia

Bajodere of Highlarches

Helios v. Siegestor

Princess v. Siemenau

Dewald v. Ludwigsburg

Asta II v.d. Sonnenhoehe
G.G.G.P.

DAM

Ch. Maida v. Coldod
NO. A336875

Ch. Corlo v. Bassewitz

Inka v. Lindenhof

Sg Boby v. Hohenzollernpark

Fiffi v. Heimfeld

Sg. Muck v. Brunia

Cora v.d. Ruppertsburg

Ch. Figaro v. Sigalsburg

Corma v. Sigalsburg

Sg. Alto v. Sigalsburg

Ursula v. Lugumklostor

Ch. Luz v. Rodeltel

Hella v.d. Winterberg

Sg. Hamlet v. Hearthasee

Ada v.d. Adolshohe

BREED Doberman Pinscher
DATE OF BIRTH August 8, 1941
SEX Male
COLOR Black & Tan
LITTER REGN. NO.

BREEDER Mrs. A. Ernest Mills & Colyer P. Dodson
ADDRESS 76 Boston Ave., W. Medford, Mass.
OWNER of SIRE E.E.H. Fleitmann
ADDRESS Far Hills, N.J.
PURCHASED
ADDRESS

Above Pedigree certified
to be correct to the best
of my knowledge and belief

Signed Alma E. Mills Date 7/10/42
BREEDER.

1. **HELLEGRAF v THUERINGEN** to Schnuppe vd Saale	1. **HELLEGRAF v THUERINGEN** to Beda Frischauf
2. **Lux Edelblut v Ilm Athen** to Lotte v Ilm Athen	2. **Lord v Ried** to Helga vd Pfalz
3. **Prinz Modern v Ilm Athen** to Sybille v Langen	3. **Prinz Leuthold v Hornegg** to Asta v Starkenburg
4. **Bayard v Silberberg** to Fee vd Boerde	4. **Achim v Langerode** to Leddy vd Blankenburg
5. **Arno vd Gluecksburg** to Gudrun v Hornegg	5. **Alex vd Finohoehe** to Dora v Wiesengrund
6. **Burschel v Simmenau** to Asta Voss	6. **Stolz v Roeneckenstein** to Ella v Siegestor
7. **Lux vd Blankenburg** to Lotte v Roeneckenstein	7. **Helios v Siegestor** to Ilisa of Westphalia
8. **Alto v Sigalsburg** to Fee vd Roedeltal	8. **Astor of Westphalia** to Anita zur Mimmermannhoehe
9. **Luz v Roedeltal** to Hella vd Winterburt	9. **Kurt vd Rheinperle-Rhinegold** to Princess Latona of Westphalia
10. **Muck v Brunia** to Cora vd Ruppertsburg	10. **Pericles of Westphalia** to Jessy vd Sonnenhoehe
11. **Bland vd Domstadt** to Ossi v Stahlhelm	11. **Westphalia's Uranus** to Maida v Coldod
12. **DICTATOR v GLENHUGEL**	12. **ALCOR v MILLSDOD**

An interesting chart showing how Dictator and Alcor, born within a day of each other in 1941, traced in male line to common ancestor in Hellegraf v Thueringen, whelped in 1904.

There is no subject in dog breeding so cloaked in mystery, glamour and fable as that which surrounds the great stud dogs. The layman is convinced that great studs become great simply because the breed's best bitches all flock to them for breeding. Yet the records of the American Kennel Club show that of the total number of litters registered with Favoriet as the sire, only one-twelfth had the assistance of bitches who were, or ever did become, champions! Of the total number of litters sired by Dictator, only one-fifth had dams who were, or ever became, champions; of the total number by Uranus, only one-fourth, and by Emperor or Rameses, one-third. Of the total number of litters by Domossi or Alcor, approximately half had dams who were, or later became, champions.

Although it has long been recognized that the better the bitch, the better the stud's opportunity to produce high-type progeny, the Seven Sires were able to produce an amazing number of champion offspring from bitches who never became champions themselves and in many cases could not even be considered show quality.

The records of Favoriet and Dictator were particularly impressive in this respect. Of the 13 champions by Favoriet, less than one-third (4) came from champion bitches. Of the 37 by Dictator, less than one-half (17) were from champion bitches. Of 14 by Uranus, 8 were from champions, and of 11 by Rameses, 7. Of 18 by Emperor, all but 3 were from champions; of 20 by Domossi, all but 2; and of 26 by Alcor, all but one were from champions.

A high proportion of the champions produced by several of these studs came from daughters of other studs included in the Famous Seven. Twelve of the 18 champions sired by Emperor were from daughters of the Seven Sires, with over half the Emperor champions from Rameses daughters alone.

One-half the 26 Alcor champions were from daughters of Dictator, Emperor and Favoriet. One-half the 20 Domossi champions were out of daughters of Emperor, Uranus and Rameses. Fourteen of the 37 Dictator champions came from daughters of Emperor, Alcor and Domossi, with ten of them from Domossi daughters only. Two of the 13 Favoriet champions were from a Uranus daughter and an Alcor daughter. One of the Uranus champions came from a Rameses daughter.

Rameses alone was never bred to any daughters of the Seven Sires, although 15 of the champions sired by the others were produced by his daughters. Ch. Dow's Illena of Marienland was not only the greatest of his offspring, but the greatest producing bitch in the history of American Dobermans. From a total of five litters by three different sires, she produced the remarkable total of 12 champions. The three sires were Domossi and his two sons, Emperor, and Ch. Dow's Dusty v Kienlesberg. There were five champions in the two Emperor litters, four in the one Domossi litter, and three in the two Dusty litters. No other American bitch even approximated this record.

Rameses was the only one of the seven who sired more female champions than males, producing 7 female champions as against 4 males. Domossi sired

Ch. Dow's Illisa of Westphalia, lovely bitch owned by Mrs. Virginia Knauer's Meadowmist Kennels in Philadelphia.

Ch. Dow's Illena of Marienland, whose progeny included five Best in Show winners.

Ch. Dow's Dodie v Kienlesburg, dam of Ch. Dow's Dame of Kilburn.

10 champions of each sex, and Illena produced 6 of each sex. Favoriet and Uranus each sired 6 female champions, with 7 male champions for Favoriet and 8 male champions for Uranus. Emperor and Alcor each sired 7 female champions, with Emperor siring 11 male champions and Alcor 19 male champions. Dictator sired 14 female and 23 male champions.

As individual specimens, Alcor, the black, and Dictator, the red, outshone all others, a fact which was reflected in their spectacular show careers. Of the other five, Favoriet was little known as a showdog, but Emperor, Domossi, Rameses and Uranus attained notable prestige both in breed and Group competition.

Five of the Seven Sires were between 27½ and 28 inches in height, Rameses being slightly over 28 and Domossi slightly under 27. All had scissors bites, and six had complete sets of teeth, the exception being Domossi who lacked one premolar. In gait and strength of quarters, Dictator and Alcor excelled the others, Dictator being noted for the strongest pasterns and Alcor for the best turn of the stifle. Uranus had the more rear angulation and Domossi, the less. The family line from which the brothers Dictator and Domossi were descended was strong in pasterns and quarters, but frequently lacked sufficient angulation. The family from which the brothers Rameses and Uranus came was often weak in pasterns and tended to have too much angulation. In Alcor and in Emperor, the two families were combined, for both of them were outcrosses.

Although none of the seven were faulty in ribspring or depth of brisket, the chests of Rameses and Dictator were the deepest, while the other five possessed greater spring of rib. Alcor had the strongest back, Dictator the highest withers, and Favoriet the most pronounced forechest. Uranus, though not the largest, was the most powerful of them all, but did not have their elegance and length of neck. The four black dogs had eyes which were various shades of brown, in the case of Rameses two-toned. Dictator, alone of the seven, had a truly dark eye, the deep shade of brown for a red dog being comparable to a black eye in a black.

Alcor, Dictator, Domossi and Emperor had excellent tailsets. Those of the other three could have been higher. The tails of Domossi and Dictator, which were always carried gaily, had a characteristic triangular shape, thick at the base and tapering to a point. The only one of the seven which could be described as a really compact short-bodied dog was Domossi. While Alcor and Dictator measured square, their backs were of medium length, and those of the other four were slightly longer.

If a composite Doberman could be made, using only one of the many qualities which each of the Seven Sires was known to possess and transmit, it might have Dictator's temperament, Favoriet's front, Rameses' chest, Uranus' ribspring, Alcor's rear quarters, Domossi's tail, and Emperor's elegance. But it would require the head of Illena, for her head was closer to perfection than any of the Seven Sires.

Not only was Illena famed for the beauty of her head and expression, but for her superb neck, shoulders and front, and the wine-red color of her markings. Her mouth was beyond criticism. She had a deep chest and excellent ribspring, but was too rounded in croup and rarely carried her tail up. Her greatest liability was a lack of showmanship and animation which often caused her assets not to be fully appreciated on first impression.

Only two studs have come within reaching distance of the Seven Sires. These are a black Emperor son, Ch. Roxanna's Emperor v Reemon, and a black Uranus son, Ch. Kama of Westphalia. Both were whelped in 1943 and are still living. Roxanna's Emperor has sired 9 black champions from six different bitches, only two of which were champions. His dam, Ch. Westphalia's Roxanna, was a litter sister of Rameses. Kama has sired 7 champions (6 black and 1 blue) from four different bitches, only one of which was a champion. His dam, Alma v Molnar, was a daughter of Rameses' litter brother, Rajah.

Among the younger sires, only three as yet have produced more than two champions: Favoriet's black son, Ch. Christie's Barrier, who died in 1951 at the age of six; Dictator's red son, Ch. Saracen of Reklaw; and Alcor's black son, Ch. Rancho Dobe's Presto. Barrier and Saracen were both whelped in 1945. Barrier has produced four champions from four different bitches, Saracen three champions from two different bitches. Neither of Saracen's mates were champions, and only one of Barrier's. Presto, whelped in 1947, has produced three champions from one champion bitch. Two of the Saracen champions were red. The Barrier and Presto champions were black. Saracen was out of an Emperor daughter, Kay of Reklaw; Presto was from a daughter of Roxanna's Emperor, Ch. Rancho Dobe's Kashmir; Barrier's dam, Ch. Christie v Klosterholz, was a daughter of Rameses' litter brother, Rajah.

Of the younger Dobermans, male or female, the greatest producer to date is the red Dictator daughter, Ch. Dow's Dame of Kilburn, whose dam was the Domossi daughter, Ch. Dow's Dodie v Kienlesberg. She was whelped in 1945, the same year as Saracen and Barrier, and in her first two litters produced seven champions (five males and two females). From the first litter, which was sired by Alcor, five became champions. From the second litter, sired by Emperor and whelped just after his death in 1949, two have already completed their championship. Her third litter, by her grandson, Ch. Berger's Bluebeard, and her fourth litter, by her own sire Dictator, are not yet of showing age. The Alcor and Emperor champions were black, the Bluebeard litter is black, and the Dictator litter is red.

Here, indeed, is an interesting fact: the six Dobermans mentioned above—Roxanna's Emperor, Kama, Barrier, Saracen, Presto, and Dame—are all sons and a daughter of the Seven Sires!

In other lands also they have enriched the breed, many of the exports being Dictator or Emperor offspring out of daughters of the Seven Sires. In 1948, the Siamese Prince Bhanuband Yukol imported a Dictator son and daughter

Ch. Walire's Roberta and Ch. Walire's Rollo I, daughter and son of Dictator.

Ch. Damasyn the Solitaire CDX and Ch. Brown's Evangeline, 49th and 50th champions of Ch. Dictator v Glenhugel, owned and handled by Peggy Adamson.

for the purpose of establishing the line in Siam. The red male, Damasyn The Shawn, was out of a daughter of Emperor. In Tokyo, Damasyn The Bat, who is by Dictator from a Domossi-Illena daughter, produced a litter sired by the Kama son, Ch. Dacki vd Elbe, whose dam was a Domossi daughter out of a Uranus daughter. One of these was awarded the 1951 title, Grand Champion of Japan. The Cuban Champion Damasyn Venture and his half-brother, Damasyn The Blade, have sired a number of litters in Havana. Both are by Dictator, Blade being a full brother of Damasyn The Bat. In Germany in 1950, Arda Lark of Inverness produced a litter by the Red Sieger Artus v Wertachbrucke. She is a red Dictator daughter out of a Domossi-Emperor granddaughter.

The most famous of all the exports is probably Ch. Kilburn Escort, the Emperor-Illena son recently sold to Hawaii. Escort is one of the few Dobermans ever to leave America after completing his championship, most Dobermans being exported as puppies. Meadowmist Barrister, by Emperor out of a Rameses daughter, has established himself as a stud in Brazil.

The Seven Sires were the backbone of the American show Doberman. Through their intermarriages with the daughters, not only of each other but of the brothers and sisters of their families, they have transmitted a productive power that makes itself evident from generation to generation. During the ten years prior to August, 1951, a total of 416 Dobermans completed their championships in the United States. One-half of these were the descendants in the first, second, or third generation of the Seven Sires. One-third of the total number were their own sons and daughters (139), sixty-two were their grandchildren, and seven were great grandchildren. Many, of course, could have fallen into several categories, but in considering these figures no dog was counted more than once.

Ch. Christie's Barrier, handled by Peter Knoop, pictured in win of the Group at Philadelphia in 1947. Barrier, by Ch. Favoriet v Franzhof ex Ch. Christie v Klosterholz, was owned by Winifred Bacon.

Ch. Venture of Jerry Run, by Ch. Axel v Gothenberg ex Quickly of Jerry Run. Venture's daughter, Venture's Blue Waltz, was the foundation bitch for the Gra-Lemor Kennels.

Ch. Arko von Adelerbe, an early 1950s winner, by Ch. Christie's Barrier ex Elva of Damhof. Owned by Mr. and Mrs. G. Hendrickson of Chicago.

Ch. Damasyn the Fiery Filly, whelped 1953, by Ch. Damasyn the Solitaire CDX ex Damsyn the April Rain. Owned by Karen Kamerer.

Ch. Berman Brier, Grand Victor 1957. A red Ch. Damasyn the Solitaire CDX son ex Berman Armina. Owned by Bernie Berman.

5

The Modern Doberman in America

I̶N FOLLOW-UP of the story of the Seven Sires, it seems appropriate to begin our account of the great American Dobermans of recent years with an updated consideration of Ch. Alcor v Millsdod and Ch. Dictator v Glenhugel. Both were not only outstanding specimens of our breed, but were also great as sires. Their names are getting further and further back in present-day pedigrees, true, but they are still there—and have had a very great influence on the breed.

Ch. Alcor v Millsdod was sired by Ch. Westphalia's Uranus and his dam was Ch. Maida v Coldod. Alcor and his brother Ch. Merak v Millsdod were from Maida's first litter and were the only two shown; the rest of the litter were sold as pets and were never bred. Alcor was the first Doberman who was twice Best of Breed at Westminster. Shown 53 times, he won 44 Bests of Breed, 15 Group firsts and 6 Bests in Show. He twice won the Doberman Pinscher Club of America Specialty, in 1946 and again in 1948. His brother Merak was the only dog to defeat him twice.

Alcor, who sired 61 litters, was a dominant black. (Merak, however, did sire reds.) Alcor's most outstanding litter contained five champions. The dam of this litter was the lovely Ch. Dow's Dame of Kilburn, who was Jack and Eleanor Brown's foundation bitch. She was sired by Dictator ex Ch. Dow's Dodie v Kienlesburg. This litter contained Champions Brown's Armand, Archer, Admiral, Achilles and Adventuress (who was retained by the Browns and lived to a ripe old age). In all, Alcor was the sire of 33 champions.

Ch. Dictator v Glenhugel was sired by Ch. Blank v Domstadt and his dam was Ch. Ossi v Stahlhelm, both of whom were German imports. Dictator was purchased from John Cholley of Glenhugel Kennels by Bob and Peggy Adam-

Ch. Berger's Bluebeard. This dog was considered quite large in the 1950s. Owned by Gilbert Berger.

Ch. Domossi of Marienland
Ch. Emperor of Marienland
Ch. Westphalia's Rembha
Ch. Roxanna's Emperor v Reemon
Ch. Kurt vd Rheinperl-Rhinegold
Ch. Westphalia's Roxanna
Ch. Jessy vd Sonnenhohe
CH. BERGER'S BLUEBEARD
Ch. Westphalia's Uranus
Ch. Alcor v Millsdod
Ch. Maida v Coldod
Ch. Brown's Adventuress
Ch. Dictator v Glenhugel
Ch. Dow's Dame of Kilburn
Ch. Dow's Dodie v Kienlesburg

Ch. Berger's Baron, litter brother to Bluebeard. Though not as well-known as his brother, Baron was equally outstanding.

son for only $150. since he was second choice in the litter. What an impact this dog was to have on the breed! From the time he was a puppy Dictator had exceptional temperament, and through his get it is being passed on. He had a short but impressive show career. At Cleveland in 1944, an unknown two year old, he went from the classes all the way to Best in Show. In just months from Cleveland through Westminster in 1945, he was Best of Breed 15 consecutive times and 5 times Best in Show.

Richard Webster of Marienland Kennels wrote this critique of him at the Cleveland show:

"Dictator von Glenhugel, winners dog, Best of Breed, Best Working and Best in Show. What a magnificent animal is this gorgeously coated red Doberman of marvelous physical stature, perfect conformation, type and balance. . . . He is a large dog, standing 27½ inches at the withers, bone yet without a single trace of coarseness. He is powerfully constructed with perfect balance throughout and with a very good head, full teeth, proper bite and beautiful colored eye that blends with his matchless coat. His neck slightly arches and flows into the high withers and shoulders as one; and the strong back, topline and tailset leave nothing to be desired.

Here too, is the temperament and nobility that a great Doberman should have. He is a master showman, alert with muscular and temperamental fire, inquisitive and bold, yet without viciousness or stupidity. I wish to make the prediction that Dictator v Glenhugel will have a most profound and vital influence in the further development of our breed. I am most pleased that he was bred and is owned in our own country and will be available to those who seek breed improvement."

How right Mr. Webster was!

As a sire, Dictator was indeed great and he went on to sire 52 champions, over half of which were red. It is interesting that today the reds are more popular than ever. Many of today's top breeders based their foundation stock on Dictator. Our own Ch. Damasyn the Waltzing Brook CD was a double Dictator granddaughter, and her son Ch. Derek of Marks-Tey (sired by Ch. Brown's Eric) had Dictator on all four sides of his pedigree in the first three generations.

Dictator died in 1951 at the age of ten, in a tragic accident that cost not only his life, but also that of Damasyn Sikhandi, his daughter. (Sikhandi was an older sister to Ch. Damasyn the Solitaire CDX.) The dogs had been left in a locked car — as they had many times before — but this time it was a brand-new car, and it was not realized that the car was air-tight.

Dictator luckily left behind a beautiful red son, Ch. Damasyn the Solitaire CDX, who was just a year old when his sire died. "Tari," as he was called, was a singleton puppy out of the Dictator-Alcor granddaughter, Ch. Damasyn the Sultry Sister. He was not shown until he was four years old. He stayed a year with Curt Sloan who had 400 acres in which he could run and develop into the working dog Nature meant him to be—galloping twenty-five miles a day, hunting and learning to be a farm dog.

Tari started his show career by winning the Indianapolis Specialty at his very first show and finished with three Bests of Breed at major shows a few months later to become Dictator's 50th champion. Tari was particularly noted for his beautiful head with its parallel planes and full muzzle. He had very dark almond shaped eyes, long arched neck and personality plus. I had the pleasure of having him in our home once, so can vouch for the fact that he was a complete gentleman. Like many Dobes, he loved to back up to a couch or chair and sit down with his rump on the chair and his front feet on the ground. He was a great Obedience worker and there is a film of him going over the jumps when he was ten years old. If one had to fault him, it would be that he was a speck long in loin but all his other qualities more than made up for this. He was the sire of 14 champions.

Ch Delegate v.d. Elbe (October, 1947–October, 1955) was a black dog bred by Hans Schmidt and owned by Mrs. Ruth Castellano. He was one of three champions from the litter sired by Ch. Kama of Westphalia out of Ch. Belydia vd Elbe. His litter brothers were Champions Dacki and Dyke. Delegate was a large dog, at least large for his time; he was 28½" and weighed 90 pounds. He had many excellent qualities—a good solid topline, good tail-set and excellent angulation, tight feet and a full mouth.

Delegate's owner was particularly proud of his fabulous temperament. To fault him, he could have had a better head, a better stop, and have been more filled in under the eye. He was also a little long in hock.

Delegate was the sire of 55 champions from just sixty litters and he died at the age of only eight. He was the top producing sire for five consecutive years, 1954–1958. He carried dilution, so sired all four colors. Of his progeny, 254 were blacks, 66 were reds, 34 were blues and five were fawns.

"Delly," as he was called, was not shown extensively. His owner would not allow a handler to take him, so he was only shown at the shows that she herself was able to attend. Notwithstanding, he had an impressive show record of 70 Bests of Breed, 21 Group firsts and 2 Bests in Show. This dog can still be found in many of today's pedigrees.

Ch. Rancho Dobe's Primo was also whelped in 1947. He was a son of the great Alcor out of Rancho Dobe's Kashmir, and represented the fourth generation of Rancho Dobe breeding for his breeders, Brint and Vivian Edwards of California. His ancestry is primarily that of Eastern and German breeding.

Primo was a slow developer and did not mature until he was three years old. (This is certainly not uncommon for males; most of us show them far too soon and before they are ready.) At two he was shown for the first time at Harbor Cities and went from the classes to Best of Breed and fourth in Group. After this win he was sold to Mr. and Mrs. James Case, but he was so homesick that he was returned to Rancho Dobe where he lived out the rest of his days.

Ch. Delegate vd Elbe (1947–1955), sire of 55 champions owned by Mrs. Ruth Castellano.

Ch. Dortmund Delly's Colonel Jet, son of Delegate and sire of Ch. Steb's Top Skipper.

He is best known as the sire of the famous Ch. Rancho Dobe's Storm who was twice Best in Show at Westminster. Storm was his sire's first Champion; he was followed by the Hardings' Opera litter of eight Champions.

Ch. Rancho Dobe's Storm was a very different type of dog from Dictator, but the combination of these two great dogs has produced much of the quality that can be seen in our Dobermans of the present.

Storm was whelped in December 1949 at the Rancho Dobe Kennels. His dam was Ch. Maedel von Randahof, who died soon after he was born. Storm was out of a litter of thirteen, of which only four survived—and two of these were later killed by cars. Storm was the only one shown.

At three months, he was sold to Len Carey, and took on the life of a city dog—getting his daily exercise in Central Park in New York City.

Storm's show career was short, but phenomenal. Shown just 25 times (he was retired at 38 months), he was never defeated in the breed. He scored 22 Group firsts and 17 all-breed Bests in Show—topping everything by twice going Best in Show at Westminster, once when he was only two, and again when he was three. He was handled by Peter Knoop, one of the top handlers of the time, and today a licensed all-breeds judge of great popularity both here and abroad.

Mr. F. F. H. Fleitmann, whose Westphalia Kennels at Far Hills, N. J. in the 1920s and '30s had brought many of the great imports to America, wrote: "The Germans have not yet produced a dog to beat Storm. But then there is quite a difference between Storm and the next-best American dog." Life magazine published a lengthy article on him at the height of his career, and brought out the fact that Storm was not only a great showman, but a personality dog as well.

The first bitch bred to Storm was Peggy Adamson's Damasyn Sikhandi, Dictator's daughter who was to tragically die along with her sire. One of the resulting puppies was the lovely Damasyn the Easter Bonnet who could not be shown due to an eye injury. She did, however, produce and was the dam of the well-known Ch. Steb's Top Skipper. The sire was Ch. Dortmund Delly's Colonel Jet, a Delegate son.

Ch. Dortmund Delly's Colonel Jet was a dog who was in several homes and as Natalie Stebbins, with whom he spent his last days, stated, "he was cheated from the day he was born; sometimes he lived like a king and was winning Bests in Show all over the country, and then he would live the life of a kennel dog or be kept in some cellar." Natalie had always loved and admired the great dog and this brings us to another tale.

It is interesting to note that some dogs had sad starts in life and went on to do great things for the breed. It was Natalie Stebbins' great love for Colonel Jet that prompted her to buy his dam, Tauzieher Lady Ambercrest, when she was ten years old. Natalie bred her back to Colonel's sire, who was Delegate.

Ch. Rancho Dobe's Primo, whelped in 1947, sire of Ch. Rancho Dobe's Storm. Bred by Brint and Vivian Edwards. Pictured at 10 years of age.

```
                              Pericles of Westphalia
                   Ch. Westphalia's Uranus
                              Sg. Ch. Jessy vd Sonnenhoehe
       Ch. Alcor v Millsdod
                              Ch. Carlo v Bassewitz
                   Ch. Maida v Coldod
                              Inka v Lindendorf
CH. RANCHO DOBE'S PRIMO
                              Ch. Emperor of Marienland
                   Ch. Roxanna's Emperor v Reemon
                              Ch. Westphalia's Roxanna
       Ch. Rancho Dobe's Kashmir
                              Ch. Mes v Sidlo
                   Rhumba of Rancho Dobe
                              Juno of Moorpark, CD
```

Ch. Rancho Dobe's Storm, only Doberman to twice win Best in Show at Westminster (1952 and 1953). Owned by Len Carey and handled by Peter Knoop.

<pre>
                              Ch. Westphalia's Uranus
                Ch. Alcor v Millsdod
                              Ch. Maida v Coldod
        Ch. Rancho Dobe's Primo
                              Ch. Roxanna's Emperor v Reemon
                Ch. Rancho Dobe's Kashmir
                              Rhumba of Rancho Dobe
CH. RANCHO DOBE'S STORM
                              Ch. Ferry v Rauhfelsen of Giralda
                Mr Butch v Rittenhouse
                              Kara v Randahof
        Ch. Maedel v Randahof
                              Ch. Sgr. Muck v Brunia
                Ch. Indra v Lindenhof
                              Mitzi of Lawnwood
</pre>

Ch. Rancho Dobe's Storm going Best in Show at Eastern Dog Club, Boston, in 1952 in followup of his first Westminster triumph. Owner Len Carey is pictured accepting the ribbon from judge Harry Peters, Jr. Storm was handled by Peter Knoop. Today, Mr. Carey and Mr. Knoop are two of only 28 judges who are approved to do all breeds at AKC shows.

Ch. Storm's Donnor, a son of Ch. Rancho Dobe's Storm ex Storm's Tempesta (a Storm daughter), winning Best in Show at Suffolk County (NY) in 1959. Donnor, a big winner of his day, was also handled by Peter Knoop.

59

This resulted in just two puppies, a red bitch who became Ch. Steb's Point of Order, and a black male they named Steb's Investigator whom she, of course, kept. This puppy was outstanding in every way and many felt he was even better than his older brother, Colonel Jet. But it was not to be, for this lovely puppy was killed in a freak accident before he was a year old. I am sure this was a loss to the breed.

The Stebbins had leased Damasyn the Easter Bonnet from Peggy Adamson and bred her to Colonel Jet. They had then given a black male puppy of this breeding to Bob Mullen (who owned Colonel at the time) as a stud fee puppy, since they felt they had the male they wanted in Investigator. He in turn sold the puppy and the owners were to bring him back for ear taping, but failed to do so.

About six months after the Stebbins lost Investigator, they got word that this puppy was in need of a home as his owner was not able to care for him and could not get his ears up. He certainly did not look like much, but when he jumped up and licked Natalie's face, she could not leave him there so took him home with them. His name was Steb's Top Skipper.

Skipper was sent to George Rood who was an expert with problem ears and after five operations, his ears were up! George entered him at a show and this was the first time the Stebbins had seen him with his ears up. But he was still out of condition from all he had gone through and they took him home to fatten him up. At his next show he went Best of Breed from the classes under the veteran authority, Mr. Fleitmann, and went on to finish his championship with four straight major wins. In 1957 he won the Top Ten in Chicago after winning Best of Breed at the Chicagoland Specialty under the English judge, Fred Curnow. The dog who was unwanted was now a great and well-known champion. He was also a much loved house pet. He was leading sire of the year for three consecutive years. He died at the early age of just six of a heart attack but even with so short a life as a stud, he sired close to 50 champions. The first of these was Ch. Alemap's Checkmate, a Best in Show winner. Skipper's next breeding, to Ebonaire's Flashing Star, resulted in the famous "Football" litter of Champions Ebonaire's Touchdown, Gridiron, Touche, Balestra and Flying Tackle.

A repeat of the breeding to Flashing Star produced Ch. Steb's Gunga Din who later joined the Stebbins household. When Gunga Din was bred to a bitch out of Ch. Patton's Ponder of Torn lines called Farley's Princess, owned by George Olenik, the breeding produced the lovely black Ch. Sultana von Marienburg, owned by Mary Rodgers, and she skyrocketed to fame and glory. She had that Top Skipper "look of eagles" and handled by Rex Vandeventer (who is now a judge) was successfully shown at major shows throughout the country.

Meadowmist Isis of Ahrtal was bred by Virginia Knauer and sired by Ch. Emperor of Marienland ex Dow's Ditty of Marienland. This black bitch pro-

Ch. Steb's Top Skipper, immortal sire.

Ch. Ebonaire's Touchdown, one of the famous "Football Litter" by Ch. Steb's Top Skipper ex Ebonaire's Flashing Star. Touchdown, a multiple Best in Show winner of the early 1960s and sire of nine champions, was owned by Charles A. T. O'Neil, currently one of the directors of the American Kennel Club, and handled by Monroe Stebbins.

duced a total of 35 puppies, of which 17 became champions; and these in turn inherited the ability to produce champions, generation after generation. All of Isis's champion children were sired by Delegate and since both carried the dilution factor, they produced 26 blacks, five reds, three blues and one fawn.

Tess Henseler can rightly be proud of this bitch who was the foundation for her Ahrtal Kennels which has produced 63 champions from 1948–1976. Dorian, from the first litter, was the first male champion that Miss Henseler kept for herself. He won a Group before he was even finished and was just eleven months old at the time. He was the sire of Ch. Willa v Ahrtal, who was the dam of the very famous all-champion litter of six that included Fidelia, Freya, Frigga, Frido, Florian and Felix. They were sired by Ch. Lakecrest Thunderstorm.

The outstanding producers of the Delegate ex Isis breeding were: Ch. Dogobert, Ch. Horst, Ch. Friederun, Ch. Frederica and Ch. Falstaff — all vom Ahrtal. Ch. Falstaff vom Ahrtal was a red owned by Tom Rae of Tulsa, Oklahoma. He was handled by Rex Vandeventer and completed his show career with one Best in Show, nine Groups and 21 Bests of Breed. Due to illness in the family this beautiful dog was almost lost to breed, as he was surrounded by stud dogs who were widely advertised and promoted at stud. He was not bred to a worthy bitch until Ch. Brown's Feegee was bred to him and the breeding produced five champions in one litter. It was this litter that included Ch. D-Dow's Bonaparte of Falstaff.

Ch. Florian vom Ahrtal CD who was black, sired a total of 14 champions, while his brother Felix, who was a blue, sired 28 champions. All the puppies out of Willa were sold except for Fidelia, who lived with Tess until she died at the age of twelve years. All had excellent homes except for poor Felix who was in first one home and then another. His second owner had to give him up when he was drafted into the service and he was left with someone who did not care for dogs, with result that poor Felix was chained and abused. He was returned to his breeder at nine months of age and as Tess herself put it, "It just about broke my heart when he came home, beaten but not broken; he had that proud defiant look. Felix had the most beautiful eyes, but now they were sad. He had in his young life experienced enough misery and rightfully should have hated people. But he never did. He was sound, and with the love he got here, came around fast." Because of his past experiences he never felt really at home in the house and was far happier in his kennel where he felt safe. However, he loved to go in the car and Tess would take him with her as much as possible. He was a great protector and all Doberman.

Felix loved dog shows and was a super showman but being a blue was a great handicap in those days, so he often lost when he should have won. He finished his championship at two years of age but was never shown again. The first champion he sired was out of Mikadobe's Flambeau, the black Ch. Alnwick's Black Fury Bismark. Out of the 29 champions he sired, 26 were black and only three were blue. The first bitch bred to him was a daughter of Ch.

A very young Jeffrey Brucker handling Ch. Ebonaire's Gridiron, one of the famous "Football Litter" sired by Ch. Steb's Top Skipper ex Ebonaire's Flashing Star. Gridiron was owned by Al and Leisel Lefkowitz of New York.

Ch. Delegate vd Elbe

Ch. Dortmund Delly's Colonel Jet

Tazieher Lady Ambercrest

Ch. Steb's Top Skipper

Ch. Rancho Dobe's Storm

Damasyn the Eastern Bonnet

Damasyn Sikhandi

EBONAIRE'S "FOOTBALL LITTER"

Ch. Damasyn the Solitaire CDX

Damasyn the Captain Sabre

Damasyn The Winter Waltz

Ebonaire's Flashing Star

Ch. Dictator v Glenhugel

Damasyn the Flash

Damasyn The Flaming Sable

Hagen vom Ahrtal named Iduna vom Ahrtal and out of three litters there were a total of seven champions. Felix died on April 18th, 1969, at the age of eleven years.

On February 20th, 1964, Ch. Juno vom Ahrtal whelped a litter of four black puppies sired by Xandu vom Ahrtal. Xandu won quite a few points from the puppy class and then was sold, but was not shown by the new owners. The only male in the litter was called Cassio and he was never offered for sale as Tess fell for him from the very start. He was the apple of her eye and at just six months he won a Best in Match. He finished at 17 months and had numerous Bests of Breed and Group placings. I got to see him at the Quaker City Doberman Specialty where he was shown under the German judge Herr Rothfuss. He won the breed and also the stud dog class and here is Herr Rothfuss's critique on Cassio;

"A powerful two and a half year old male of elegance (*Adel*), well-knit in body, with good build, strong bone, true front, tight feet, firm back, good tail-set, angulated hindquarters, short coat and dark markings. Shown in good condition. Free gait. Good temperament."

For those who think one must have a handler in order to win, Miss Henseler is a good example of an owner-handler who has "made it". Circumstances did not allow her to show her dogs extensively and she has always handled them herself. She may not be able to boast of great show records but she has still managed to breed more champions than anyone else. Cassio died at the age of ten in January, 1974. He and Felix tied for the honor of being leading sire in 1968; in 1969, they tied for third place and in 1970 Cassio was leading sire. He sired a total of 37 Champions.

Ch. Defender of Jan-Har was a red dog with plenty of bone and substance. He was sired by Ch. Saracen of Reklaw ex Ch. Cissi of Jan-Har, who was a Saracen granddaughter. He was the winner of the Top Ten award at the Chicagoland Speciality in 1956. Defender was later sold to Canada to the well-known judge, Dr. Wilfrid E. Shute and he had a great show career in that country also.

Of the first two litters he sired, one consisted of 13 puppies and the other of 12, and all were reds since they were out of red bitches. One of these bitches was the lovely Ch. Damasyn the Fiery Filly.

Ch. Brown's Eric was, without a doubt, Dictator's most outstanding and top producing son. His dam was the Dictator daughter, Ch. Dow's Dame of Kilburn, who was Jack and Eleanor Brown's foundation bitch. Unlike his famous sire, Eric was not a great showman; he was not shown after he finished as he did not care for the ring. But at home he was a joy to live with and he was Eleanor's constant companion. His greatness was as a sire and he was able to pass on his great heritage to his get. He sired 28 champions and many of his children became top producers in their own right.

64

Ch. Felix vom Ahrtal, sire of 28 champions. Bred by Tess Henseler.

<pre>
                              Ch. Rancho Dobe's Primo
                 Ch. Rancho Dobe's Storm
                              Ch. Maedel v Randahof
       Ch. Lakecrest's Thunderstorm
                              Westphalia's Cavalier
                 Ch. Apache Lady of Lakecrest
                              Emma of Blue Top
CH. FELIX VOM AHRTAL
                              Ch. Delegate vd Elbe
                 Ch Dorian v Ahrtal, CD
                              Meadowmist Isis of Ahrtal
       Ch. Willa v Ahrtal
                              Ch. Dagobert v Ahartl
                 Ch. Elektra v Ahrtal, CD
                              Meadowmist Belladonna
</pre>

Ch. Alnwick's Black Fury Bismark CD, (1961–1970), the first champion sired by the blue Ch. Felix vom Ahrtal. Owned by Marjorie Brooks Anagnost.

65

Ch. Cassio vom Ahrtal (1964–1974), sire of 37 champions. Bred and owned by Tess Henseler.

```
                                    Ch. Delegate vd Elbe
                     Ch. Hagen v Ahrtal
                                    Meadowmist Isis of Ahrtal
            Xandu vom Ahrtal
                                    Ch. Lakecrest's Thunderstorm
                     Ch. Fidelia vom Ahrtal
                                    Ch. Willa v Ahrtal
CH. CASSIO VOM AHRTAL
                                    Ch. Berger's Bluebeard
                     Ch. Fortuna's Maestro
                                    Ch. Anona v Tamara
            Ch. Juno vom Ahrtal
                                    Alaric v Ahrtal, CDX, TD
                     Ch. Zessica v Ahrtal
                                    Ch. Friederun v Ahrtal
```

Ch. Juno vom Ahrtal, Cassio's dam.

David and Helen Dow of Kansas City, Missouri, purchased the lovely black Brown's Feegee from the Browns and after finishing her championship, bred her to Eric. This breeding produced Champions D-Dow's Aladdin v Riecke, D-Dow's Anchor v Riecke, D-Dow's Anoree v Riecke and D-Dow's Erica v Riecke. Aladdin and Anchor were both Best in Show winners. Another from this breeding was Ajax and it is possible that he too finished. Feegee, who was sired by Ch. Kilburn Cameron ex Ch. Brown's Belinda, was the dam of ten champions. Erica was a particularly lovely black bitch and she had some great wins, but she belonged to a busy doctor and it is sad that she was never bred.

Aladdin was within a point of his title in 1956 when he was very badly burned in his crate while out with his handler. It was a freak accident and only his handler's quick action saved him—when led from his burning crate he never uttered a cry. For thirty days it was touch and go but although he was scarred slightly, five months later he went on to win back-to-back Bests in Show.

Ch. Brown's Eric was also the sire of the lovely Ch. Brown's Bridget who was red, and her black brother Ch. Brown's Dion. When the Browns obtained Dion, as a stud fee puppy, they found the litter being raised under appalling conditions, in nothing larger than a baby's playpen. The rest of the litter was sold to a Chicago puppy-factory but one little red bitch was rejected as too sickly. The bitch, Bridget, was boarded with a veterinarian for treatment, ran up a big bill and it was decided to put her to sleep. Jack Brown heard of the dilemma and drove 250 miles to see if he could save her. He paid the veterinarian's bill and took little Bridget home to Eleanor who nursed her along and gave her every possible care. All she hoped to do was to save her, so she could at least be sold to a loving pet home. I saw her at this time and she was so tiny she could walk under her brother Dion!

She more than repaid the Browns' kindness as she grew into a lovely bitch and was sold to the McFaddens of St. Louis. Bridget finished her championship in style by going Best of Breed from the classes, handled by Jack Brown. However, life was never really smooth for Bridget as she was in several homes although loved by each of her owners. Her last owner was Ruth Bell who purchased her for $500, plus three of her puppies yet to be produced. Alas, Bridget was bred three times but did not conceive. The McFaddens sued and were awarded $750. So, with legal costs, Mrs. Bell figured she ended up paying $3000 for Bridget. While all this was going on Bridget was out racking up the wins with ten Bests in Show and was also Best of Breed at the National Specialty.

It was then decided to have one last try at breeding her and since her owner realized that most stud owners could not be expected to service a bitch as often as the veterinarians felt she should be mated, Eleanor suggested they try her with her brother Dion. Luckily, this breeding did take and six were whelped. This gave the Browns their Ch. Brown's Gigi of Ar-Bel, a lovely

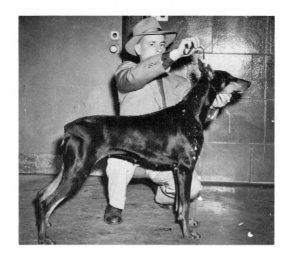

Ch. Brown's Feegee
with owner David Dow.

		Ch. Westphalia's Uranus
	Ch. Alcor v Millsdod	
		Ch. Maida v Coldod
Ch. Kilburn Cameron		
		Ch. Emperor of Marienland
	Ch. Kilburn Audacity	
		Ch. Dow's Illena of Marienland
CH. BROWN'S FEEGEE		
		Ch. Domossi of Marienland
	Ch. Emperor of Marienland	
		Ch. Westphalia's Rembha
Ch. Brown's Belinda		
		Ch. Dictator v Glenhugel
	Ch. Dow's Dame of Kilburn	
		Ch. Dow's Dodie v Kienlesburg

Ch. D-Dow's Anoree v Reicke,
wh. 1956, by Ch. Brown's Eric ex
Ch. Brown's Feegee. Bred by
David and Helen Dow.

Ch. Brown's Eric, with
handler Johnny Schmitt.

                                Ch. Blank v Domstadt
                        Ch. Dictator v Glenhugel
                                Ch. Ossi v Stahlhelm
                Ch. Brown's Eric
                                Ch. Dictator v Glenhugel
                        Ch. Dow's Dame of Kilburn
                                Ch. Dow's Dodie v Kienlesburg
CH. BROWN'S DION
CH. BROWN'S BRIDGET
                                Ch. Torn's Desert Gold
                        Ch. Patton's Ponder of Torn
                                Ch. Meadowmist Berenike
                West Begins Dagmar
                                Ch. Smerk's Pride of Torn
                        Ch. Cochise's Black Magic
                                Darkee's Hi-Jerrie

Ch. Brown's Dion, outstanding
sire of 35 Champions. Dion,
black brother of Ch. Brown's
Bridget, was owned by Eleanor
Brown.

Ch. Brown's Belinda in 1961 win under judge Alva Rosenberg. Belinda, by Ch. Emperor of Marienland ex Ch. Dow's Dame of Kilburn, was owned by Eleanor Brown.

Ch. Brown's Bridget winning Best of Breed at the 1961 Doberman Pinscher Club of America Specialty under Frank L. Grant. Bridget was considered by many to be one of the greatest bitches of all time.—*Bushman*

red who was whelped January, 1965. She became the dam of two DPCA Best of Breed winners, Ch. Brown's A-Amanda and Ch. Brown's B-Brian. The dam of Dion and Bridget was the black West Begins Dagmar, a Patton's Ponder of Torn daughter.

Ch. Brown's Dion was a black dog, 27½ inches tall, and with excellent temperament. He was the sire of 35 champions. At this time the Browns had three champion studs in their home—Eric, Dion and Kevin (who was Jack's special pet). They used to leave notes to let each other know which male was out in the yard for exercise!

Ch. Borong The Warlock CD and Henry Frampton were a team that were almost unbeatable in the '50s and '60s. This black son of the German imported Ch. Astor von Grenzweg ex Ch. Florowill Allure CDX was whelped in January of 1955 and died in 1965. He was indeed a legend in his time. With 234 Best of Breed wins, he won the DPCA Specialty no less than three times, the first with a CD title to win the Specialty. At the grand old age of eleven years he won a Group first and over a four year period (1957-1960) Warlock was America's number one winning Doberman.

Yet once when Warlock was but a puppy, he was offered for sale for the price of just $100, but the buyer would go no higher than $90. So Henry, being the stubborn man he was, turned it down and decided that he was a pretty darn nice puppy and kept Warlock for himself. Rather a wise move, to say the least.

In the beginning Henry and Theodosia Frampton were looking for a short-haired dog and like many of us, were enchanted with the Doberman. They were lucky enough to be able to purchase Ch. Damasyn the Pert Patrice from Florence and Ed Williams, and they also acquired her daughter by Damasyn the Sage. This puppy was named Florowill Allure and she was their constant companion and bedmate for the rest of her life. As Luri was growing up they began to think about breeding her and decided to bring new blood into their line, so imported a young black male called Astor v Grenzweg, who descended from a long line of siegers and grand-siegers. After Luri finished her championship, she was bred to Astor.

On January 5, 1955 Luri produced a litter of seven, two males and five bitches. The male they ended up keeping was named Warlock which means "male witch." He was a particularly smart and very affectionate puppy and he grew into a true "gentleman" with perfect manners. At three months Henry started Warlock in Obedience and he got his C.D. degree in three straight shows.

At a year old Warlock started his show career on the Florida circuit and won his majors and all but two of his points. Two months later, he picked up these two points and finished with his first Best of Breed. By the time he was two years old, Warlock had added International titles to his name, finishing championships in Canada and Cuba.

Ch. Patton's Ponder of Torn, important sire. Pictured here being handled by his owner, James Patton, the Best of Winners at the DPCA National Sepcialty.

                              Ch. Emperor of Marienland
              Ch. Roxanna's Emperor v Reemon
                              Ch. Westphalia's Roxanna
        Ch. Torn's Desert Gold
                              Ch. Dictator v Glenhugel
              Ch. Gretchen v Torn
                              Laura v Torn
CH. PATTON'S PONDER OF TORN
                              Ch. Domossi of Marienland
              Ch. Emperor of Marienland
                              Ch. Westphalia's Rembha
        Ch. Meadowmist Berenike
                              Ch. Westphalia's Rameses
              Ch. Dow's Illisa of Westphalia
                              Ch. Dow's Cora v Kienlesberg

Ch. Kurt von Vulcan, by Ch. Brown's Archer ex Jetney v Carlo, owned by James Katcher and handled by Jack Brown.

Ch. Bordo vd Engelsburg, German Sieger import, owned by F.F.H. Fleitman and handled by Peter Knoop, pictured going Best in Show at Ox Ridge Kennel Club in 1953 under judge Mrs. Hayes B. Hoyt.

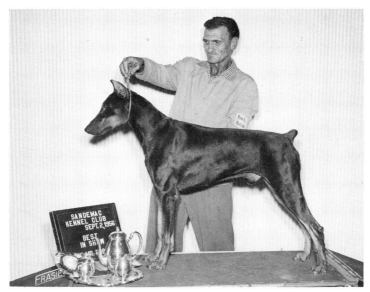

Ch. D-Dow's Alladin v Riecke, a 1956 Best in Show winner, sired by Ch. Brown's Eric ex Ch. Brown's Feegee. Bred by David and Helen Dow and handled by Harold Hardin, who later became a much respected judge.

It was at the age of two that Henry took him to Germany for the annual Sieger show and he went Reserve there for the simple reason that he refused to attack the judges when they charged him with sticks, simply holding his ground and cocking his head as if to say, "What's this all about?" As an American Doberman he had been taught to behave in the ring, not charge the judge and try to bite him, so it was a bit much to expect him to act otherwise.

Warlock was retired from showing at eleven and a half and by then his lovely black daughter (he was a dominant black) had started to make a name for herself. She was Ch. Jem's Amythest v Warlock CD, and was number one Doberman in 1964. She also won the DPCA Specialty that year and she twice won the breed at Westminster. She was beautifully handled by Joe Gregory.

Amy was at center of one of dogdom's most dramatic happenings. Henry Frampton was showing her at Greenville, South Carolina in 1966, when he was stricken with a fatal heart attack. Joe took over, and Amy went all the way to Best in Show. The show world was shocked at the passing of this great man but most who knew him agreed that he would rather go this way than any other, doing what he loved most, showing his beautiful Dobermans.

Three days later Warlock who had been having prostate trouble for some time, quietly passed away also.

Warlock retired with 234 Bests of Breed, 75 Group firsts and 7 All-Breed and 61 Specialty Bests in Show, and was the first three time winner of the National Specialty. He was always handled by his owner Henry Frampton and the two of them were a joy to behold. Warlock was the sire of 39 champions.

Ch. Damasyn the Waltzing Brook CD was the foundation for the Marks-Tey Kennels. She was sired by Ch. Damasyn the Solitaire CDX ex Damasyn the Winter Waltz. "Mitzi" as she was called, produced a total of only ten puppies and she outlived all of them. Luckily, several of these were far more prolific than their dam. Her owners were complete novices but managed to complete her championship owner-handled with four majors, and her Obedience degree was acquired at some of the same shows where she won her points. She was a very dark red and very much showed the strong concentration of Dictator in her pedigree. She particularly excelled in head and this she passed on to her descendants. She also had the "Dictator" temperament and while a good guard, made friends wherever she went.

Her first litter was sired by Ch. D-Dow's Anchor v Riecke, who was an Eric son, and while this did not produce any champions, the litter of four did contain Marks-Tey's Mischief Maker and Marks-Tey's Magic Maker, two bitches who produced several champions. Mischief Maker was a beautiful black bitch and a great show dog. At barely six months she was Best Puppy at the St. Louis Specialty with a very large puppy entry. A week later she went Reserve. She was undefeated in puppy class and took points her first time in Open class. After she had acquired twelve points she was injured while playing with her dam and a front leg damaged so was not able to be finished.

Ch. Borong the Warlock CD, owned by Henry Frampton.
One of the all-time greats of the breed.

                                Casso v Kleinwaldheim
                    Ch. Bordo vd Angelburg of Westphalia
                                Hertha vd Brunoburg
        Ch. Astor v Grenzweg
                                Derby vd Brunoburg
                    Illa vd Leinenstadt
                                Grafin v Paulinenhof
CH. BORONG THE WARLOCK, CD
                                Ch. Dictator v Glenhugel
                    Ch. Damasyn the Sage
                                Damasyn the Song
        Ch. Florowill Allure, CDX
                                Ch. Meadowmist Elegy
                    Ch. Damasyn The Pert Patrice
                                Ch. Damasyn the Sonnet

Bred to Ch. Ebonaire's Gridiron she became the dam of Ch. Marks-Tey's High Hat, Ch. Marks-Tey's Hanover and Ch. Marks-Tey's Hondo. High Hat and Hanover were reds; Hondo was black. Hondo won 7 Bests in Show and 27 Groups. He was owned by Allen and France Shi of Atlanta.

Waltzing Brook's second litter was sired by the Dictator son, Ch. Brown's Eric and contained just four puppies, all reds. The only male Ch. Derek of Marks-Tey was kept by his breeders, while Ch. Dodie of Marks-Tey was co-owned. The pick bitch of the litter, Darinda of Marks-Tey was particularly outstanding and it was most unfortunate that she was lost from her owner's car while traveling to the National Specialty when she was just a year old. She was never heard of again.

Derek was the sire of ten champions, but was not used a great deal due to the fact that he carried the dilution factor and at this time, blues and fawns were not looked on with favor, many being destroyed at birth. It was not until he was seven that Derek's true value was realized and at this point his owner was not willing to allow him to be used to any great extent. He was a big and impressive dog, well angulated front and rear, lovely head and very dark eyes much like his grandsire Solitaire. He could have been a little tighter in shoulders but he had bone and substance and good depth of brisket. He was a fearless guard but never forgot who his friends were.

Ch. Marks-Tey Melanie was a black bitch sired by Ch. Marks-Tey's Hanover out of the Ch. Felix vom Ahrtal daughter, Halcyon Impala. Her dam was co-owned with Joanna Walker, and Melanie was her pick of the litter; she went home to Marks-Tey in Illinois when she was just six weeks of age. However, she had been promised before she was whelped, so at nine weeks she went to her new home. At six months her breeder had a chance to buy her back and she came home with one ear completely down! Luckily, with just a few weeks of taping, the ear was made to stand. At six months it was obvious that this bitch had great potential as a show dog, for she was a natural showman and loved the ring. Shown 16 times in puppy class, she came home with the blue each time and was never defeated as a puppy. She won Best Puppy awards at the two Specialties in which she was entered and at eight months went Best of Winners and Best of Opposite Sex over top champions for a four point major.

Melanie moved beautifully and showed on a very loose lead. To fault her she could have had more rear angulation; she also lacked a little in forechest but she had a beautiful head, iron strong topline with good tail-set, very tight feet and elegance. Also a perfect mouth. She was handled throughout her career by Keith Walker, whom she adored. Melanie died in 1976, in her twelfth year. She stands as the dam of eight champions and the granddam of 37 champions to date, but this last number could go much higher.

Her first litter was sired by Ch. Derek of Marks-Tey, a dog very strongly linebred to Dictator. Derek had Dictator on all four sides of his pedigree in the

Ch. Damasyn the Waltzing Brook CD, the foundation bitch for Marks-Tey Kennels, known for her outstanding head and very dark eye. Bred by Peggy Adamson and owned by Joanna Walker, she lived to be 14½ years.

Lovely headstudy of the black bitch, Ch. Marks-Tey Shay, owned by Fay Wathen Dorval of Louisville. Shay was Top Winning Bitch—Phillips System in 1969, and in 1972 won the Doberman Pinscher Club of America Award for Top Producing Dam. She is one of the very few to have won both honors. Shay was handled to her title by Keith Walker, and then campaigned in the Midwest and California by Gene Haupt.

Ch. Derek of Marks-Tey. A very dark red, Derek was sire of 10 champions.

           Ch. Blank Domstadt
        Ch. Dictator v Glenhugel
           Ch. Ossi Stahlhelm
     Ch. Brown's Eric
           Ch. Dictator v Glenhugel
       Ch. Dow's Dame of Kilburn
           Ch. Dow's Dodie v Kienlesburg
CH. DEREK OF MARKS-TEY
           Ch. Dictator v Glenhugel
       Ch. Damasyn the Solitaire, CDX
           Ch. Damasyn the Sultry Sister
    Ch. Damasyn the Waltzing Brook, CD
           Ch. Dictator v Glenhugel
       Damasyn the Winter Waltz
           Damasyn the Wild Wing

Ch. Marks-Tey Hanover, red male out of the famous "H" litter by Ch. Ebonaire's Gridiron ex Marks-Tey's Mischief Maker. Hanover was sire of Ch. Marks-Tey Melanie.

Ch. Marks-Tey Melanie, pictured at 10 years of age. Melanie was dam of 8 champions and granddam of 37.

```
                                        Ch. Steb's Top Skipper
                        Ch. Ebonaire's Gridiron
                                        Ebonaire's Flashing Star
            Ch. Marks-Tey's Hanover
                                        Ch. D-Dow's Anchor v Riecke
                        Marks-Tey's Mischief Maker
                                        Ch. Damasyn the Waltzing Brook, CD
CH. MARKS-TEY MELANIE
                                        Ch. Lakecrest Thunderstorm
                        Ch. Felix vom Ahrtal
                                        Ch. Willa v Ahrtal
            Halcyon Impala
                                        Ch. Steb's Diablo of the Seven Seas
                        Ch. Lauwick Champagne
                                        Ch. Steb's Sparkling Burgandy
```

Ch. Marks-Tey Vixen, red bitch, a full sister to Chs. Vale and Valika CDX. By Ch. Gra-Lemor Demetrius vd Victor ex Ch. Marks-Tey Melanie.

first three generations. This breeding produced three champions, Ch. Marks-Tey Shawn C.D. who was kept by his breeder, Ch. Marks-Tey Sonnet, and Ch. Marks-Tey Shay. It also produced Marks-Tey Stacy who produced six champions, all sired by Ch. Gra-Lemor Demetrius v.d. Victor.

Shay was also a great producer and is the dam of eight champions. She was the top winning bitch in 1969 and won the DPCA award for Top Producing Bitch in 1972. Seven of her champions were sired by Ch. Highbriar Bandana and were from her first litter; one was sired by Demetrius. Shay was shown to her title by Keith Walker and then campaigned by the well-known handler, Gene Haupt. She is owned by Fay Dorval of Louisville, Kentucky.

Shawn was a big red dog with a personality that made many friends for the breed. He was shown very little as a puppy due to a hairline facture in his shoulder from an injury at five months. He did, however, win several large puppy classes and took his first points at just a year old when he was Best of Winners at the Kansas City Specialty under Tess Henseler for a five point major, and again the following day at Heart of America under Forest Hall. Shortly after he picked up another five point major. He was never campaigned as a Special due to the fact that his owners had other dogs to show for clients.

The first bitch to be bred to Shawn was his aunt, Ch. Hanover's Amsel C.D., and this breeding produced three Champions. He was just a year old at the time.

Shawn was only eight and a half when he died in June of 1975. He stands as sire of 16 champions, but several of his get are still being shown and some have major points and are expected to finish. He left his mark on the breed passing on lovely heads, very tight compact feet with nails that stay short with little trimming, and above all, his puppies have temperaments that are a credit to him and to the breed.

Melanie was bred to Ch. Gra-Lemor Demetrius v.d Victor for her second litter. Her breeder had judged Demetrius at the Quaker City Futurity when he was just a puppy of eleven months of age and had been very impressed by this lovely black dog. This breeding produced three champions: Ch. Marks-Tey Vixen, Ch. Marks-Tey Valika CDX and Ch. Marks-Tey Vale.

Vixen, an outstanding red bitch, took most of her points from puppy and American-Bred class where she kept beating her handler's Open bitch. It is sad that she died young after her first and only litter. Valika was black and she, too, was an elegant showman and a real clown. She also produced three champions in her first litter, which was sired by Shawn's son Ch. Laur-ik Procyon of Marks-Tey. She was then bred to Shawn's son Ch. Lisitza's Buccaneer and this produced the lovely black bitch Ch. Mikater Brisen of Marks-Tey. Brisen has, for the most part been novice owner-handled and has done very well; she finished very young and has several Bests of Breed to her credit.

Ch. Jem's Amythest v Warlock CD, whelped 1960, by Ch. Borong the Warlock CD ex Ch. Hi Dave's Korry's Kay Ingraham.
Amy was the nation's top Doberman of 1964, and in a 2-year
span scored 8 BIS and 33 Groups. Like her great sire, she won
the National Specialty three times. Bred by Mr. and Mrs. Joe
Babcock, she was owned by the Framptons.

Ch. Dobe Acres Cinnamon, a multi Best in Show winner of
the mid-1950's and the important sire of 19 champions.
Cinnamon, son of Ch. Patton's Ponder Torn, was bred by
R. B. Hoover, owned by Harley Plummer. Pictured here
with handler Dick Salter.

Great rivals and also great friends! Henry Frampton with Ch. Borong the Warlock CD and Johnny Davis handling Ch. Val-Eric's Slip Stitch. The judge is John Cholley (breeder of Dictator) and Slip Stitch's owner, Pepper Baron, holds the trophy.

Ch. Storm's Pogo Nip of Kia Ora, a Storm son, owned by H. J. Caro and handled by Peter Knoop, pictured scoring Best in Show under Mrs. M. Hartley Dodge (second from right). Pogo and the great Warlock were often shown against each other and during the late 1950s *Dog News* magazine carried amusing advertisements from one dog to the other!—*Shafer*

Ch. Marks-Tey Vale was kept by her breeders and was without a doubt the best moving bitch of the three, but did not like dog shows particularly. She was very elegant with a lovely head, correct eye and excellent angulation. She finished with four majors but was never shown after this. Her first litter was sired by the Derek son, Walkaways Ablaze of Marks-Tey, a dog who was not shown as he lost part of a toe as a young puppy. This produced a red male, Ch. Marks-Tey Alfie of Rads, who finished by winning four majors in four consecutive days. Also Ch. Marks-Tey Blue Velvet U.D. who was black and who set a record by winning all his Obedience degrees in just five and a half months. Vale was twice bred to Shawn and from the first breeding came Ch. Marks-Tey Shalimar, Ch. Marks-Tey Windsong and Ch. Marks-Tey My Sin. Puppies from the second breeding are now being shown and some are pointed and should finish. In 1975 Vale won the DPCA award for Top Producing Bitch.

Melanie was also bred to Ch. Marks-Tey Hondo and produced another record maker. Ch. Marks-Tey Waystar, who at just eight months of age went Best of Winners at the National Specialty in 1969. She was also Best Puppy. She is owned by Richard Brue of New Orleans and co-owned by Ray Bailes with whom she still lives. Waystar is the dam of several champions including a Best in Show winner.

A breeding of Melanie with Ch. Damasyn the Troycen produced Ch. Marks-Tey Chelsea and a red male Marks-Tey London Pride, who was close to the title with both majors when he was hit by a car and so badly injured he could not be shown further.

Ch. Val-Eric's Slip Stitch CD was a red bitch who went by the unlikely name of Pumkin. She was owned by Carl and Pepper Barron and sired by their Ch. Wil-Ruf's Rowdy Roger ex J'Ore Storm Girl (who was a Ch. Agitator of Doberland daughter ex Ch. Aida's Duchess).

Slip Stitch was handled beautifully by the late Johnny Davis, who was also her breeder. In 1964 she and Warlock became great rivals in the ring but even though the competition between the dogs was really hot, their owners became the best of friends as they had great respect for each other and for each other's dogs. Remarkably, the two dogs won their first Best in Shows on the same day in different parts of the country. It was Slip Stitch's first time out as a Special, so it was a real thrill for her owners. I personally saw Johnny Davis show her and he always had her on a very long loose lead; he was a great handler and she would give her all for him. It was a great loss to the handling profession when Johnny suddenly died of a heart attack.

An incident on the Florida circuit testified to the great friendship that existed between the Framptons, owners of Warlock, and the Barrons, owners of Slip Stitch. When a judge excused Slip Stitch from the ring at one of the shows, Henry Frampton was so insulted that he, too, left the ring with Warlock, stating that if Slip Stitch was not good enough, neither was Warlock!

For her first littler Slip Stitch was bred to Top Skipper and ten puppies resulted from the breeding. However, disaster struck and all but one puppy died of hardpad; this lovely survivor had 14 points when he, too, met his death. After this, it seemed only right that Slip Stitch should be bred to her old rival, Warlock.

Just a few days after the passing of Henry and Warlock, the lovely red bitch was also gone. Slip Stitch was ten years old and had been her owners' constant companion as had Warlock—which goes to prove that the best show dogs are also those that are loved house pets, NOT kennel dogs. To put out that extra something in the show-ring, a dog needs personality—and that he can only acquire if he is close to those he loves.

Ch. Kay Hill's Paint the Town Red, or "Red" as she was fondly called, was a striking bitch of medium size—26″ tall. She was sired by Ch. Defender of Jan-Har out of Jane Kay's foundation bitch, Ch. Westerholz Elita. Red was a controversial bitch at times due to the fact that she had two missing teeth, a fact her owner-breeder never tried to hide or make excuses for. But she had many other qualities to make up for this and as a producer she was one of the best the breed has seen. She finished very fast, handled by her owner and by George Rood. George had advised Jane to try Elita with Defender, after her first litter (sired by Ch. Gaylord of Westphalia) had proved disastrous. This breeding had looked beautiful on paper, and Gaylord was a truly beautiful dog, but the breeding was too close and as Jane herself put it, "all the faults of Westphalia joined forces and came forth."

Elita was bred twice to Defender and this time the results were far more pleasing. The first breeding produced the lovely "Red" and also Ch. Kay Hill's Black Enchantress and Ch. Kay Hill's Ebonette (who made a name for herself as a show dog and brood bitch in Canada). From the second breeding came Ch. Kay Hill's Something Special and Kay Hill's Slightly Scarlet. Scarlet was the dam of Ch. Kay Hill's Siegfried v. Hagen, who in turn was the sire of Jane's first Grand Prize Futurity winner, Ch. Kay Hill's Study in Wine.

Elita was then bred to Ch. Dobe Acres Cinnamon who was a cousin to Defender. Again she hit the jackpot and there were four champions, namely Champions Kay Hill's Rubietta, Fiddler's Folly, Mandarin Red CDX and Amador Allegre.

Red's first litter was sired by the black Ch. Patton's Ponder of Torn and it was an all champion litter of three—Champions Kay Hill's Caroletta, Gold Braid and Painted Coquette. Jane had hoped to repeat this breeding but Ponder died before this could be done, so Red was bred to Ch. Borong the Warlock, thus starting the famous "Witch" litters. This breeding to Warlock was repeated three times with champions in each litter. The second litter produced three Best in Show winners in the one litter! In all, Red produced a total of twelve champions. From the first of these breedings came, Champions Kay Hill's Witch Hunt, Bewitch Inge, Witch Power and The Merrye Witch. From

84

Ch. Westerholz Elita, pictured finishing to her championship in 1955, handled by George Rood. Elita was the foundation bitch for the Kay Hills Kennels, owned by Jane Kay.

Sgr. Ch. Bordo vd Agnelburg
Ch. Astor v Grenzweg
Illa vd Leinenstadt SCH II
Ch. Borong The Warlock
Ch. Damasyn the Sage
Ch. Florowill Allure, CDX
Ch. Damasyn the Pert Patrice
CH. KAY HILL'S WITCH SOUBRETTA
Ch. Saracen of Reklaw
Ch. Defender of Jan-Har
Ch. Cissi of Jan-Har
Ch. Kay Hill's Paint the Town Red
Ch. Beltane of Tamarack
Ch. Westerholz Elita
Ch. Ericka of Damhof

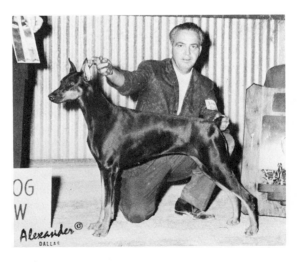

Ch. Kay Hill's Witch Soubretta, Best in Show winning dam of 18 champions, and the foundation bitch for the Tannenwald Kennels, owned by Charles and Kay Etner.

the second came Champions Kay Hill's Shadow Witch, The Wizard Witch, Witch Soubretta and Witch Sprite. The third breeding produced Ch. Kay Hill's The Moon Witch. Since Warlock was a dominant black, all the Witch puppies were also black.

Jane much preferred bitches to males and the only male she kept was Ch. Kay Hill's Takeswon to Nowon. This red dog was sold to Mrs. Michael Pym, but returned to Jane when Mrs. Pym retired. He was the only dog in the history of the Doberman Pinscher Club of America to be an all-breed Best in Show winner before becoming Grand Prize Futurity Winner at the National Specialty. He was sired by Ch. Kay Hill's The Wizard Witch ex Ch. Rubigold's Harmony of Kay Hill, a full sister to Ch. Rubigold's Dentuda who was a Group and Best in Show winner. Many of us who attended the DPCA at Pittsburgh, Pennsylvania in 1965, well remember the excitement when Toppy, as he was called, won the Futurity and how he jumped up on Jane as the crowd applauded their approval. Some felt he should not have been shown since he was already a champion but he was certainly eligible and it was to his credit that he finished so young.

Ch. Kay Hill's Witch Soubretta, who was whelped in May 1960 and died in October 1972, holds the record as the top producing bitch in the history of the breed, having produced 18 champions, five of which were Best in Show winners. She was the foundation for the Tannenwald Kennels of Charles and Kay Etner of Houston, Texas. Soubretta was described by John Phelps Wagner as one of the most perfect Working dogs he had ever judged. She had a particularly beautiful temperament. She was not a large bitch; all her teeth were correctly placed; she had an iron strong topline, well-angulated rear, and a lovely driving gait. If one was to fault her, she could have had a better eye and been a little better filled in under the eyes.

Her first litter was sired by Ch. D-Dow's Bonaparte of Falstaff, also owned by the Etners. This lovely dog was bred by David and Helen Dow in 1956. He was one of five champions and won his title in his first five shows, finishing at just fifteen months of age. He was sired by Ch. Falstaff v Ahrtal and his dam was the lovely Ch. Brown's Feegee. Bonaparte sired a total of eleven champions, seven of which were out of Soubretta.

The best known of Soubretta's children is, without a doubt, Ch. Axel von Tannenwald, owned by Norton and Betty Moore of Houston, who are both well known professional handlers. Axel won 18 Bests in Show, five of which were all-breed shows and 13 Specialties. He won 29 Group firsts and 105 Bests of Breed, and was a Top Ten Doberman for five consecutive years. He was the sire of seven champions.

Another dog from Texas who was well known in the mid-1960s was Ch. Audrey's Orbital Fancy. This flashy black male was finished at just 13 months of age by his novice handler, with two five point majors, a four and a three in

Ch. Kay Hill's Paint the Town Red, owned by Jane Kay. An excellent picture of this lovely bitch.—*Shafer*

Ch. Dictator v Glenhugel
Ch. Saracen of Reklaw
Kay of Reklaw
Ch. Defender of Jan-Har
Ch. Brigum of Jan-Har
Ch. Cissi of Jan-Har
Kilburn Jiffy
CH. KAY HILL'S PAINT THE TOWN RED
Ch. Ximenes of Elblac
Ch. Beltane of Tamarack
Zita of Elblac
Ch. Westerholz Elita
Ch. Kama of Westphalia
Ch. Ericka of Damhof
Topaz of Westphalia

Ch. Kay Hill's Takeswon to No-won, 1964–1972, bred and owned by Jane Kay. Topper, pictured at eight years, was a multi Best in Show and Group winner.—*Shafer*

just three weekends of showing. As a Special he was shown by Stanley Flowers and won six Bests In Show, 19 Groups and 75 Bests of Breed. Fancy was owned by Audrey Schambon.

Ch. Singenwalds Prince Kuhio was bred by Chris and Barbara Harris and purchased by Dale and Bea Rickert of Indianapolis, Indiana in 1960. This black male was three and a half months at the time and his ears had not yet been trimmed, so they had this done at once. It was unfortunate that they were cut far too short; it is probable that the vet was afraid a longer trim would not stand since they were cut so late. Prince's sire was Ch. Ravensburg Bert and his dam (who was bred by the Rickerts) was Singendwalds Jelissa. At six months they showed him to George Rood who was disappointed at his short ears, but agreed to show him. For a dog with ears too short, he did not do badly; luckily the judges realized this was a man-made fault, and he finished from the puppy class with five majors and in just ten shows.

Prince's most outstanding quality was an excellent lay back of shoulder that was in balance with his rear, giving him beautiful movement with plenty of drive. He also had a good topline and level head planes and a very dark eye. His markings were, if anything, a little too dark and small, particularly on his chest. He is another dog I had the pleasure of meeting in his home and he was a gentleman always and beautifully behaved. Dale died in 1964 and shortly after this Prince started to get nose bleeds and his one eye was inflamed. He was X-rayed and a tumor was found behind that eye. He was operated on at Auburn University and the tumor was removed along with the eye.

Prince died very suddenly in July of 1968. His show career was outstanding with 8 Bests in Show, 16 Specialty Bests of Breed, 28 Group firsts and 132 Bests of Breed. He won the DPCA Specialty in 1962 and again in 1963.

Prince was also a great sire, and had 36 champion get. Two of his grandchildren, Ch. Hollyhigh's Drumfire and Stefanbets Eclair, were Best in Show winners. He will certainly go down as one of the great dogs of the breed.

Ch. Jo's Brandy Alexander (February 1960—March 1969) was a red male sired by Ch. Thunder von Adelstadt ex Ch. Katrina von Vulcan. He was bred by Jo Acuff, owned by Fred and Jackie Kortright of St. Louis, and handled by William Kramer. Brandy was a very fiery showman, and did not much care for other males. He finished at just 15 months, with three majors at five consecutive shows held on three consecutive weekends.

Brandy was the sire of twelve champions plus one Canadian Champion. He was the sire of Ch. Brown's A-Amanda ex Ch. Brown's Gigi of Ar-Bel. Amanda won Best of Breed at the 1971 DPCA Specialty. He was also the sire of: Ch. Elfred's Nikki, 1969 DPCA Grand Futurity winner; Ch. Barryton's Elisa, 1965 DPCA Best of Winners; and Ch. Black Bacardi of Philcra Lane, who in 1965 was the DPCA Best Futurity Puppy, and came back in 1966 to go Winners Dog.

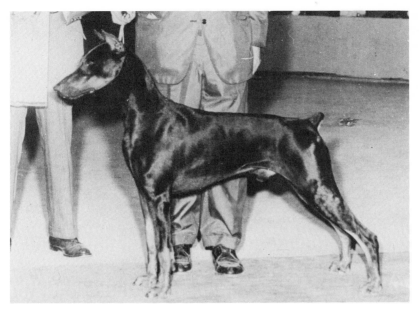

Ch. Singendwald's Prince Kuhio, oustanding winner and sire of the mid-60s. Owned by Mr. and Mrs. Dale Rickert, and handled by George Rood.

Ch. Gra-Lemor Demetrius vd Victor, black son of Ch. Damasyn Derringer ex Jerry Run's Boo Sprite, whelped in 1966. A Best in Show and Group winner, and one of the most important sires of the breed. Bred and owned by Grace Moore.

Ch. Jo's Brandy Alexander, 1960-1969, one of the breed's outstanding sires. This handsome red was owned by Fred and Jackie Kortright.

```
                                        Ch. Kurt von Vulcan
                        Ch. Storm von Vulcan
                                        Ch. Brown's Hildegarde
        Ch. Thunder von Adelstadt
                                        Ch. Brown's Eric
                        Brown's Jezebel
                                        Debony Von Carlo
CH. JO'S BRANDY ALEXANDER
                                        Ch. Brown's Archer
                        Ch. Kurt Von Vulcan
                                        Jetney Von Carlo
        Ch. Katrina Von Vulcan
                                        Ch. Brown's Eric
                        Ch. Brown's Hildegarde
                                        Ch. Brown's Adventuress
```

Ch. Tevrac's Top of the Mark CD, red, owned by Joanne Fisher of Dallas, Texas. Topper is the sire of 18 champions including Ch. Brown's B. Brian, two-time DPCA Specialty winner.

Ch. El Dorado Black Magic, sired by Ch. Wilmar's Arrow ex Regalaire's Eloise, bred by Ruth McCourt and owned by Virginia Sweems. Black Magic was handled by the late Harry Sangster, one of the country's great handlers.

Ch. D-Dow's Bonaparte of Falstaff, black male sired by Ch. Falstaff vom Ahrtal ex Ch. Brown's Feegee. Bred by David and Helen Dow and owned by Charles and Kay Etner's Tannenwald Kennels.

Ch. Kama of Westphalia

Ch. Delegate vd Elbe

Ch. Belydia vd Elbe

Ch. Falstaff v Ahrtal

Ch. Emperor of Marienland

Meadowmist Isis of Ahrtal

Dow's Ditty of Mairenland

CH. D-DOW'S BONAPARTE OF FALSTAFF

Ch. Alcor v Millsdod

Ch. Kilburn Cameron

Ch. Kilburn Audacity

Ch. Brown's Feegee

Ch. Emperor of Marienland

Ch. Brown's Belinda

Ch. Dow's Dame of Kilburn

91

Ch. Haydenhill's Hurrah, or the "Great Hurrah" as he was affectionately called by his owner Dick Souders, was whelped in April 1961 and died in April 1971. This lovely black dog was sired by Ch. Hallmark of Naumanheim ex Ch. Haydenhill's Diana. His breeder was Myrtle Hayden of California.

Hurrah was the sire of 28 champions, of which many were Best in Show and Group winners. He was only used at stud thirty times. His show record was also tops and he had 21 Bests in Show, 56 Group firsts and 141 Bests of Breed. He was owner-handled except for a nine month period during which he was handled by Harry Sangster.

Ch. Alnwick's Black Fury Bismarck CD was the first Doberman owned by Marjorie Brooks Anagnost. He was bred by Joanne Boiger of Pennsylvania and sired by the blue Ch. Felix v Ahrtal out of Mikadobe's Flambeau. His owner is one of the very few who has been honest about the shortcomings of her dog as a stud and she wrote about this in the 1971 issue of *Doberman Quarterly*. In this article she admitted that he did not have the best mouth and had two extra and two missing teeth. She even considered not using him further for this reason, but he had already sired some excellent puppies and she never tried to hide the fact that on occasion he sired get with missing teeth. To offset this he had many outstanding qualities to offer.

Bismarck had simply beautiful tight cat's feet, very well laid back shoulders and a strong topline. He had good angulation in rear, so therefore moved with correct drive. He was a number four black so could sire all four colors. His owner describes his temperament as bold and very intelligent, well mannered and obedient.

He was bred 86 times, but 15 of these breedings did not result in puppies. The beautiful Ch. Highbriar Jasmine was the first champion to be bred to him and this breeding produced five champions out of six puppies, one of which died at a young age and so did not have a chance to finish. He sired a total of 26 champions. Bismarck was a good-sized dog, standing 28½ inches at the shoulder and was 28 inches long. In many ways he was a very controversial dog, probably because his owner had been willing to state in print the faults that had been sired by him as well as the virtues.

Among his outstanding get were: Ch. Weichardt's Rosen Cavalier CD, Ch. Devrin's Black Candy Bismarck, Ch. Peroma's Aztec, Ch. Daredobe's Santonio, Ch. Daredobe's Kash and Ch. Daredobe's Macho CD.

Ch. Highbriar Blackbird CD was the first champion owned by Theodora ("Ted") Linck. Blackbird was purchased from Betsy Thomas as a very young puppy and was from the last litter sired by Ch. Jet v.d. Ravensburg, a big winner in his day. Her dam was Highbriar Stormette CDX, one of the top Obedience Dobes in the country.

Handled by George Rood, Blackbird finished for the title in January of 1960 at the Miami Specialty. She went into Obedience training soon afterward, finishing the C.D. requirements in four shows.

Ch. Haydenhill's Hurrah, 1961–1971, black male owned by R. E. Souders. "The Great Hurrah" is pictured winning Best in Show at Beverly-Riviera show under judge Len Carey, handled by his proud owner. In all, Hurrah won 21 Bests in Show and he was the sire of 28 champions.—*Ludwig*

                                   Ch. Rancho Dobe's Riff
                 Ch. Quo Vadis of Naumanheim
                                 Ch. Hildegarde v. Naumanheim
         Ch. Hallmark of Naumanheim
                                 Ch. Rancho Dobe's Riff
                 Ch. Cinderella of Naumanheim
                                 Ch. Hildegarde v Naumanheim
CH. HAYDENHILL'S HURRAH
                                 Ch. Torn's Desert Gold
                 Ch. Patton's Ponder of Torn
                                 Ch. Meadowmist Berenike
         Ch. Haydenhill's Diana
                                 Ch. Rancho Dobe's Riff
                 Ch. Rancho Dobe's Cointreau
                                 Ch. Rancho Dobe's Roulette

Bred only three times, she produced five Champions, all with the Highbriar prefix, since she was in co-ownership with Betsy Thomas. From her litters by Ch. Florian v. Ahrtal she produced Ch. Highbriar Halla CD, Ch. Highbriar Hasty Road, and Ch. Highbriar Rock Sand. From one litter by Ch. Singendwald's Prince Kuhio she produced Ch. Highbriar American Flag and Ch. Highbriar American Emblem. Hasty Road, owned by Marlyn and Bob Woodside of Pittsburgh, gained his championship in only six shows, being defeated only once. Later he became a Group winner and was Best Opposite Sex to the great Ch. Ru-Mar's Tsushima at the DPCA in 1965. Ch. Highbriar Halla CD was named for a famous horse—as were all eight of the champions co-bred by Ted and Betsy Thomas. Halla the horse had been a world champion jumping mare. At ten months of age the Doberman Halla was the 1961 DPCA Grand Prize Futurity winner and Best Puppy. She finished in short order thereafter, with a Best of Breed from the classes. Shown sparingly as a Special, she then went into Obedience training and gained her C.D. degree in four shows, as her dam had done.

Halla's full sister, Ch. Highbriar Rock Sand was bred to Ch. Ravensburg Falsta and produced the lovely Ch. Highbriar Piping Rock, who in turn was bred to the Felix son, Ch. Tarrado's Corry and produced for her breeder Shirley McCoy, the good sire Ch. Tarrado's Flair.

Ch. Highbriar Valencia was owned by Joe Worman of Columbus, Ohio but due to his work, Ted undertook to get her to the shows for George Rood to handle. Not shown until Open class, Valencia went Best of Breed her first time out and finished in just five weekends.

Ted was able to lease Valencia for two litters and had picked Ch. Cassio v Ahrtal as the sire when he himself was but a puppy. From these two breedings came three champions: Ch. Tedell Red Carpet, owned by Barbara Shourt Hendley, who also went Best of Breed his first time out as a puppy; and two black males, Ch. Tedell Private Label and Ch. Tedell Eleventh Hour, both of whom went on to become Best in Show winners.

Eleventh Hour was purchased as a young puppy by Nancy and Jim Kibiloski of Michigan. He shortly proved his importance to the breed by going Best in Show all-breeds at the tender age of only eight months and eleven days, a record for the breed that still stands. Realizing his potential, Nancy then gave co-ownership to Ted Linck and the campaign began.

Handled as a youngster and finished for the title by William T. Haines, Eleventh Hour then went to Jane Kay in his young adulthood for "the woman's touch." With Jane he topped many Specialties and Groups.

In his full maturity, he went to George Rood, who handled him until his retirement at age five. At his first show with George he went to Best in Show and this was followed by many prestige wins of Groups and Best in Shows.

Among his fourteen champion get to date are many that also accounted for gratifying wins. His blue daughter, Ch. Silent Sentry's Bikini, was best pup-

Ch. Tedell Eleventh Hour, the youngest Doberman to ever go Best in Show—he was just over eight months old! Handled by George Rood for owner Ted Linck.

Ch. Silent Sentry's Bikini, blue daughter of Ch. Tedell's Eleventh Hour ex High Halo's Camelot. Bred by Betty Brockman James, and co-owned by Mrs. James with Karen Wright, who is pictured handling her. Bikini was Best Puppy at the 1968 DPCA Specialty.

py at the DPCA in Houston in 1968. His red son Ch. Misti Morn's Stormi Knight CD was a Canadian Best in Show winner and took major points at the Chicago International the same day that Eleventh Hour topped the breed there. A final count of Eleventh Hour's champion get will be a while coming as puppies from his last litters are just now starting their show careers. His son, Ch. Tedell Indulto v. Ri-Jan's, has had some nice wins and is currently being campaigned.

Early in 1965 Ted Linck acquired from Bill Haines the exquisite black, Ch. Checkmate's Flower Girl, who accounted for many Specialties and Group wins and this bitch was Ted's first Best in Show winner. Flower Girl was sired by Ch. Checkmate's Beau Geste and her dam was Ch. Alemap's Glamour Girl CD. It was a great shame that this lovely bitch was only able to have one litter.

Kilburn Kit, who was Betsy Thomas's foundation bitch, was just bred once and was six years old at the time of her only litter. The sire was Ch. Rancho Dobe's Storm and the litter produced Ch. Highbriar Typhoon CD, whom Betsy kept for herself, and Ch. Highbriar Monsoon CD, who was to compete in the first Top Ten Exhibition held in Chicago in 1957, being rated third in the event.

There was also a litter sister, Stormette, who did not become a champion but was a great Obedience worker. Betsy gave this bitch to her daughter Nancy, and until she died on Christmas day at eleven and a half, she was Nancy's constant companion. Stormette was bred four times; the first was to Ch. Figaro von Mannerheim, who was owned by Frank Mayville, who also trained Stormette for the Obedience title; her second and third litters were sired by Ch. Jet vd Ravensburg, who was owned by Walter and Mae Dencker; and her fourth litter was sired by Ch. Steb's Top Skipper. Stormette was the dam of five champions: Ch. Highbriar Commanche, Ch. Highbriar Seneca, Ch. Highbriar Blackbird—all sired by Jet; and Ch. Highbriar Easy to Love and Ch. Highbriar Tea for Two UD—sired by Top Skipper.

Ch. Highbriar Tea For Two UD was the dam of Ch. Highbriar Jasmine, who became the foundation for Nancy Jo Simons Tarrado's Kennels. Tea for Two was owned by Harold Schobel who trained her for her U.D. degree. She was bred just the one time, to Ch. Florian v. Ahrtal. The other bitch from the litter was Ch. Highbriar Constant Comment, who in turn produced Ch. Highbriar Bandana, the sire of 26 champions.

Jasmine, who like Comment was a black, was the top Working dam of 1967 and her first litter sired by Ch. Alnwick's Black Fury Bismarck was an all-champion litter. She was then bred to Ch. Highbriar Hasty Road for her second litter, and to Ch. Felix v. Ahrtal for her third and fourth litters.

The best known of all the Highbriar dogs is the lovely black Ch. Highbriar Willo of Allenwood, co-bred by Betsy Thomas and Mr. and Mrs. Charles Allen of Ohio. Whelped in 1963, she was sired by Ch. Ravensburg Falsta out of

96

Ch. Highbriar Tea for Two UD, a Top Skipper daugher, owned by Harold Schobel. Dam of Ch. Highbriar Jasmine.

<pre>
                              Ch. Rancho Dobe's Storm
                  Ch. Lakecrest's Thunderstorm
                              Ch. Apache Lady of Lakecrest
          Ch. Florian v Ahrtal
                              Ch. Dorian Ahrtal, CD
                  Ch. Willa v Ahrtal
                              Ch. Elektra v Ahrtal, CD
CH. HIGHBRIAR JASMINE
                              Ch. Dortmund Delly's Colonel Jet
                  Ch. Steb's Top Skipper
                              Damasyn the Easter Bonnet
          Ch. Highbriar Tea For Two, UD
                              Ch. Rancho Dobe's Storm
                  Highbriar Stormette, CDX
                              Kilburn Kit
</pre>

Ch. Highbriar Jasmine, foundation bitch of the Tarrado Kennels, owned by Nancy Jo Simons. Jasmine's first litter was an all-champion litter.

Ch. Highbriar Blackbird CD, the first champion owned by Ted Linck. Blackbird was sired by Ch. Jet vd Ravensburg ex Highbriar Stormette CDX.

Ch. Highbriar Bandana, black sire of 26 champions, owned by Virginia Markley's Hotai Kennels. Shown being handled by Bill Haines to win under judge Derek Rayne.

Ch. Highbriar Easy To Love. The Walter Denckers, who owned the sire, took Willo as a stud fee puppy, but sold her to Betsy when Willo was just four months old, as they were not in a position to keep her at the time.

Willo was handled by Gene Haupt and what a team these two made. She loved him best of all and lived with him and his wife Betty most of her life, only going back to Betsy to whelp her litters. She flew all over the country in Gene's plane and she moved to California with them after they moved there from Ohio. She was retired at the age of three and a half years after winning her 100th Best of Breed, with 42 Group firsts and 8 Bests in Show. She lived to a ripe old age and was with Gene and Betty at her death in 1975.

Ch. El Campeon's Diosa was a black bitch sired by Ch. Dobe Acres Cinnamon ex Ch. Singendwalds Demitasse. Demitasse was a full sister to Ch. Singendwalds Delisal CD, who was a blue. The two sisters did not get along so the Rickerts put her up for sale and she was purchased by some Boxer breeders who bred her to Cinnamon, and she produced a litter of three, all of whom became champions: Diosa, Gallito and Tentadora. However, the people who owned her were then divorced and Tassy was passed from pillar to post until she was rescued by Betsy Thomas. Betsy then repeated the breeding to Cinnamon and this produced two good bitches, Ch. Aphrodite and Ch. Cassandra.

Diosa was purchased by Janie Forbes as a six-week-old puppy and handled to her title by her owner. She finished at just eleven months of age, undefeated in her sex. She won the DPCA once.

Ch. Ru-Mar's Tsushima CD or "Tish" as she was known to all, never had a chance to prove what she could do in the whelping box; she died whelping her one and only litter, the result of being given a drug called Promone that was used in the 1960s to prevent bitches from coming into heat. Many good bitches were lost as a result of this drug or were unable to whelp normal litters. We personally had a bitch who never came into heat again after being on the drug for a short time and she died at age five. The drug was taken off the market, but for Tish it was too late. She died due to uterine inertia following a Caesarian and with her went her eight puppies. She was not quite five years old—what a heart-breaking waste and what a loss to the breed.

However, those of us who were lucky enough to see Tsushima, can never forget her. She was a lovely show bitch and gave her all to her handler Bob Hastings. She was whelped in May 1962 and died April 1967. Her sire was Ch. Rancho Dobes Cello and her dam Ch. Jessamyn II vom Ahrtal. Her breeders were Rudy and Marie Wagner and she was owned by Margaret Carveth. Tish was a personality dog and how could she help it—she came by it honestly. I knew her sire Cello very well since I was friends with his owners, Bob and Connie Sigler, while we were both living in Texas. Cello was a clown to say the least. He was finished very quickly by Rex Vandeventer, who once confided to me "The dog is nuts! Why at the motel, he just stands in front of the bathtub and barks at it." I informed him that all he wanted was for someone to turn on the tap so he could get a drink, "Cello has to drink from a running tap!" He also used to bark at the TV if he wanted it turned off so he could be the center of attention, and he had to have ketchup on his feed. Yes, Cello was a little spoiled, but he was a fun dog.

Tish was shown 170 times, 24 times in the classes and 146 times as a Special. She won 13 Bests in Show all-breeds plus 9 Specialties, 92 Bests of Breed, 43 Groups, and topped the DPCA Specialty in 1965. She won Best in Show at the International in Chicago under Joseph Quirk, who was quoted: "I believe I have judged all the great ones—old Jessy of Fleitmann's, Ferry, Storm and many others and Tish compares most favorably with them."

I have mentioned Tsushima's sire but it would be unforgivable not to also mention her dam, the lovely black Ch. Jessamyn II vom Ahrtal. In 1968 she was rated the Top Producing Working Dam and third Top Producing Dam of All Breeds. She produced 13 champions in four litters by three different sires. Bred first to Cello, this breeding not only produced Tsushima but also Ch. Ru-Mar's Morgansonne CD. She was then bred to Ch. Ebonaire's Gridiron and this produced Ch. Ru-Mar's Pandora CD and Ch. Ru-Mar's Regan v Dartshire.

Jessamyn was owned by Rudy Wagner of Auburn, California, but she was leased for her next two litters by Rod and Margaret Carveth of Tevrac Dobermans. They bred her to Ch. Cassio vom Ahrtal twice and she produced the following champions: Champions Tevrac's Thelonius CD, Tycoon v Ru-Mar CD, Intrepid v Ru-Mar, Tahita CDX, Top of the Mark CD, Triton CD, Miss Tangerine, Titan, Heidi. Several of these were Best in Show winners and also produced Best in Show winners.

Ch. Sultana von Marienburg was the only bitch in a litter bred by George Olenik out of Farley's Princess. Her sire was Ch. Steb's Gunga Din. The litter was whelped in May of 1963 and the lovely black Sultana was sold to Mary Rodgers of California. Even as a small puppy, she was an outstanding example of the breed, and she never went through the awkward stage that most puppies seem to go through while growing up. She was not a large bitch, just 25½" at the shoulder, very short coupled and beautifully balanced. I had the pleasure of seeing her many times both in and out of the ring and she was a joy to watch. She was described by one judge thus, "She is a medium-sized bitch with a delightful personality; she moved expertly and handled on a loose lead, with the ability to set herself up in a correct position without being 'sculptured' in the ring by the person handling her. The practice of hanging a Doberman by its neck and holding the tail while pushing it to make the body appear shorter and change the balance of weight, is one of the most unappealing sights." Her handler Rex Vandeventer would make the most of her showmanship by standing several feet away from her. They were indeed a team and his love for this great bitch was obvious.

Ch. Ru-Mar's Tsushima CD, 1962–1967, whose fantastic winning included 13 Bests in Show and the DPCA Specialty in 1965. Pictured going Best of Breed at Santa Barbara, 1964, under judge C. Ross Hamilton, with Bob Hastings handling. "Tish" was bred by Rudy Wagner, and owned by Margaret Carveth.

				Ch. Rancho Dobe's Riff
			Ch. Rancho Dobe's Bach	
				Ch. Rancho Dobe's Roulette
		Ch. Rancho Dobe's Cello		
				Ch. Rancho Dobe's Primo
			Hannah of Adobe Hill	
				Christina of Adobe Hill
CH. RU-MAR'S TSUSHIMA, CD				
				Ch. Berger's Bluebeard
			Ch. Fortuna's Maestro	
				Ch. Anona von Tamara
		Ch. Jessamyn II vom Ahrtal		
				Alaric v Ahrtal, CDX, TD
			Ch. Zessica vom Ahrtal	
				Ch. Friederun vom Ahrtal

Ch. Rancho Dobe's Cello, black, sire of the great Tsushima. Bred by Brint and Vivian Edwards, and owned by Bob and Connie Sigler.

Ch. Ru-Mar's Morgansonne CD, brother of Tsushima by Ch. Rancho Dobe's Cello ex Ch. Jessamyn II v Ahrtal. Owned and handled by Ruth Morgan.

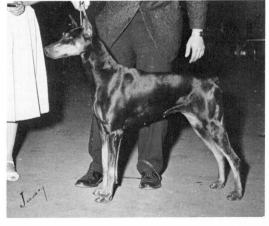

Ch. Jessamyn II v Ahrtal, dam of 13 champions including Tsushima and Morgansonne. Top Producing Working Group dam of 1968. Bred by Tess Henseler, and owned by Rudy Wagner.

Ch. Rudy's Holli-Berri Florowill, a top producing bitch owned by Edward and Florence Williams.

                              Ch. Rancho Dobe's Bach
                    Ch. Rancho Dobe's Cello
                              Hannah of Adobe Hill
          Ch. Ru-Mar's Morgansonne, CD
                              Ch. Fortuna's Maestro
                    Ch. Jessamyn II v Ahrtal
                              Ch. Zessica v Ahrtal
CH. RUDY'S HOLLI-BERRI FLOROWILL
                              Ch. Steb's Top Skipper
                    Ch. Ebonaire's Touchdown
                              Ebonaire's Flashing Star
          Rudy's Miss Samdown
                              Ch. Florian v Ahrtal, CD
                    Samantha v Ahrtal
                              Ch. Zessica v Ahrtal

Ch. Castle Lanes Quereda Miranda, lovely red bitch, Best Puppy at the 1972 DPCA Specialty. Bred by Larry Clardy, Miranda is a daughter of Ch. Damasyn Carley of Jerseystone.

103

Sultana's sire, Gunga Din, was a dog with a great personality and he was really smart with a fantastic ability to open doors and latches, something his daughter inherited from him; she also had a great sense of humor. It was a shame that Gunga Din died just before Sultana was whelped, so the breeding could not be repeated.

As a show dog Sultana was one of the best the breed has ever seen and her show record is most impressive. She won the Group from the Open class at the Northwestern Connecticut Dog Club in September 1964 under William Kendrick and completed her championship two months later by going Best of Breed from Open for a three point major. In August of 1965 she completed her Canadian championship by going all the way to Best In Show for a five point major. In September of the same year she was shown in Mexico where she won the Group. Later in her career, at age of seven, she returned to Mexico and completed her championship there by going to Best in Show.

Sultana had many handlers. She was shown by Jane Forsyth in the classes, by Ellen Hoffman in Canada, and was also handled by her owner Mary Rodgers, by Dick Sufficool, Jack Dexter, Larry Downey and finally by Rex Vandeventer and his wife Leota. With Rex she skyrocketed to the top of the standings in 1967. She had 26 Bests in Show, 58 Group firsts, and won the National Speciality in 1967 and again in 1968. This last win was particularly outstanding for Sultana as her first litter was just three months old.

While she was a sensation in the show ring, as a producer Sultana only had a total of ten puppies in four litters. Her first litter in July of 1968 was sired by Ch. Marienburg's Maximillian. And although Max was a red dog, her puppies were all black and rust. Out of these five puppies came three champion daughters: Ch. Marienburg's Copy of Sultana, Ch. Marienburg's Black Onyx and Ch. Marienburg's Portrait in Black. Mary Rodgers kept Portrait and Copy. Sultana's second litter of three whelped in September 1969 was sired by Ch. Gra-Lemor Demetrius vd Victor. Some of these died at an early age for one reason or another. The breeding to Max was repeated for her third litter and produced just one puppy, Marienburg's Unique d'Sultana. Sultana was then bred to Ch. Marienburg's Red Baron and again produced just one puppy, a lovely black bitch, Ch. Marienburg's Only One. This bitch was also kept by her breeder and at the 1972 National Speciality was selected Best Junior in the Futurity.

Sultana died at the age of eleven years with the cancer that had spread all through her body. Her total show record was 37 all breed Bests in Show, 94 Group firsts, and 148 Bests of Breed including ten Specialties. In answer to all the questions that are asked pertaining to the "cowlick" — "Doesn't that count against them in the ring?" — Sultana had a rather prominent cowlick down the back of her neck!

Ch. Rancho Dobe's Maestro (April 1964-February 1972), was the most famous of Ch. Haydenhill's Hurrah's get. A black dog, Maestro was out of

Ch. Sultana v Marienburg, 1963–1974, bred by George Olenik and owned by Mary Rodgers, winner of 26 Bests in Show. Pictured here in her win of the Group at Del Monte, 1967, under judge Phil Marsh, with Rex Vandeventer handling.

<pre>
                              Ch. Dortmund Delly's Colonel Jet
              Ch. Steb's Top Skipper
                              Damasyn the Eastern Bonnet
       Ch. Steb's Gunga Din
                              Damasyn the Captain Sabre
              Ebonaire's Flashing Star
                              Damasyn the Flash
CH. SULTANA VON MARIENBURG
                              Haydenhill's Dedicate
              Ch. Patton's Prince Quillo
                              Ch. Haydenhill's Delight
       Farley's Princess
                              Aristo von Gotenberg
              Gerda von Juareg
                              Doberman Down's Foli
</pre>

Rancho Dobe's Lotto, and was owned by Karen and Corky Vroom. He was always beautifully handled by Corky and was the winner of 17 Bests in Show, 4 Specialties and 68 Group firsts.

Dick Souders, owner of Hurrah, had leased Lotto from Vivian and Brint Edwards of Rancho Dobe fame, so she could be bred to Hurrah. Dick sold Maestro to Karen Vroom (then Karen McClary) and he took his first points at his first two shows, from the puppy class. He was handled to his title by C.D. Lawrence who also handled him to his first Best in Show win.

After Karen's marriage to Corky, "Mo" as he was called, was handled by Corky and the two chalked up quite a record. He was initially retired at the end of 1968, but in June of 1969 his owner brought him out again and he went Best in Show at the Kennel Club of Pasadena. In only five months of showing that year he was the No. 2 Top Winning Doberman. In 1970 Maestro really hit a winning streak and was the Number One Working dog. It is also interesting that he tied with his son Ch. The Maestro's Reflection for the DPCA award for "Most Specialties Won". His last win was Group first at Antelope Valley Kennel Club in December of 1970 when he was close to seven years old. He was in superb condition and still sound as a bell. He seemed to have lost none of his elegance. Unfortunately, like so many of his breed, this great dog was lost to cancer just before his eighth birthday. He was the sire of eight champions.

Ch. Dolph von Tannenwald was bred by Charles and Kay Etner and sold as a young puppy to Virginia Gaddis of Atlanta. He was handled to his title by Michele Leathers. This handsome black dog was small by comparison to most top winning males. He was just 27¼" inches at the shoulder, but he was well put together and a very sound moving dog. He was sired by Ch. Ambradobe's Choirmaster and his dam was the lovely top producing Ch. Kay Hill's Witch Soubretta. It was Soubretta's breeder Jane Kay who suggested the breeding to Choirmaster.

In the fall of 1969 George and Sheila West asked their young handler Jeffrey Brucker to find them a top champion male good enough to campaign. Jeff had first seen Dolph at the National Specialty in Houston and liked everything about him except his size, as he looked small against the rest of the Specials. But he was impressed with his flawless gait and when he heard that the dog might be for sale, he flew to Atlanta with George West to take another look at the dog. A few days later Dolph was shipped to his new home in New York and he became part of the West family.

Dolph started his show career with Jeff on the 1970 Florida circuit. He certainly proved that even a small dog can win if he is also sound, as he won 28 Bests in Show, 78 Group firsts and 209 Bests of Breed, along with six specialty Bests of Breed. He was also Best of Breed at Westminster.

In 1971, Dolph was not only the top winning dog but also the top sire for that year. He spent a great deal of his life with Jeff and Betty Brucker, even

Ch. Rancho Dobe's Maestro, 1964–1972, sired by Ch. Haydenhill's Hurrah ex Rancho Dobe's Lotto. Winner of 17 Bests in Show, 4 Specialties and 68 Groups. Owned by Corky and Karen Vroom. (Pictured being handled by Corky to win under judge O. C. Harriman.)

Ch. Audrey's Orbital Fancy, winner of 6 Bests in Show in the 1960s, pictured winning Best of Breed under G. Plaga. Fancy was owned by Audrey Schambon and handled by Stanley Flowers.

107

going on their honeymoon! He always slept on their bed so it seemed fitting when it was found that he had cancer, that he be allowed to spend his last days with them. He died in June of 1972.

As previously stated, I first saw Ch. Gra-Lemor Demetrius v.d. Victor when I judged the Quaker City Futurity in Philadelphia in December of 1966. This gorgeous black dog was then but an eleven month old puppy and when he walked into the ring with his handler, Monroe Stebbins, I could not take my eyes off him. I knew right then that it would take a mighty good one to beat him that day and he was my Grand Prize Futurity winner. In the regular classes he won the puppy class under the German judge Herr Willi Rothfuss. He finished his championship very quickly.

Demetri was whelped in February of 1966; he was sired by Ch. Damasyn Derringer ex Jerry Run's Boo Sprite. His breeder-owner is Grace Moore of Pennsylvania. He is a large dog, 29" at the shoulders; he has great substance coupled with elegance, an iron strong topline, excellent angulation both front and rear, a deep brisket and full forechest, and a lovely head and long elegant neck. To fault him, he could have slightly better feet. Some have stated that he has bad temperament as he is a male who hates other males and he has shown this at times. However, he has lived all his life in a home full of children with whom he has gotten along beautifully. I have personally had several litters sired by him and the temperament of his puppies has always been ideal.

Demetrius was shown to his title in the East handled by Monroe Stebbins, who is now a field representative for the American Kennel Club. So that he could be used at stud on the West Coast, he was then sent to California, where he was handled by Mike Shea. He is a Best in Show and Group winner. To date he has sired forty champions but this number will no doubt be increased as he is still at limited stud.

The list could go on and on, and fill many books. I have tried here to pick from among the great ones, those that have had strongest impact on our breed. In addition, some whose renown is more recent, are pictured throughout the book with fuller captions that tell their story. I fully realize that there have been many others deserving of recognition, and apologize that the limitation of space has denied them mention.

108

Ch. Dolph von Tannenwald, top Doberman winner and sire of 1971, whose career winning includes 28 Bests in Show, 78 Groups and 6 Specialties. Bred by Charles and Kay Etner, owned by George and Sheila West, and handled by Jeffrey Brucker.

Ch. Axel von Tannenwald, 1960s winner of 5 all-breed Bests in Show and 13 Specialties, and sire of 7 champions. Owned by Norton and Betty Moore.

Miss Tess Henseler in 1975 with two of her Ahrtal puppies.

Meadowmist Isis of Ahrtal, 1948–1957, pictured at seven years of age. Isis, foundation bitch of Ahrtal Kennels, was dam of 17 champions.

6

Current Doberman Kennels of the United States

In THE PRECEDING CHAPTER, we have saluted some of the outstanding dogs—let us now turn to the kennels.

The demand for a good guard type dog in America has never been so great
as it is today. At the same time, people still want the type of dog that can be a
family pet as well, and the Doberman certainly fits the bill. Luckily, there are
still breeders who are deeply concerned with the preservation of this wonderful breed and are trying their best to see that it does not "go down the drain,"
as has been the fate of so many other breeds when they became too popular.

It is quite impossible to cover all the many kennels and individuals that
have helped—and are helping—make the breed what it is today, but we will
try to note the more prominent ones.

Tess Henseler's Ahrtal Kennels have so far produced 64 chamipions. Tess
came over from Germany to manage a horse farm and acquired her first Doberman in the early 1940s. He was named Hasso vom Ahrtal and Tess bought
him as a six-month-old puppy simply with the idea that he would be a good
farm dog. Horses were her whole life and she was an excellent rider and trainer, and at that time had no intention of breeding dogs. However, she did become very interested in Obedience training and Hasso was trained to his
C.D.X. A serious riding accident ended her career in large animal husbandry,
so she turned to training dogs. In 1947 she bought a two year old bitch and
named her Kriemhild v Ahrtal. This bitch was sired by Ch. Favoriet v Franzhof and became Tess's constant companion for nearly fourteen years. She
made her C.D. in three shows and then was shown some in conformation but
did not finish her championship. She was bred to Ch. Emperor of Marienland
owned by Virginia Knauer and from this breeding, which resulted in just three

puppies, came Tess's first homebred champion and the only one not carrying the Ahrtal name. This was Ch. Meadowmist Elegy owned by Mrs. Knauer. (Mrs. Knauer, a past president of the Doberman Pinscher Club of America, has attained national prominence in other areas—at this writing, she is Assistant to the President of the United States in charge of consumer affairs.)

Tess conducted classes in Obedience at Moravian College in Bethlehem, Pennsylvania for eight years plus classes for various dog clubs. Having watched the famous Lippinzaner horses of Vienna, Austria, she got the idea of a dog drill team and her first team consisted of twenty dogs of different breeds. They gave performances at children's hospitals and other institutions and also each year at the Rittenhouse Square, Philadelphia dog show. Then the idea struck her that an all-Doberman team performing in time to music, would come even closer to the performance of the Lippinzaners. She had 16 Dobermans in this team, with one extra stand-in. Only four of these dogs were owned by the handlers. She was then asked to bring the team to the Westminster show and this performance brought much favorable publicity for our breed. The evening performance was televised for the full twenty minutes.

Tess Henseler has been the leading breeder eight times over the years and is still breeding on a limited basis, as well as being a respected judge.

There is a new Drill Team now, the Northern California Drill Team with Rosalie Simpson at the helm. They put on a different type of performance, with the Dobermans doing such feats as going over a very high jump with a raw egg in their mouths, and then going through a tunnel and finally bringing the egg to the handler who breaks it in a bowl to prove that it is still intact! Dogs and handlers alike wear beautiful blue and white uniforms and a performance that I got to see at the Doberman Pinscher Club of America Specialty in San Diego was very impressive and enjoyed by everyone who was lucky enough to attend. It is hoped that more teams of this type will be organized, for they show that our breed has brains as well as beauty.

In the Midwest is the kennel of Jack and Eleanor Brown of St. Charles, Missouri. Their first Doberman was named Hallwyre's Herr Klown CD and he came from the kennel of Forest Hall in Texas, a kennel better known for Wire Fox Terriers. (Mr. Hall was an all-breeds judge for many years.) Then in 1945 Jack gave Eleanor a Christmas present that was to change both their lives. This was the lovely red bitch, Ch. Dow's Dame of Kilburn, who was sired by Ch. Dictator v. Glenhugel ex Ch. Dows Dodie v Kienlesburg. (Dame was bred by Marge Kilburn, who had leased Dodie from Bert Dow and bred her to Dictator. Dame went to Mr. Dow as part of the lease agreement.) Dame was already ten years old when I first saw her and even at that age she was lovely.

The Browns have produced a total of 41 champions. They have always given much of their time and efforts to helping the novice owners and breeders

112

Hallwyre's Herr Klown CD and Ch. Dow's Dame of Kilburn, the first Dobermans owned by Jack and Eleanor Brown of St. Charles, Missouri. Dame, sired by Ch. Dictator v Glenhugel ex Ch. Dow's Dodie v Kienlesburg, was the Brown's foundation bitch.

Ch. Brown's Adventuress, by Ch. Alcor v Millsdod ex Ch. Dow's Dame of Kilburn. This lovely black bitch, bred and owned by Eleanor Brown, was the dam of eight champions.

113

and their home was always open to anyone who needed help or advice. Jack used to handle most of their dogs and did a beautiful job. He was a hard one to beat back in the 1950s and 1960s.

With notable kennels in the Midwest we must include Marks-Tey Kennels at Centralia, Illinois, owned by my husband Keith and myself. Like the Browns, we have based our breeding on a strong concentration of Dictator. Keith is an all-breeds handler and he has finished many of the over forty champions who carry the Marks-Tey prefix. I have been involved with dogs in one way or another, both in my native England and here, for most of my life. Our foundation bitch was the lovely Ch. Damasyn the Waltzing Brook CD, purchased from Peggy Adamson as a nine-week-old puppy in 1955. Keith and I are convinced that the good temperament for which Marks-Tey dogs are noted, comes from our foundation bitch.

D-Dow's Dobermans was owned by David and Helen Dow of Kansas City, Missouri and this couple, who are now gone, certainly did their share for the breed in the Midwest. Helen did a great deal of research on pedigrees and worked hard to perfect the best guidelines methods of raising and feeding puppies. She helped many novices with advice on puppy care and I for one learned a great deal from her. They purchased Ch. Brown's Feegee from Jack and Eleanor Brown and she proved to be one of the breed's great producers.

Other kennels in this area who have also done some excellent breeding include: Centre Dobes of Francis and Phyllis Willmeth, Castle Lane owned by Larry and Shirley Clardy and Kismet owned by Don and Dee Roberts. And, of course, there are others.

The well-known Damasyn Kennels of Peggy Adamson is in Long Island, New York. A kennel is usually founded on a top bitch but it has to be the great Ch. Dictator v Glenhugel who really put this kennel on the map. Over the years, Mrs. Adamson has worked as much towards temperament as she has for conformation, and believes as I do, that a Doberman should have brains as well as beauty and that these brains should be put to use. All her dogs are trained and beautifully behaved. She has been assisted for some years by Carol Selzle who is a top handler. Damasyn has produced 32 champions since 1955 alone. (I do not have a record of how many were finished before that time.) She is not only a licensed judge for several breeds who has judged in many countries around the world, but is also a writer of great merit and her articles have appeared in all the leading dog magazines at home and abroad. Mrs. Adamson is also a past President of the Doberman Pinscher Club of America.

Ebonaire Kennels is also located in New York and is owned by Edward and Judy Weiss. Their dogs are also founded on the Dictator lines and over twenty champions have been bred by them. Their Ebonaire's Flashing Star was the

114

Ch. Wilmar's Arrow, an older brother of Chs. Brown's Dion and Bridget, owned by Wilma Anderson.

Ch. Checkmate's Beau Geste, a Ch. Brown's Dion son. This big impressive dog was owned and handled by Bill Haines.

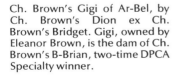

Ch. Brown's Gigi of Ar-Bel, by Ch. Brown's Dion ex Ch. Brown's Bridget. Gigi, owned by Eleanor Brown, is the dam of Ch. Brown's B-Brian, two-time DPCA Specialty winner.

115

dam of the famous football litter of five champions. They have sent several good dogs overseas to help the breeding programs in other countries.

Elfred Kennels, also in New York, is owned by Ellen Hoffman, who is a professional handler. Her homebred Ch. Elfred's Spark Plug was also a Bermudian, Canadian, Mexican, Colombian and CACIB champion. "Sparky", as he was called, was a dominant black, and the sire of several champions. He finished his American title at just 13 months of age with two 5-point majors at Specialty shows, and was the first Doberman to earn three titles before he was two years old. A large, impressive dog, "Sparky" did a lot of winning for his owner-handler.

An up and coming new kennel in this area is Alisation, owned by the young mother and daughter duo, JoAnn and Gwen Satalino. Few of us will forget the thrill we shared with Gwen when her lovely young bitch, just a year old and shown by her in the Bred by Exhibitor class, won the points at the National Specialty in Washington, D.C. in 1973. This was her lovely Ch. Alisation's Kinderwicke, who jumped right up into her young owner's arms when the judge pointed to her for Winners, as the crowd roared their approval. Some lovely dogs are being bred by these two ladies.

Other kennels that have done well in the East include: Gemae, owned by George and Mae White; Triadel owned by Jeanne Hendricks, who is one of our newer handlers; Barricade, owned by Agnes Johnson; Biggin Hill, owned by Norman and Phyllis Biggin. The Biggins moved to the United States from England several years ago and have introduced German blood into their line through their Ch. Biggin Hill's Alarich who was sired by Ch. Cassio v Ahrtal out of the German bitch Citta vom Sirrahwald, who goes back to the Furstenfeld line. Norman is also a judge.

Rosemond Valentine's Rosevale Kennels has bred several champions of note and are active in breeding and showing. Srigo Kennel of Mrs. Felicia Luburich breed Rottweillers as well as Dobermans and have had success with both. Barbara Kirfel's Arabar Kennels, Kay Martin's Civetta Kennels and Dr. Arnold Orlander's Kami Kennels are making a good impression. Marilyn Meshirer of Brandendorf has bred several good blues and done well with them. Of particular note is her Ch. Brandendorf Periwinkle. Marilyn is also a judge.

Jane Kay is another breeder who has turned from breeding and handling to judging. Her Kay Hill Kennels are known the world over and have produced some outstanding records. Jane was for many years one of our most successful all-breed handlers. She was first located in Harrisburg, Pennsylvania and then in Virginia where she owned a real show place of a kennel with 300 runs. She handled many of the country's top dogs of many different breeds, at all the major shows. She retired from handling in 1970 and she and her husband Harold moved to Florida, where they still live and Jane is busy judging. Jane

Ch. Ebonaire's Flying Tackle, another of the famous "Football Litter" sired by Ch. Steb's Top Skipper ex Ebonaire's Flashing Star. Owned by Sue Neville, Shinya Kennels. Pictured being handled by Johnny Long to win under judge Charles Hamilton.

Ch. Ebonaire's Balestra, another of the famous "Football Litter" who was a constant companion for her owner-breeders, Edward and Judy Weiss. Yet another sister was sent to Australia.

Ch. Wahlmar's Baroness CD (1957–1966), by Ch. Brown's Hobgoblin ex Barbarosa v Siegerstadt. This lovely bitch was the foundation for Pat and Judy Doniere's Toledobe Kennels. She produced six champions sired by Ch. Brown's Dion and Ch. Alemaps Checkmate.

Ch. Toledobe's Linebacker, 1966 DPCA Specialty winner. By Ch. Ebonaire's Touchdown ex Ch. Toledobe's Covergirl, this outstanding black was bred by Pat and Judy Doniere and owned by Loren Nichols.

Ch. Damsyn Carly of Jerseystone, black male sired by Ch. Damasyn Derringer ex Toledobe's Misty Moonlight. Owned by Pat and Judy Doniere.

was the breeder of 39 champions and since these came out of just 21 litters, percentage-wise she bred more champions for the number of litters whelped than any breeder in the United States.

Toledobe Kennels is owned by Pat and Judy Doniere of Toledo, Ohio. Judy started in Dobermans at an early age with an unregistered bitch by the name of "Champ" who lived to be 15 years old. When Champ was about eleven, Judy married Pat and it was a case of "Love me, love my dog!" — and soon Pat was handling Dobermans for Judy. Their first champion was purchased from Bob and Peggy Wahl. (Bob has also turned to judging.) This bitch was Ch. Wahlmar's Baroness and Judy handled this one herself. Baroness was almost pure Brown's breeding so it was only natural that Jack and Eleanor Brown should influence their breeding program. Baroness was bred to Ch. Alemaps Checkmate, but this first litter was a disaster as they came down with the dreaded hardpad. However, one bitch was able to finish her championship and this was Ch. Toledobe's Barbiturate. The breeding was then repeated and produced four champions: Checkmates Chessman, Toledobe Classic Cameo, T. Chancellor and T. Covergirl. Covergirl was the only black; the rest were all reds.

The top winning Doberman bred by the Donieres was Ch. Toledobe's Linebacker, a son of Ch. Ebonaire's Touchdown ex Ch. Toledobe's Covergirl. In 1966, Linebacker won Best of Breed at the Doberman Pinscher Club of America in Kansas City and his brother Quarterback was the Grand Prize Futurity Winner at the same show. When Quarterback suddenly died, the Donieres were able to acquire Ch. Damasyn Carly of Jerseystone from Peggy Adamson. Carly was four and a half years old and Peggy did not have time to campaign him. Carly adjusted perfectly to the new home with children including a baby of five months. By the time he was five years old he was a champion.

Carly became the sire of another dog that gave Judy a great thrill, the lovely red bitch Ch. Castle Lane's Querida Miranda, bred by Larry Clardy. Miranda won the Futurity at the 1972 National Specialty and went on to finish her title at just twelve months of age, with all but two points from the puppy class! Pat is a judge and Judy has just been awarded her provisional judge's license.

Bill Haines and Jack Hronek were the joint owners of Checkmate Kennels in Ohio. Twenty-four champions have come from this kennel thus far. Bill is a professional handler and has carried on alone after Jack's tragic death. More recently Bill's home was burnt down but luckily none of his dogs were lost. He lost many of his records and personal effects but fortunately his photo albums were on loan to the DPCA and were saved. They contain many lovely pictures of Ch. Alemaps Checkmate and his get.

Another Ohio breeder is Betsy Thomas of Highbriar fame. This kennel has produced over 25 champions to date and no doubt more will be added to this list. Betsy's foundation bitch was Kilburn Kit. Betsy Thomas and Ted Linck

Ch. Alemaps Checkmate, by Ch. Steb's Top Skipper ex Brooknelle Roxanne. This top winning black male of the mid-1960s was owned by Bill Haines.

Ch. Delegate vd Elbe
Ch. Dortmund Delly's Colonel Jet
Tauzieher Lady Ambercrest
Ch. Steb's Top Skipper
Ch. Rancho Dobe's Storm
Damasyn the Easter Bonnet
Damasyn Sikhandi
CH. ALEMAPS CHECKMATE
Ch. Delegate vd Elbe
Ch. Dortmund Delly's Colonel Jet
Tauzieher Lady Ambercrest
Brooknelle Roxanne
Ch. Brown's Eric
Brown's Lydia
Ch. Brown's Adventuress

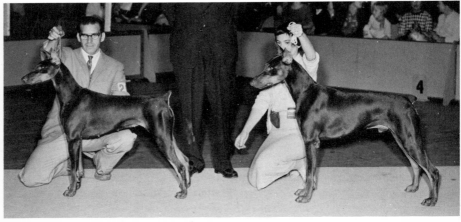

Sister and brother—Ch. Toledobe's Barbiturate (at 1½ years) and Ch. Checkmate's Chessman (at 8 months)—winning Best of Breed and Best Opposite. They were from matings of Ch. Alemaps Checkmate ex Ch. Wahlmar's Baroness, and were bred by Pat and Judy Doniere.

were co-breeders for several years, until Ted branched out to breed under the Tedell name.

Ted Linck, like a great many people, started out by being interested in Obedience. In 1955, she joined the Toledo Kennel Club for which she became an Obedience instructor for many years. She then became director of conformation training. She was a founding member and active in the Maumee Valley Doberman Pinscher Club, and has served as President and in other offices for this club. She is also on the board of the DPCA and twice was the chairman of the committee that put out the Breeders Directory.

Tarrado Kennels, owned by Nancy Simons, was founded on Highbriar dogs and her foundation bitch was the lovely Ch. Highbriar Jasmine. This kennel has produced several good champions including the well-known Ch. Tarrado's Corry who has been an excellent sire.

Singendwalds Kennels was owned by Dale and Bea Rickert of Indianapolis, Indiana. Dale has been dead for several years and Bea now lives in Florida. This kennel has bred some excellent dogs, including the great winner and sire of the early '60s, Ch. Singendwalds Prince Kuhio. Also well remembered are the litter sisters, the black Ch. Singendwalds Demitasse and the blue Ch. Singendwalds Delisal CD, shown in the mid-50s. They were sired by Ch. Delegate vd Elbe out of the blue bitch, Ch. Lydeomel's Azure of Gracewood.

Mae Downing's Mikadobe's Kennels have produced close to twenty champions over the years. This kennel is located in Georgia and was another founded on Dictator breeding. The Downings lived in Japan for several years and had their Ch. Mikado vd Elbe there with them. He was sired by Ch. Dacki vd Elbe ex the Dictator daughter, Damasyn the Bat, whom they also owned. Ch. Mikadobe's Cupid is one of our more recent winners and he is the sire of several champions.

Grace Moore, who is now a judge, is the owner of the Gra-Lemor kennels near Philadelphia. Her foundation bitch was a blue, Venture's Blue Waltz, whom she acquired from Mrs. Eleanor Carpenter of the famous Jerry-Run Kennels. (Mrs. Carpenter is no longer breeding, but has in past years done a great deal for the breed. This lovely lady has been very active in the National Breed Club, and helped write the Standard that we now have. She helped Grace Moore plan her breedings when she first started out.) Ch. Gra-Lemor Demetrius v.d. Victor is a product of Jerry-Run and Damasyn breeding, and many other top dogs and bitches have followed.

The largest kennel on the West Coast at this time is the Marienburg Kennels owned by Mary Rodgers of El Cajon, California. Her dogs are always beautifully handled by Moe Miyagawa. This kennel has produced at least twenty champions with many more on the way. Ch. Marienburg Sun Hawk, a lovely red dog is doing his share of winning Groups and Bests in Show and proving to be a good sire, too.

121

Commander Kennels, owned by Mr and Mrs Bob Bender, has produced quite a few champions, plus dogs with Obedience degrees. Bob is a member of the Sacramento Police Department and uses his Dobermans in his work. He is also a licensed breed judge.

Tamarak, owned by Doris Nemeth; Amor Nature Kennels, owned by Gerry and Barbara Gains who are both professional handlers; Montwood Kennels, owned by Vic Monteleon, who is a very active member of NASA (North American Working Dog Association) the governing and licensing body for all Schutzhund Trials in the United States and North America, are all still active and breeding some top Dobermans.

Rancho Dobe and Haydenhill are names that cannot be forgotten as both have produced many outstanding winners and producers over the years. The great Ch. Rancho Dobe's Storm appears in many of our pedigrees. This kennel was owned by Brint and Vivian Edwards who started out in the breed way back in 1939. Their foundation bitch was Juno of Moorpark C.D. and her first litter was sired by the German import Ch. Ferry v Rauhfelsen of Giralda. The Edwards started to use the kennel prefix of Rancho Dobe in 1943; prior to that they used Moorpark.

Ch. Rancho Dobe's Cointreau was the foundation bitch for the Haydenhill Kennels, owned by Barney and Myrtle Hayden. Ch. Haydenhill's Hurrah was one of the best known dogs from this kennel.

Kamric is the prefix used by Nancy Hogans of Carmel Valley, California. Nancy is the daughter of the well known Dick and Helen Kamerer who formerly lived in Illinois and bred under the Damasyn prefix for several years. Helen is a judge and she has judged the National Specialty several times. Her Ch. Loron's Aviator won the DPCA Specialty in 1974, handled by Nancy. He is sired by Ch. Marks-Tey Shawn CD ex Ch. Rosevale's Little Nip of Loron and his breeders are Ronald and Loretta Batacao. The Kamerers purchased this dog as a puppy after Helen judged the DPCA in Miami, Florida where she put up his dam for Best of Breed. When she found out that Little Nip was to be bred to Shawn, whom she had always admired greatly, she had to have one of the puppies. Since there were only two in the litter, both males, Helen picked "Ricky" as he is called. He finished his championship very fast.

Nancy Hogans is Chairman of the DPCA Archives and has done a fantastic job of presenting them each year at the National Specialty. She has recently followed in her mother's footsteps and is now a judge. She is the owner of Shawn's full sister, Ch. Marks-Tey Sonnet.

Other well-known kennels in California are: Karellmar, owned by Thoral (Brick) and Marie Warner; Rehli, owned by Anne Woodruff; Annheim, owned by Ann Mayer; Morgansonne, owned by Ruth Morgan; Shinya, owned by Sue Neville. This last kennel has produced more than ten champions, some of which were sent to Sue's home-land of Japan. Barbara Flores was tied with Joanna Walker for leading breeder in 1975.

Ch. Loron's Aviator, Best of Breed at the 1974 Doberman Pinscher Club of America Specialty. "Ricky" (as he is known to his owners) is by Ch. Marks-Tey Shawn CD ex Ch. Rosevale's Little Nip of Loron. Bred by Ronald Batacao, he is owned by Helen Kamerer and Nancy Hogans and handled by Gene Haupt (pictured).

Ch. Rosevale's Little Nip of Loron, dam of Ch. Loron's Aviator, and like him a DPCA Best of Breed winner. This black bitch, sired by Ch. Marks-Tey's High Hat ex Rosevale's Velvet Lady, was handled by Al Kirby.

123

In Hawaii we have Mary Leser, owner of Von Cort Kennels and Hanadobe owned by Ken and Aileen Hanaumi. Both of these kennels are active in breeding and showing. Mary has done a lot of humane work on the island.

Kay and Charles Etner are the owners of Tannenwald Kennels in Houston, Texas. "Chuck" was recently President of the Doberman Pinscher Club of America and is also a licensed judge. Their kennel has produced many champions over the years and they are still breeding, but on a small scale due to Kay's ill health.

In Dallas, Texas is the Florowill Kennels of Ed and Florence Williams. They were the leading breeders in 1974. In the 1950s they were fairly active in showing and breeding and then had to quit due to Florence's ill health. They owned Ch. Damasyn the Pert Patrice and Ch. West Begins Sabrina. In 1966 they purchased Ch. Rudy's Holli-Berri Florowill from Rudy Proffitt, and she finished at eighteen months with three majors, handled by Ed Bracy who was one of our top handlers for many years and is now a respected judge. Holli proved to be a wonderful producer and to date is the dam of 15 champions with more on the way. She was first bred to Ch. Cassio v Ahrtal and this produced two champions; then to Ch. Gra-Lemor Demetrius vd Victor and this produced three champions; her third litter was by Ch. Highland Satan's Image and this has so far produced five champions; her fourth litter was by Ch. Gambolwood's Hellelujah and this, too, has produced five champions. A repeat of this breeding was made, and the puppies are just starting to be shown.

Also in Dallas is Dobereich owned by John and Joanie Fisher, owners of Ch. Tevrac's Top of the Mark CD, a lovely red Cassio son ex Ch. Jessamyn II vom Ahrtal. This dog has sired many champions including Ch. Brown's B-Brian, who won the DPCA twice. This kennel has so far produced 12 champions, and as it is one of the newer kennels, no doubt more are on the way.

Virginia Markley of Hotai Kennels is located in Ohio. This kennel is best known for the black dog, Ch. Highbriar Bandana, who has proven to be a top sire, with 26 champion offspring already to his credit. The foundation for this kennel was Tamerlane Alert Abbie, a Ch. Derek of Marks-Tey daughter ex Ch. Ladaska's Ebony Charm. Mrs. Markley's kennel has bred more than 12 champions to date.

In Florida is the Kai Esa Kennels of Mrs. Tommie Jones. Her Ch. Dobedach's Kai Esa is the dam of five champions, sired by Ch. Agony Acres Devotee of Zeno, who is owned by Nancy Wood of Maine. Zeno, a Ch. Singendwalds Prince Kuhio son, who was whelped in 1966 and died in 1971, stands as the sire of eleven champions.

Also in Florida are the kennels of Grace Apollony, who breeds under the prefix of Invicta Dobes; Arjean, owned by Arthur and Jean Conwell, which has produced over ten champions; Belbravo, owned by Luis and Connie Beltran; Bar-Lock, owned by Vic and Donna Blackburn; Roy El owned by Roy and Evelyn Smith; and Hollywoods, owned by Dean Fike.

124

A trio of top Highbriar bitches: *Right,* Ch. Highbriar Halla CD, co-bred by Ted Linck and Betsy Thomas, pictured going Best Puppy at DPC of Michigan Specialty under judge Denver Dale, with George Rood handling. Halla was also best puppy and Futurity winner at the 1961 Doberman Pinscher Club of America Specialty.

Ch. Highbriar Constant Comment (dam of the famous sire Ch. Highbriar Bandana) is pictured winning her first major from the puppy class in 1963, under judge Robert Waters, with George Rood handling.

Ch. Highbriar Valencia, owned by Joe Warman and handled by George Rood, being shown to win under Mrs. Bea Godsol. Valencia, who became the dam of Best in Show winners Ch. Tedell's Eleventh Hour and Ch. Tedell's Private Label, was Best of Breed her first time in the ring, and finished in just five weekends.

125

There are many, many more good kennels, names such as Encore, Mattappany, Gayamon, Gambolwoods, Shadow Run, Pamelot, Ri-Jan, Redjack, High Halo, Lujac, Moorwood Manor, Housecarl, Windrush, Silent Sentry—the list goes on and each year new names are added as new stars appear. But let us not forget the kennels of the past who are gone or no longer active, names such as Colstar, Runicast, Elblac, Ravensburg, Jan-Har, Meadowmist, Dobe-Acres, Dows, and breeders such as Bill Roach, Glenn Staines, Helen Rundle to name just a few, for they gave a great contribution to this wonderful breed.

Ch. Egothel's All American, black male, sired by Ch. Steb's Top Skipper ex Donar the Windstorm, a top winner and top sire of the 1960s. Owned by Bernard J. Gallagher of Philadelphia, and handled by Monroe Stebbins.

7

Official AKC Standard for the Doberman Pinscher

General Conformation and Appearance—The appearance is that of a dog of medium size, with a body that is square; the height, measured vertically from the ground to the highest point of the withers, equalling the length measured horizontally from the forechest to the rear projection of the upper thigh.

Height—at the withers—**Dogs**—26 to 28 inches, ideal about $27^1/2$ inches; **Bitches**—24 to 26 inches, ideal about $25^1/2$ inches. Length of head, neck and legs in proportion to length and depth of body. Compactly built, muscular and powerful, for great endurance and speed. Elegant in appearance, of proud carriage, reflecting great nobility and temperament. Energetic, watchful, determined, alert, fearless, loyal and obedient.

The judge shall dismiss from the ring any shy or vicious Doberman.
Shyness—A dog shall be judged fundamentally shy if, refusing to stand for examination, it shrinks away from the judge; if it fears an approach from the rear; if it shies at sudden and unusual noises to a marked degree.
Viciousness—A dog that attacks or attempts to attack either the judge or its handler, is definitely vicious. An aggressive or belligerent attitude towards other dogs shall not be deemed viciousness.

Head—Long and dry, resembling a blunt wedge in both frontal and profile views. When seen from the front, the head widens gradually toward the base of the ears in a practically unbroken line. Top of skull flat, turning with slight stop to bridge of muzzle, with muzzle line extending parallel to top line of skull. Cheeks flat and muscular. Lips lying close to jaws. Jaws full and powerful, well filled under the eyes.

127

Eyes—Almond shaped, moderately deep set, with vigorous, energetic expression. Iris, of uniform color, ranging from medium to darkest brown in black dogs; in reds, blues, and fawns the color of the iris blends with that of the markings, the darkest shade being preferable in every case.

Teeth—Strongly developed and white. Lower incisors upright and touching inside of upper incisors—a true scissors bite. *42 correctly placed teeth*, 22 in the lower, 20 in the upper jaw. Distemper teeth shall not be penalized. *Disqualifying Faults*—Overshot more than 3/16 of an inch. Undershot more than 1/8 of an inch. Four or more missing teeth.

Ears—Normally cropped and carried erect. The upper attachment of the ear, when held erect, is on a level with the top of the skull.

Neck—Proudly carried, well muscled and dry. Well arched, with nape of neck widening gradually toward body. Length of neck proportioned to body and head.

Body—Back short, firm, of sufficient width, and muscular at the loins, extending in a straight line from withers to the *slightly* rounded croup. *Withers*—pronounced and forming the highest point of the body. *Brisket*—reaching deep to the elbow. *Chest*—broad with forechest well defined. *Ribs*—well sprung from the spine, but flattened in lower end to permit elbow clearance. *Belly*—well tucked up, extending in a curved line from the brisket. *Loins*—wide and muscled. *Hips*—broad and in proportion to body, breadth of hips being approximately equal to breadth of body at rib cage and shoulders.

Tail—Docked at approximately second joint, appears to be a continuation of the spine, and is carried only slightly above the horizontal when the dog is alert.

Forequarters—*Shoulder Blade*—sloping forward and downward at a 45-degree angle to the ground meets the upper arm at an angle of 90 degrees. Length of shoulder blade and upper arm are equal. Height from elbow to withers approximately equals height from ground to elbow. *Legs*—seen from front and side, perfectly straight and parallel to each other from elbow to pastern; muscled and sinewy, with heavy bone. In normal pose and when gaiting, the elbows lie close to the brisket. *Pasterns*—firm and almost perpendicular to the ground. *Feet*—well arched, compact, and catlike, turning neither in nor out. Dewclaws may be removed.

Hindquarters—The angulation of the hindquarters balances that of the forequarters. *Hip Bone*—falls away from spinal column at an angle of about 30 degrees, producing a slightly rounded, well-filled-out croup. *Upper Shanks*—at right angles to the hip bones, are long, wide, and well muscled on both sides of thigh, with clearly defined stifles. Upper and lower shanks are of equal length. While the dog is at rest, hock to heel is perpendicular to the ground. Viewed from the rear, the legs are straight, parallel to each other, and wide enough apart to fit in with a properly built body. *Cat Feet*—as on front legs, turning neither in nor out. Dewclaws, if any, are generally removed.

Gait—Free, balanced, and vigorous, with good reach in the forequarters and good driving power in the hindquarters. When trotting, there is strong rear-action drive. Each rear leg moves in line with the foreleg on the same side. Rear and front legs are thrown neither in nor out. Back remains strong and firm. When moving at a fast trot, a properly built dog will single-track.

Coat, Color, Markings—*Coat,* smooth-haired, short, hard, thick and close lying. Invisible gray undercoat on neck permissible. *Allowed Colors*—Black, red, blue, and fawn (Isabella). *Markings*—Rust, sharply defined, appearing above each eye and on muzzle, throat and forechest, on all legs and feet, and below tail. *Nose*—Solid black on black dogs, dark brown on red ones, dark gray on blue ones, dark tan on fawns. White patch on chest, not exceeding 1/2 square inch, permissible.

FAULTS
The foregoing description is that of the ideal Doberman Pinscher. Any deviation from the above described dog must be penalized to the extent of the deviation.

DISQUALIFICATIONS

Overshot more than 3/16 of an inch; undershot more than 1/8 of an inch. Four or more missing teeth.

Approved October 14, 1969

HEAD long, dry, as blunt wedge; widening toward base of ears; skull top flat, muzzle line parallel to skull top

TEETH strongly developed; scissors bite

EYES almond-shaped, moderately deep-set; dark color desirable

STOP slight

NOSE solid black, dark brown, dark gray, dark tan, according to coat color

LIPS close to jaws

JAWS full, powerful, well-filled under eyes

CHEEKS flat, muscular

SHOULDERS: Blades slope forward and downward 45°; meet upper arm at 90° angle

CHEST broad; forechest well-defined; brisket reaching deep to elbow

RIBS well-sprung from spine

LEGS straight; parallel, muscled, sinewy; bone heavy; elbow close to brisket

FEET well-arched, compact, catlike; turning neither in nor out

HEIGHT: Males 26″-28″ (ideal 27½″); Females 24″-26″ (ideal 25½″)

EARS normally cropped, carried erect; upper attachment on level with top of skull when erect

NECK upright, well-muscled, dry; arched, nape widening gradually toward body; length proportioned to body and head

WITHERS pronounced, forming highest point of body

BACK short, firm, sufficient width; muscular at loin; straight line from withers to slightly rounded croup

LOINS wide muscular

HIPS broad in proportion to body; hip bone falling away from spinal column at 30° angle

TAIL docked at approx. second joint, set on line with spine

HINDQUARTERS: Shanks long, wide, well-muscled; stifles clearly defined, parallel; upper and lower shanks of equal length

HOCKS turning neither in or out; hock to heel perpendicular to ground

COAT smooth, short, hard; thick, close-lying

COLORS: black, red, blue, fawn (Isabella); markings—rust, well-defined

BELLY well tucked up

BODY square, medium size. Compactly built, muscular, powerful. Height at withers equals length.

PASTERNS firm; almost perpendicular to ground

DISQUALIFICATIONS: Shyness, viciousness; overshot more than 3/16″; undershot more than 1/8″; four or more missing teeth.

Visualization of the Doberman Pinscher standard. (With permission from *Dog Standards Illustrated*, © 1975 by Howell Book House Inc.)

130

8

An In-Depth Look
at the Standard

by Ruth McCourt

THE BREEDERS are the artists who strive for perfection in what they create; the judges are the evaluators of their success. Both must have a thorough knowledge of the Standard and learn through experience to apply that Standard to the living dog. Both also need to have "an eye for a dog" that distinguishes what is quality and what is not.

The novice has the same road to follow. He must study, continually educate his eye by looking at a great number of dogs, talk to as many knowledgeable people as possible, and read all available books.

Most people are not even "novices" to start. They have bought a Doberman simply because they liked his looks and wanted a pet, a companion and a guard. Then they become attached to the dog, meet other people who have Dobermans, learn about shows, perhaps win a ribbon, and are on their way to a lifetime of fun and/or disappointment in the sport of showing dogs. On the other hand, there is the buyer who *knows* he wants a good dog to exhibit. He looks around, visits several reliable breeders, takes his time in finding the right one, relies on the breeder's advice and is set on the right road.

From these two catagories come the novices and they are the lifeblood of the dog game. Every effort should be made to encourage them, enlighten them, guide them. Everyone has started as a novice; we should remember how much we learned, and how much we appreciated the help and advice of other Doberman owners and breeders.

Every dog owner can begin learning by trying to evaluate his own dog. Obviously there is much to learn; first, we must study to acquire the information, and then—through experience—learn to apply what we have learned. Educa-

131

tion continues by watching the show ring, by continued discussion with knowledgeable owners and breeders, and by reading—reading about all breeds, not just one.

The mechanical laws of power, weight and motion are applicable to all dogs. They all have the same bones and the same muscles; the differences between breeds exist in the relationship of the parts and in the characteristics required to do the work for which each was bred. The perfection with which his anatomy and his breed characteristics are blended constitute the beauty and artistic quality of each animal.

Everyone interested in breeding, exhibiting or judging Dobermans has one basic set of rules to learn, the Standard. The Standard represents a consensus of the knowledge gained over the years by breeders working together in the National Club, which has then been accepted by the American Kennel Club as representing the correct Doberman. Naturally there are differences of opinion on various points but the Standard represents the majority opinion at any given time.

The Standard is not static; over the years there have been changes in aesthetic features to meet the style demands of changing times. The Doberman which originally had many of the characteristics of the Rottweiler, is today a svelte and elegant animal of graceful lines. Beauty has been added but the request for the structure that makes him a good working animal has remained intact.

The work a dog does dictates how he is built. All dogs have the same number of bones, held together by the same ligaments and activated by the same muscles, but certain variations in size and proportions have proven to be the most efficient for certain types of work. For instance, the Sporting dogs work feathers on land or water; the Hounds follow fur by scent or sight and some go to ground after their prey; Terriers go to ground in most cases and are built to contend with that kind of antagonist. The Working dogs, of which of course the Doberman is a prime example, are used for draft, herding, guarding, army and police work.

The structure for use is the architecture of the dog. The Standard is equivalent to the blueprint that the engineer follows in building his machine, or the architect in building his house. An animal must not only be functionally correct but must be strong in those features considered by the Standard to be characteristic of his breed, distinguishing that breed from any other. The art is expressed in the beauty and perfection with which all of these factors are assembled.

Perhaps an explanation of the "why" behind the request for each feature in the Doberman Standard will help those striving to apply that Standard. The Doberman is an elegant dog, carrying himself with pride and an air of nobility. The refinement that has been added by the breeders over years has created

Ch. Highbriar Willo of Allenwood, with her handler and
friend Gene Haupt, for whom
she was a constant companion.

Ch. El Campeon's Diosa, owned
and handled by Janie Forbes. Diosa finished at just 11 months,
undefeated in her sex.

this noble appearance without in the least detracting from his power and endurance. It is a smoothing of his outline which adds grace and artistic beauty while leaving the working structure as strong as ever. His physical makeup is "medium" in every characteristic. In no way is he overdone. Every line flows smoothly into every other line, making an harmonious whole. He is a dry (no flabbiness or loose skin), compact, solidly packed dog, hard muscled, built for both speed and endurance—medium. He has a long neck and head for speed; cat feet for endurance; deep brisket, good tuckup for endurance; short, strong loin and good angulation for power. As a protector he can turn with great agility and put on short bursts of great speed. His general outline is one of *equal balance;* height to length, depth of brisket to length of leg, shoulder blade to upper arm, front angulation to rear angulation, upper shank to lower shank, pastern to hock. His general appearance is that of an energetic dog of symmetrical lines that is capable of handling any situation.

The Head

It is in the head that many of the breed characteristics exemplifying type are displayed. The molding of the skull and muzzle, the placement and carriage of the ears, the color and set of the eyes together form the typical breed expression. "Long head resembling a blunt wedge" describes a muzzle longer than the distance from the occiput to stop, with skull and muzzle in parallel planes; jaws full and powerful, width and depth within the meaning of "wedge." Fill under the eyes is essential to provide a good foundation for the molars as the maxillary bone on each side of the bridge of the nose backs up these teeth. A snipy face will not have a good foundation for the stresses imposed by a hard bite.

The requested shape of head would of necessity have to have the almond eye, so if the eye is too large or round, the skull shape is not correct. The eyes should have an alert, intelligent expression. The color is an aesthetic factor but it is interesting to note that a very light eye is very seldom of the proper shape and placement. As stated, the set and carriage of the ears is important to the breed expression. They are usually cropped, set level with the top of the skull and carried erect, adding much to the elegance of the animal. Cropped ears contribute to good hearing and are less vulnerable to injury. The thickness or thinness of the ear leather is important; thick enough to house good erectile muscles but not so heavy as to fall of their own weight.

Since four or more missing teeth, or undershot or overshot bite, are disqualifications, great attention must be paid to the Doberman's mouth. A powerful jaw with a full set of 42 teeth is the Doberman's fighting and protection equipment. As the head has lengthened, spaces and missing teeth have appeared and in time the jaw itself may become weak and unserviceable. Since

134

Ch. Ebonaire's Scarlet Chutist, by Ebonaire's Entertainer ex Ebonaire's Colonel Lady. This lovely red bitch, owned by Judy Weiss, finished with four majors and Winners Bitch at Westminster in 1966. Pictured being handled by Monroe Stebbins to win under Dr. Wilfrid Shute, a past president of the DPCA.

Ch. Ebonaire's Puma, red bitch sired by Ch. Brown's Dion ex Ch. Ebonaire's Balestra. Owned by Judy Weiss and A. DeSousa, and handled by Monroe Stebbins.—*Gilbert*

missing teeth is a genetic mutation, breeders must consider this in planning their programs. The incisors are the tearing teeth (the canine's weapons of battle), the pre-molars are for cutting and the molars for grinding. A deep underjaw or mandibles adds to the secondary leverage that makes for a hard bite. An overshot bite is completely unserviceable and unacceptable in any breed. Some breeds call for an undershot bite, but for the Doberman the scissors bite is the most serviceable. Large, strong teeth also indicate good bone texture in the skeleton.

The proudly carried, well-arched neck, its length in proportion to the length of body and head, is a thing of beauty. However, this carriage and beauty is dependent on a strong, well-anchored cervical ligament. This ligament, according to McDowell Lyon (*The Dog In Action,* Howell Book House, New York, N.Y.) "supports the long neck and head, governs head carriage, and stabilizes the base attachments of the muscles that move the leg forward and rotate the crown of the shoulder blade forward as the leg moves backward." This is quite an assignment but on it depends much of the activity and beauty of the dog. A ewe neck is evidence of a weak ligament. So the Standard asks for the proudly carried, well-arched neck, not for beauty but because it is an evidence of strength.

Body

The topline is composed of the withers, the back, the loin and the croup, with the withers being the highest point and giving a gentle slope to the topline. The withers which are usually spoken of as the highest point of the shoulder blade, really consist of the span of the back half of the trapezus muscle as well, which muscle is attached to long vertical spires of the vertebrae. We occasionally see a small thickness at back of the shoulder blade where this muscle attaches itself and a slight drop to the five level vertebrae of the back proper. This structure is anatomically correct. The short firm back is necessary for proper transmission of power from the rear quarters to the front assembly. The loin is strong and muscled, as it is the keystone arch through which passes the driving power of the rear quarters. The loin also supports the rearing muscles which enable the dog to lift his center of gravity and to rear and jump. The slightly rounded croup adds strength to this keystone arch.

The statement "broad chest" can be confusing. How broad is broad in a dog that is supposed to be the same width at shoulders, rib cage and thighs? His chest can't be any broader than the rest of him. And as for a well defined forechest, that again calls for judgment, as a pigeon breast is not wanted. All must be looked at within the concept of the Doberman being a dog of smooth, graceful lines in which nothing is exaggerated or overbuilt.

Having the brisket to the elbow gives heartroom, and it should extend level to the ground for some distance back of the front legs. Ribs which are well

136

Ch. Majakens Little Apache, sired by Ch. Ebonaire's Entertainer ex Majaken's Joyous Gypsy. Bred by Marlene Kennels and owned by Sam Means, Apache is pictured being handled by Ellen Hoffman to win under Herman L. Fellton, current president of the Doberman Pinscher Club of America.

Ch. Ebonaire's Mr. Esquire, a Best in Show winner by Ch. Ebonaire's Entertainer ex Ebonaire's Joyeuse Noel, owned by Lee Wagner. Mr. Esquire was handled by Monroe Stebbins (pictured).

sprung from the spine, yet flattened at the lower end, allow elbow clearance. Barrel ribs cause the dog to bend the column of his leg and throw out his elbows—"out at elbows." Depth, not width, gives heart and lung room. The last two floating ribs will tell us about the rest of the rib cage. If they are long, strong and properly angled, so are the rest of the ribs. The tuck up should be confined to the abdominal section only and is controlled by a wide, powerful muscle extending from the pelvis to the base of the ribs and sternum. It must be strong and straight, or else the dog is potgutted with no staying power. The curved line which we see is caused by the skin of the flank.

The tail, like the ears, was probably docked originally to prevent injury in a fight and to remove a handhold when Dobermans were used as a protection against man. It adds to the beautiful outline but also gives us information about the size of the spinal column and the set of the croup. If it is carried straight up on the top of the back like a terrier, the croup is probably too flat; if carried too low, the croup is probably too long or set at too steep an angle. The steep croup prevents the final straightening of the back leg and cuts the amount of power produced.

The shoulder blade is the foundation of the front assembly and affects every movement of the dog. It supports and lifts weight, absorbs concussion, propels on turns and offsets lateral displacement. It is a mechanical truth that a blade that has a 45° layback is more efficient than one at any other angle, as this permits the widest and longest muscle and so is the strongest. The loaded shoulder with its solumnar muscle placement is weak; the Bulldog is a good example of this. The 45° layback of shoulder blade, upper arm of equal length meeting the shoulder blade at as nearly 90° as possible, the slightly bent pastern, together place the heel of the pad directly under the center of gravity for good static balance. This combination of angles, together with the rotating shoulder blade, also allows a long ground-covering reach. The slightly bent pastern works like a hinge to cusion the shock as the heel pad hits the ground and prevents knuckling over. The short, tight cat feet are attributes of endurance. They conserve energy and are least subject to injury.

The forequarters balance and use the power provided by the hindquarters. Having no collarbone the front assembly is not firmly based but is held by muscles and ligaments and is flexible, whereas in the hindquarters the pelvis is fixed firmly to the spinal column. The hindquarters carry little weight but provide the power. The 30° pelvis with the upper thigh at the same angle as the shoulder blade, the lower thigh at the same angle as the upper arm (these bones of equal length), create a good turn of stifle, the whole assembly capable of delivering great power. This power depends upon the angulation, the muscles, the set of the croup and the ability of the hock to straighten in that last push.

What has been explained so far has been in relation to the dog standing still, the static dog. It is evident that there is a mechanical law governing the re-

h. Marienburg Sun Hawk, owned by Mary Rodgers and handled by Moe Miyagawa. This red male homebred, whelped January 12, 1973, was the No. 1 Doberman in the United States in 1975, and was in the lead for 1976 when he mysteriously disappeared from his owner's motor home at a dog show in Portland, Oregon on July 4. For one month, Hawk's whereabouts were unknown and it will probably be never known where he spent that time. However, he is back home with those who love him, and it is still undecided at this writing whether they will risk showing him again. Hawk's wins include 4 allbreed Bests in Show, 23 Group Firsts and over a hundred Bests of Breed including Westminister 1976. His 13 Specialty Bests include the Doberman Pinscher Club of America, and he was winner of the 1975 Top Twenty event. He is pictured here in win under Mrs. Helen Wittrig, with Moe Miyagawa handling.

Ch. Electra's High Voltage, black male owned by Judith Bingham of California. This lovely dog was at height of his show career when he was tragically killed at age of 2½, and would have been eligible for the Top Twenty competition of 1976. Volt was by Gra-Lemor Hannibal d'El Dorado (a Demetrius son) ex Brown's Tasha (a Ch. Patton's Chateugay daughter). Already in his short life he had won 2 all-breed Bests in Show, 2 Specialties, 5 Group Firsts and 30 Bests of Breed. His passing is a great loss to the breed but happily he did leave behind some excellent sons and daughters. He is seen here being handled by Mike Shea to win under Mrs. Bernard Freeman.

quest for every part of the dog, which law is applied and tested when he moves. The proof of good construction comes in movement. If the dog moves in accordance with the Standard of his breed, he is a good mover and typical of his breed in action. This movement should be free, balanced, and vigorous with good reach in the forequarters and good drive in the hindquarters. The Doberman has a distinctive gait, neither the long reach of the German Shepherd nor the short reach of the terrier. As a result of his square, compact body and particular angulation he moves all of a piece with a somewhat medium reaching stride. Front and rear legs move in line with each other, all moving toward the center line at a fast trot in order to counteract lateral displacement. Any fault in skeletal structure, any weakness of muscles or ligaments, will show up when the dog is moving. The whole structure of the skeleton is to enable the dog to get maximum movement with the least loss of energy and the least wear and tear on the parts. Doberman gait is discussed more fully in the chapter that follows.

The coat is short, hard and thick to give weather protection. It should be shiny, showing good health but not silky. The small white spot on the chest which the Standard still allows is hardly ever seen anymore. The accepted colors are the genetic inheritance from the breeds used in developing the Doberman. The rust markings are an essential breed characteristic, without which the dog is not a Doberman.

What the Judges Look For

Study of the Standard has given us a mental picture of the ideal. Now it becomes necessary to evaluate each dog in relationship to that image. Does the dog fit? If not, why not? This is the process each judge goes through in selecting just which dogs in his opinion deserve awards on any particular day. Bear in mind that the selections made on one day may be entirely different on another, even by the same judge. The competition is different, the dog may not feel well, the weather may be too hot or too cold; any number of variables occur. Also, it is true that each judge has his own personal appreciation of the points of the Standard and since no dog is perfect, each judge places the emphasis on the characteristics that seem most important to him, that fit *his* mental picture of the Standard. Since neither dogs nor people are stamped out with a cookie cutter, this personal element is always present; and the fancy should be glad of it, for—even as in medicine—a second or confirming opinion is reassuring.

All judges look for type, balance, soundness, style and condition. An experienced judge with "an eye for a dog" can recognize the dogs with these potentials at a glance, but he must check each feature required by the Standard and gait all dogs under him in order to verify his impressions. The problem

140

Ch. Weichardt's A-Go-Go CD, one of the breed's great show bitches. By Ch. Hayden-kirk's Gallant Warrior CD ex Weichardt's Champagne. Bred by Jack Weichardt and owned by Joan Barrett. "Go-Go", handled by Gene Haupt, is pictured winning the Group at Richland County 1971 show under judge Glen Sommers.

Ch. Weichardt's Rosen Cavalier CD, handsome red male, pictured at age of 9½ years winning the Veterans Class at the 1975 Doberman Pinscher Club of America Specialty under judge Derek Rayne, handled as always by Marge Anognost. By Ch. Alnwicks Black Fury Bismarck CD ex Weichardt's Princess Athena, Cavalier was bred by Jack Weichardt and is owned by Denyse Lee, California. A Best in Show winner in both the United States and Canada, he has nine Specialty wins among his many Best of Breed and was in the Top Ten during his prize years.

becomes one of the degree with which the Standard requirements are met and the relative importance of each feature to type and the dog's working ability.

Type is adherence to breed characteristics as outlined by the Standard, those combined features which distinguish a particular breed from any other. Type is the hardest of all to learn to evaluate, as it is composed of a combination of a number of variable breed characteristics of both mind and body. The judge must evaluate each feature, point for point, faults and virtues, in comparing dogs for "type." One hears some judges called "head hunters," when what they are really doing is looking for characteristic breed expression. Just think of how many dogs are built a great deal alike in body, but vary drastically in head type. The word "type" is a much abused word being applied in many cases to personal preferences, large, small, heavy boned, over-refined. There is only one correct type in each breed and differences of size and conformation are individual variations only. *A dog that lacks type can be a good dog, but never a good specimen of his breed.*

Balance is a matter of proportion, the look of all parts being in proper relationship to each other and to the whole, with each part conforming to the Standard. It is not enough for each part to be good in itself; it must fit and be in balance with every other part. This is where the artist's eye is invaluable. Style is displayed in balance, proud carriage, alertness and showmanship. The stylish dog expresses personality and has the silhouette of the modern Doberman.

Soundness consists of all physical parts being present and in good working order. The word "sound" is most often used in connection with gait. A dog that moves properly in accordance with the requirements of his Standard is spoken of as sound. Condition means that the dog is in proper weight for his breed, clean, well-groomed and showing by his eyes and coat that he is healthy and well cared for.

Ring Procedures in Judging the Doberman

The following are the procedures which judges usually use to assay all of the previously mentioned physical characteristics in the show ring. The dogs are moved in a large circle around the ring which enables the judge to get his first impression of style, balance, soundness, reach and drive. Then they are set up one behind the other, all facing the same direction. It is at this time that the judge examines each dog in detail, comparing each feature with the Standard. He looks carefully at the shape of skull and muzzle, ear placement, set and color of eyes, and checks breed expression. Is the head long and dry, the eye of proper shape? Is the top of the skull flat with slight stop? Are there the required number of teeth with scissors bite? What of the markings?

The neck is examined for length and dryness. Does it have an arch? Does it gradually widen toward the chest and flow gracefully into the withers, which should be set high and close together? Is the shoulder blade long and sloping? Is the upper arm of equal length and at the proper angle? The bone of the forelegs is checked for shape and substance. Are the pasterns only slightly bent? Cat feet with good thick pads? The topline should be firm and slightly sloping from withers to croup. What of the brisket, does it reach the elbow? Is the loin well-muscled and the tuck up correct? The hindquarters are handled to check the musculature and angulation. Is the tail placement and carriage correct? What of the coat length and texture?

Some judges gait each dog right after they have examined it; some examine the entire class and then gait the dogs. The dog is sent down the ring and back, either straight back in a "T" or "L" formation or in a triangle, depending on the judge's preference. At this time he is checking for sound, typical movement and overall balance. Do the dog's hind legs travel in the same plane as the front legs? Does he "wing," "pound," "crab," move too close or too wide? Is he cowhocked? Does he have good reach in the forequarters and good drive in the hindquarters? Is he out at elbows or loose in shoulders? Are the legs in a straight column from shoulder joint and hip joint to pad as he moves? Does he lose his symmetry when he moves? The judge will probably line up his dogs again for re-checking, place those he considers best in the center of the ring, send them around again and make his final placings. There will be many variations of this procedure, depending on the judge, but these are the basics.

Out of this process the cream rises to the top. Not every dog is going to win every day, nor does losing mean that the dog is not good. The value judgments of many judges will eventually bring to the fore the better dogs as examples for breeders and exhibitors.

The kind of dog that the general public will finally have available is dependent upon the dedication of breeders and judges. If they are producing and recognizing physically and mentally sound dogs that are good representatives of their breed, the buyers of puppies will end up with good dogs. Unfortunately, as a breed becomes popular, too many people who are breeders in name only raise puppies, and the breed deteriorates. The true breeder must have a knowledge of genetics and be familiar with the great producers (and what made them great). And the true breeder must know the Standard requirements and the why of them as thoroughly as a judge. Dedicated breeders and knowledgeable judges alike must firmly hold the line on these requirements.

The Doberman's physical characteristics have been discussed at some length, but it doesn't matter what he is physically if he does not have the temperament, character and disposition of a true Doberman. He is then just another dog. There is very little in the Standard regarding temperament, for very few of the qualities that make up temperament are evident under the controlled conditions of the show ring. Energy and alertness can be seen, viciousness toward people and shyness can be evidenced, but how about watchfulness, determination, fearlessness, loyalty and obedience? These are facets of character and temperament displayed only toward his own family and loved ones. And in them the true Doberman cannot be excelled.

Mr. John T. Brueggeman, one of the fancy's respected old-timers, says that true Doberman temperament is: "Circumspection of strangers; loyalty to and willingness to please the master; shrewdness; uncanny intelligence; fearlessness; desire to protect the master and his family; ability to cope with any emergency; and general dignity." This covers it very well. Most Dobermans are loving and protective but understand when they are told everything is all right. They know old friends and will greet new ones; however, they do not like undue familiarity. So much depends on an intelligent owner who knows how and when to correct, and is firm and consistent about it.

Dobermans will not stand abuse and while an occasional dog will have a bad disposition, most of them bite only when mistreated or the occasion demands it. The Doberman temperament on the whole is very solid. We have today a much less aggressive dog than in the past. This change was essential to accord with the general temperament of the American people and to make it possible for the dogs to live in urban surroundings. The overly aggressive dog or trained guard dog is safe only in the hands of a very knowledgeable handler.

Obedience is the field for testing trainability. Most people enter into the training of their dog to make him a more enjoyable, obedient companion; some to eradicate bad habits which have been allowed to develop. Character traits are developed and ingrained through training. The dog that has learned to obey the command "Heel" is a joy to take any place. The dog that has developed a conditioned response to "come" may be saved from many dangerous situations. Is he erratic, easily distracted or does he think before he acts? These character traits and habits show during training; the good ones becomes strengthened, the bad ones eradicated. The dog is taught to tend to business and do as he is told. Training gives him confidence, improves his conduct and makes him a better citizen. If he is to be a good "working" dog, his mind must be trained as well as his body.

The Doberman Pinscher Club of America has underway a Temperament Testing program which subjects the dog to various conditions in which his reactions are graded. These tests are described in another chapter. The goal of the program is to create a Register of Merit Award for dogs meeting requirements of conformation, temperament and trainability—to have Standards by which to evaluate and maintain the total Doberman. This is a valuable and ambitious program which should do much to maintain the Doberman's place as unexcelled loving companion and reliable guard of person and property.

One last word to the Doberman owner. Before there is a grown dog to which to apply the Standard, there is a puppy which must have "Tender, loving care." Presumably the novice has a puppy from good stock with the potential of being a fine specimen of the breed. He must then have good food with vitamins and minerals to sustain his rapid growth; exercise to build and strengthen muscles; and above all, he must have continued contact with people. The Doberman is too personal to thrive living in a kennel but must be one of the family and have somebody to love and obey. His great intelligence and capacity for attachment are brought to flower by personal contact and training. Early training on the lead, and in stacking, condition him for the later rigors of the show ring. Matches give him experience with other dogs and ring procedure so that he is not presented with an entirely new experience when the owner decides to try his luck in point shows. The owner, in the meantime, is learning from breeders, exhibitors and working with his own dog.

Ch. Brown's Feegee
and young friend.

9

Characteristic Movement in Dobermans

by Frank Grover

Nᴏᴛ ᴍᴜᴄʜ has been written about the way Dobermans move. There are a few intriguing paragraphs in the old and honored Gruenig book and the exciting and interesting photographs and diagrams in the first edition of Denlinger that are reproduced here in the next chapter. But the special characteristics of Doberman movement have not been discussed in print at any length in English. So it is that most of what we think we know about Doberman movement is derived from literature about dog movement in general. This literature has done much to clarify questions about the mechanics of dogs in action and the relationships of certain structural types to movement "faults." Most of this applies to Dobermans; but Dobermans are a unique breed with unique proportions and structure, hence also certain unique characteristics in movement. This chapter will be confined to a discussion of those unique or special characteristics of Dobermans in action.

These characteristics are best observed by taking a mature Doberman out in a field and turning him loose and studying how he moves and what he does when he moves. If this is done often enough and with enough Dobermans, two generalizations will stand out: first, Dobermans gallop; second, Dobermans maneuver.

Give a Doberman a chance to move as he wants to and usually he will quickly begin to gallop. He may start at a gallop from a stop; he may gallop and stop seemingly in the middle of a stride. He may gallop very slowly and leisurely; or he may gallop fast, laying out almost flat. He may gallop carelessly, seeming to swing from side to side; he may gallop smoothly and effortlessly. But if he has a choice of gaits, he will gallop. If you can get to the side and watch him gallop across a field, you will see one of the most beautiful of sights: he will seem to float across—his back level and not appearing to rise and fall with his stride. All movement seems beneath his body. Typically, his head is high. While he can move at other gaits, the gallop is what the Doberman does when he has the option.

The other aspect of his movement is his ability to change speed and direction with agility. He is a dog that can and does maneuver. He can gallop at a breakneck speed in one direction and turn without seeming to break stride and gallop just as fast in the opposite direction. He can change from a slow-lazy gallop to a long, ground covering gallop in one stride. He can start from a stop and seem to take off at full speed. Even when standing, he can whirl and turn much too fast for us to see all the actions.

These two characteristics typify Dobermans in action. Both are related to the work of the breed and to the physical proportions as conceived by the originators of the breed. Our earliest literature refers to the Doberman as a "short-backed galloper" as distinct from a longer backed trotting dog. The Doberman gallops naturally because of his proportions. He is a quick reacting dog with such balance as to be able to handle himself in all sorts of "man work" and guarding. He must be able to maneuver to do this work well.

At galloping and maneuvering a good Doberman should excel. Unfortunately, in the showing of Dobermans, these are not characteristics we can test directly in the show ring. Instead, we must observe what we can with the Dobermans performing within the limitations of the show conditions. From what we see, we must infer the dog's ability to gallop and maneuver. The tests we use in the show ring consist in watching the dog at a trot; going away from the judge; coming into the judge; and moving in profile. These views give us considerable information useful in evaluating the dog. But this movement in the show ring cannot be a final test of the dog's ability to function as his breed should. Unlike the German Shepherd, where in the show we are observing the dog at his natural gait, we are studying the Doberman at a second best gait . . . often a forced gait. We can use the information we gain, but not without translating it to relate to the dog's natural or characteristic movements of galloping and maneuvering.

We can use the trotting of a Doberman to assess his balance and his soundness of joints. We can also use it to check excesses of handlers in posing the dogs in the ring, to check our observations of some aspects of structure, to relay the dogs and handlers, to show different aspects of the judging process to the ringside, etc. But, the chief values of trotting the Dobermans in the ring are to observe balance and soundness.

In checking balance and soundness, we are dealing with questions very similar to those we check in other breeds — though Doberman balance is of its own character. Emphasis is a little different in Dobermans for reasons we will get to in a moment.

Most Dobermans when considered as a whole in regard to angulation are out of balance . . . the rear quarters carry more angulation than the front quarters. Place this out of balance angulation on a square dog, and the problems of balance in trotting are exaggerated when compared to the same out of balance angulation on a longer dog. So it is that we often find in our well-proportioned Dobermans just about every out of balance adaptation in moving. One dog may dip his back; another may lift it; another may move wide in the rear and close in front; another wide in front and close in rear; many will "sidewind"; some will lift the rear legs high behind and slice down with them instead of reaching under; many will over-reach with the rear legs. All of these are signs of the out of balance angulation of the animai. In Doberman judging it is not too much of a chore to detect that the dogs are out of balance; the problem is to assess the degree of the problem. It is also to remember that the judge should not forsake the ideal of the breed . . . a short-backed galloper . . . in favor of a longer dog that is able to accomodate his out of balance angulation a little better when he trots. The short dog will gallop well and be better at maneuvering.

Two additional faults are common among Dobermans. The first is toeing in, in front. As the dog comes into the judge, one or both front feet will toe in. The problem is usually more marked in the left front leg. It appears to begin in the pastern and to affect the way the foot lands. It may be a problem stemming from shoulder placement. But whatever the reason, it is a very common problem; indeed it is rare not to see it in some degree.

The second problem is in the rear quarters. A marked difference may appear in the action of the right rear leg. A careful examination will usually show that one of the legs is larger, longer, or appreciably stronger than the other. The variance is not easily detected when the dog is standing still, but it is apparent in the odd swing of the right leg. This fault has been diminishing in the last fifteen years, and is not found in most of our dogs now. It does occur frequently, however.

To gain a clear concept of balanced and sound trotting in Dobermans, the descriptions in the Standard should be reviewed, the photographs and diagrams in this book (reprinted from the first edition) should be examined, the books on movement should be studied, and in particular many Dobermans should be watched trotting. Out of these will emerge the particular characteristics of Doberman balance when trotting.

As the concept of balance and sound trotting is clarified, you will realize how few of our Dobermans trot in this manner . . . and are also square dogs. The reasons are many; first, perfection is rare; second, we are asking our dogs to demonstrate a gait that is second best to them; third, our breed has not yet achieved the perfection of joint and balance we want; fourth, the trotting must be taught and taught very carefully to our dogs if they are to do it "at the best"; fifth, the conditions must be right for the dog . . . his attention must be in the right place, and his health must be right.

148

For, what a Doberman demonstrates in the ring is a combination of structure, health, habits, and attention. It a dog's attention is straight ahead, he will tend to move more nearly straight and in better balance than if his attention is to one side or the other. A Doberman can twist himself to watch the liver in the handler's pocket and "sidewind" all the way across the ring. This sidewind looks (from the judge's point of view) exactly like the dog that "sidewinds" because he is out of balance structurally. When a Doberman trots in the ring, he demonstrates the habits he has formed, as well as his structure. Many Dobermans have formed habits of adjusting reach and drive when on leash . . . so the head reaches forward but the front leg does not reach as far, and the rear minces. Such a dog may be able to reach out; or he may not. If his shoulder is set straight, the chances are good that he can't reach much further in front.

So it is that a judge must use observations of structure when a dog is standing to check what he sees when the dog moves, just as he uses movement to check what he sees when the dog is still.

In most judging situations today, the Doberman that demonstrates an acceptable trot has shown that he is built so he can gallop and maneuver. What is an acceptable trot? It is one in which the Doberman moves in balance at least at one speed in a trot, in which his joints are free and his movements are true. He may not demonstrate as much reach nor as much drive as we wish, but when standing his shoulders are laid back and his rear angulation is not overly extreme.

About once or twice in a decade, a well-proportioned Doberman appears that is also able to trot beautifully. His structure is in excellent balance; his training has been top notch; and his handling is first rate as far as movement is concerned. This dog will stretch out with his front legs, his front feet landing directly beneath the nose of the dog as it extends forward; the rear reaches under and the rear foot lands in the track left by the front foot on the same side. Such dogs do appear; but they are rare and almost not typical of the breed. They are recognized when they do appear, and it is good to remember that it is possible for a square Doberman to be able to trot at almost all speeds in balance and with soundness.

To the Doberman fancier, the trot of the dog must be remembered as a test by which we get clues to how well the dog can gallop and maneuver. To the Doberman judge, gait in the ring is a challenge as well as a tool. It is a challenge to use gaiting and at the same time to keep it in perspective. To the exhibitor, getting his Doberman to demonstrate an acceptable trot may be a tremendous task — of observing, of training, of learning and inventing skills to get the best from the dog. To the breeder, gaiting at a trot is an excellent check on soundness and balance . . . but it is not a goal. Proportions with a Doberman head, character and temperament, and a dog able to maneuver and gallop — these are the Doberman ideal.

10

A Pictorial Study of Doberman Gait

by Curtice W. Sloan

Doberman Trotting

THIS SERIES of thirteen pictures was selected from a strip of movie film taken in slow motion at the rate of sixty-four pictures per second. They show the extreme accuracy of the movements of a properly angulated Doberman while trotting.

Although it cannot be seen in these pictures, as they are all taken from the side, the dog is single tracking; that is, all four feet, when placed on the ground during trotting, are placed on a single line the same as the dog would have to do if he was trotting along a tight rope suspended above the ground.

The time interval of the pictures has been given in 64ths of a second and it should be noted that each full step required 17/64ths of a second or a total of 34/64ths of a second for the dog to take two full steps and return his legs to the starting position as shown in Picture # 1.

Inasmuch as all of this action takes place in just a little over one-half second, it is not surprising that many of our owners and even some judges do not know exactly what a dog does do with his feet because the movement takes place entirely too rapidly for the eye to follow.

There are, however, other means than the slow motion camera for checking the proper movement of a dog and that is to observe the tracks he leaves behind him when trotting. A properly angulated dog, carrying himself in good balance, will leave behind him a single line of tracks which are in a straight line.

150

EXAMPLES

Front Foot—O   Hind Foot—H

1 (H)   (H)   (H)   (H)   (H)   (H)   (H)   (H)

This is the correct gait when single tracking. Notice the hind foot print is directly on top of the front foot print.

2   O H   O H   O H   O H   O H   O H

Correct gait flying trot — also single tracking. Notice that the tracks are still on
a straight line but that the dog's body moved forward in the air in that split second between the front foot movement and the hind foot placement so that the
hind foot places in front of the front foot track. However, the tracks are still on a
straight line.

3   O   O   O   O   O   O   O   O
       H   H   H   H   H   H   H   H

The dog is side gaiting and although he makes a straight line of tracks with both
his front feet and his hind feet, they are in two different planes. Some people,
without distinguishing between front foot prints and hind foot prints, have con-
cluded that the dog is gaiting with his right hand legs in one vertical plane and
his left hand legs in a parallel vertical plane.

4   O   O   O   O   O   O   O   O
         H   H   H   H   H   H   H   H

The dog is still single tracking independently with his front and hind legs but is
side gaiting to prevent his hind feet hitting his front feet because he is over-step-
ping. This dog probably has too much angulation in the rear to match his front
angulation.

5

Some dogs actually do move with the right hand legs in one vertical plane and the left hand legs in a parallel vertical plane separated by the full width of the dog. These dogs leave tracks behind them as shown above.

6   ○   ○   ○   ○   ○
       H   H   H   H   H   H   H   H   H
          ○   ○   ○   ○

This dog is single tracking with the hind feet but moving the two front feet directly fore and aft in two parallel vertical planes.

7   H   H   H   H   H
       ○   ○   ○   ○   ○   ○   ○   ○   ○
          H   H   H   H

This dog is single tracking with its front feet and moving its hind feet in two parallel vertical planes.

152

Trotting Movements of a Properly Angulated Doberman

Picture # 1 —

The series starts at the point where the right front foot and left hind foot have been just put down on the ground and where the left front foot and right hind foot have just completed their turn of carrying the weight of the dog.

Picture # 2,

taken 2/64ths of a second after picture # 1, illustrates the follow through of the hind feet. The right hind foot has continued backward after leaving the ground and at this point is at its farthest rearward position. Follow through is as important a factor in dog movement as it is in a golf stroke.

153

Picture # 3,

taken 6/64ths of a second after picture # 2, shows the right hind hock lifted well up to pass the right hind foot over the left hind foot as is necessary when a dog is single tracking.

Picture # 4,

taken 3/64ths of a second after picture # 3, shows the start of the reach forward of the left front foot and the right hind foot.

154

:ture # 5,

en 3/64ths of a second after picture
4, shows the feet approaching the max-
um reaching position.

:ture # 6,

en 2/64ths of a second after picture
5, shows the feet in the maximum
ching position. Please observe that the
t are just barely above the ground in
s position so that the feet meet the
und at exactly the end of the reach
thout shock. This is especially impor-
t in the front feet. Pictures of dogs with
much rear angulation show that the
d legs have driven the dog's body for-
rd further than he can step with his
nt legs and at the end of his front reach
front foot is still two or three inches
ove the ground so that he lands on the
nt feet with a shock at each step.
ase note that the right front foot is
ving just a split second ahead of the
ht hind foot which is moving forward
be put down exactly in the track of the
ht front foot as shown in Picture # 7.

Picture # 7,

taken 1/64th of a second after picture # 6, shows the reach completed and the left front foot and the right hind foot now on the ground carrying the weight of the dog. Please observe that in this picture a line drawn through the left front foot and the center line of the shoulder blade makes a 45° angle with the ground. Also, that a line drawn through the right hind foot and the ball and socket hip joint of the hind leg also makes a 45° angle with the ground. These angles represent any dog's maximum possible forward reach which reach is controlled by the angle of the shoulder blade.

It is anatomically impossible for the shoulder blade to be laid back any farther than a 45° angle to the ground. It is possible, however, for a dog to be over-angulated in the hind legs so that he could reach considerably farther with his hinds legs than with his front legs. Consequently, when overangulated in the rear, he has to stilt the movement of his hind legs in order to keep his hindquarters from trying to go faster than his forequarters.

This is the main reason why dogs that are too well angulated in the rear have poor gaits since it is anatomically impossible to put a matching angulation in the forequarters.

The dog shown in these pictures has a rear angulation which matches his front angulation. If this dog had any more rear angulation he would not be able to gait with the extreme accuracy shown in these pictures. Everyone should study carefully the skeleton drawing of the Doberman standard which is so drawn as to give the dog maximum possible front angulation and a rear angulation which exactly matches the front. Dogs with more rear angulation than the one in the standard are, of necessity, over-angulated as it is impossible to put more angulation in front. Most Dobermans do not have as well laid back shoulder blades as the one in the drawing and, therefore, should have steep or slightly angulated hind legs to match their steep fronts so they can move in balance. It is always better to have matching angulation fore and aft, be it much or little, than to have different angulation at each end of the dog. Any dog with matching angulation fore and aft will move better than one whose angulations do not match. Naturally, the optimum anatomical construction for a dog is to have the full front angulation and the matching rear angulation as called for in the drawing of the skeleton in the Doberman standard.

156

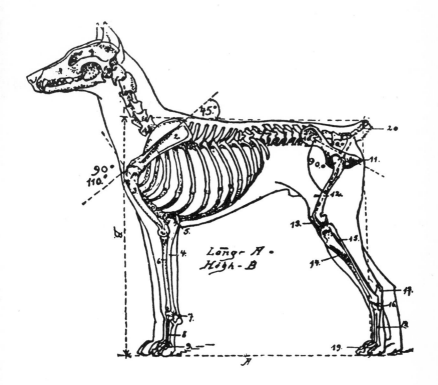

A is the length from the juncture of the shoulder blade and arm bone to the most extreme point of the hump of the ischium. B is the height from the highest point of the shoulder blade (withers to the level base on which the dog stands).

1. Head. 2. Shoulder blade. 3. Arm bone. 4. Elbow bone. 5. Elbow hump. 6. Radius. 7. Pastern. 8. Front middle foot. 9. Toes. 10. Pelvis. 11. Hump of the ischium. 12. Upper thigh bone. 13. Kneecap. 14. Lower thigh bone. 15. Fibula or shin. 16. Hock. 17. Ankle bone hump. 18. Hind middle foot. 19. Toes. 20. Ball and socket joint of the tail.

Picture # 8,

taken 2/64ths of a second after picture # 7, shows the follow through of the left hind foot in its farthest back position.

Picture # 9,

taken 6/64ths of a second after picture # 8, shows the left hind hock up to carry the left hind foot over the right hind foot which is on the ground.

158

cture # 10,

ken 3/64ths of a second after picture # 9, shows the start of the reach and is mparable to picture # 4 only this time is the right front leg and the left hind leg at are doing the reaching.

icture # 11,

ken 3/64ths of a second after picture # 10, is comparable to picture # 5 where e left front and right hind feet are ap-roaching maximum reach.

159

Picture # 12,

taken 2/64ths of a second after picture # 11, is comparable to picture # 6 wherein again the front foot is moving a split second ahead of the oncoming hind foot so that it may be placed on the ground in the left front foot track. This is the maximum reaching position of the right front and left hind legs.

Picture # 13,

taken 1/64th of a second after picture # 12, shows the dog's feet again returned to the same position they were in picture # 1; that is, the right front foot and left hind foot have been just placed on the ground to carry the weight of the dog.

160

Doberman Galloping

The high speed gait of a Doberman is the double suspension gallop as shown in the following series of fifteen pictures. These pictures were also taken at the rate of sixty-four pictures per second with the slow motion camera. So that you may be able to follow the pictures more closely, below is a diagram of the tracks made by the dog during galloping.

EXAMPLES

 # 1—Full Gallop—Top Speed

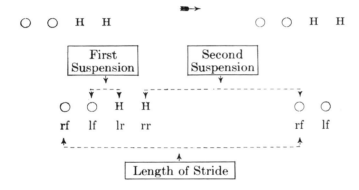

This shows the full stride tracks left by the dog at his maximum speed. It will be noted that the tracks appear in groups of four and that the hind foot tracks are in front of the front foot tracks in the direction in which the dog is going. This shows what is called the double suspension or that the dog has all four feet off the ground twice during the complete cycle of his galloping stride, the first suspension taking place between the front foot tracks and the hind foot tracks of a group of tracks and the second taking place between the two groups of four tracks which complete the cycle. The letter notations on the last group (rf—lf—lr—rr) indicate the placement of the right and left front and hind feet.

2—Starting the Gallop

H			H				H					H	
○	○		○	○			○	○				○	○	H
○				H					H			rf	lf	lr rr
H														

This shows the tracks that are quite likely to be left behind by a Doberman getting up to speed on his gallop. You will notice that in the first few strides the tracks are not on a line as he is using the power of both hind legs simultaneously to overcome the inertia of the weight of his body and get him under way. As his speed increases, the feet are placed more nearly on a straight line.

Some dogs will continue to gallop moderately with their feet placed as shown in the last group of tracks; that is, with the left rear foot a little off the line. It will be noted, however, that the two front feet and the right rear foot are on a line inasmuch as the dog is right galloping and using his right hind leg primarily in his spring forward which he carefully places on the center line of his travel forward.

Picture 1 shows the right front foot about to touch the ground at the end of one stride and the beginning of another.

162

Picture 2, taken 3/64ths of a second after Picture 1, shows the full weight of the dog now on the right front foot with the pastern bent back to cushion the shock of landing.

Picture 3, taken 1/64th of a second after Picture 2, shows the left front foot just touching the ground directly in front of the right front foot as the dog moves forward.

Picture 4, taken 1/64th of a second after Picture 3, shows the left front foot now taking the load.

Picture 5, taken 3/64ths of a second after Picture 4, shows the left front foot now carrying the full load and the pastern fully bent to cushion the shock. The loin is arching and the hind feet are coming forward.

164

Picture 6, taken 1/64th of a second after Picture 5, shows the left front pastern now completely straightened out and ready to leave the ground for the first suspension.

Picture 7, taken 2/64ths of a second after Picture 6, shows all four feet off the ground with the hind feet moving forward to meet the ground. The dog is now in the first or minor suspension of the galloping stride.

165

Picture 8, taken 2/64ths of a second after Picture 7, shows the front feet picked up out of the way of the hind feet, the left hind foot just about to touch the ground ahead of where the front feet were. This is the end of the first suspension. It is interesting to note here that the cross relation of leg action maintains in the gallop as well as in the trot; that is, the right front foot was placed down first (Pictures 1 and 2) and now it is the diagonal or left hind leg which is being put down first.

Picture 9, taken 2/64ths of a second after Picture 8, shows the left hind leg now carrying the full weight of the dog with the hock nearly touching the ground.

166

Picture 10, taken 1/64th of a second after Picture 9, shows the right hind foot now about to touch the ground ahead of the left hind foot and directly in front of it. Notice that the loin is fully arched ready for the rearing action to get the forequarters of the dog up and contribute to the next spring forward by the hind legs.

Picture 11, taken 1/64th of a second after Picture 10, shows both hind feet on the ground and the start of the rearing action. Notice the front legs by this time have moved forward, starting to get into position for a landing at the end of the next suspension.

167

Picture 12, taken 1/64th of a second after Picture 11, shows the beginning of the spring forward.

Picture 13, taken 5/64ths of a second after Picture 12, shows the completion of the hind leg thrust in giving the spring forward on the second or major suspension. Notice that the loin is now nearly completely straightened out.

168

Picture 14, taken 1/64th of a second after Picture 13, shows the dog in the second or major suspension period with all four feet off the ground and the loin completely straightened out as a result of the hind leg follow through.

Picture 15, taken 1/64th of a second after Picture 14, shows the end of the major suspension period and the end of the stride. Picture 16 is comparable to the starting Picture 1.

Picture 16   **Picture 17**

Just in case you find it hard to visualize a dog's ability to place his feet on a line one in front of the other, Pictures 16 and 17 have been added showing first the dog's two front feet placed on the ground one in front of the other followed by the two hind feet on the ground one in front of the other.

The entire sequence from Picture 1 to Picture 15 required 25/64ths of a second. Inasmuch as the dog's length of stride (that is, from one right front foot paw print to the next) is a distance of fourteen feet, the rate of speed can be calculated at twenty-four and one-half miles per hour. With the dog going by at this rate of speed and the foot sequences requiring from 1/64th to 3/64ths of a second, it is impossible for the naked eye to see exactly what the dog did with his feet. Here again, however, one may check his dog by observing footprints in light snow at a full gallop.

In order to do this one must first learn to distinguish between front foot tracks and hind foot tracks which can easily be done due to the fact that the front feet are considerably larger than the hind feet and make a correspondingly larger print.

170

11

Doberman Color

by Anita and Robert W. Silman

Some dog people say that a good dog comes in any color. In many breeds this is true for their standards state not what color a dog should be, but rather what colors the dog should *not* be. On the other hand, some standards are so explicit on color that certain colors will disqualify a dog completely from being shown. The standards of the German Shepherd Dog and Boxer allow white dogs to be registered but not shown.

Coat Color and the Standard

Color plays an important part in the popularity of many breeds. In many people's minds there is only one Doberman—the black and tan—even though four colors, black, red, blue, and fawn (*Isabella*) are recognized as acceptable colors in the standard. The original standard of 1899 recognized only one color, black and tan, but by 1901 two other colors were recognized, the red and tan, and blue and tan. It wasn't until October 14, 1969, that the fawn became an accepted color. The fawn was not mentioned as a fault or a color in 1899; it wasn't mentioned at all. The name *Isabella* seems to have been derived from Latin through through the French word "sable" which means sand. Therefore the word suggests being sand colored.

Early breeders believed that the fawn color indicated weakness and deterioration of body structure and temperament, and it should not be encouraged. In German stud books of the 1950s only 25 registrations of fawn colored Dobermans were listed out of about 900 entries. Of course, it is possible that many fawns were registered as reds or destroyed at birth and so never registered. The older German breeders claimed that the fawn was the result of too close

171

inbreeding. They declared that the dogs were susceptible to disease, had bad coats and weak light eyes. We now know that the color is due to genetic inheritance rather than inbreeding.

The first fawn Doberman to win a ribbon higher than a class win at a regular American Kennel Club point show was High Halo's Calypso, bred by Mildred Dold and owned by Annlee Konneker and Mildred Dold. Calypso was Reserve Winners Bitch at the Mississippi Valley Kennel Club show in 1966. The judge was Major Bryant Godsol, and Calypso was handled by Keith Walker. The bitch was by Ch. Marks-Tey Hanover ex Ch. High Halo's Brooke of Kondo.

At the time of this win the *Isabella* color was not mentioned in the standard, and there was some confusion as to whether a fawn could be shown. The AKC was asked for a ruling on the subject, and the reply was "The standard for the Doberman Pinscher breed does not state that an Isabella color is disqualifying: [sic] therefore you would be permitted to show such a color." And further "a protest could not be lodged against an Isabella because of its color."

It wasn't until September 1972 that the first *Isabella* became a finished champion of record under the revised standard. The dog was Ch. Aventine's Gabrielle, bred by Edward and Mary Bowell. She is by Ch. Tarrado's Corry out of Bachtel's Pepsi and is owned by Frank Di'Amico and Don Saslow.

The colors as stated in the revised standard are black, red, blue, and fawn (*Isabella*), all with rust markings. This statement can leave one mystified. Although black is always black, what is red when applied to the Doberman?

Black can actually be two shades. The first is a very shiny coal black. The second is deep black with a slightly reddish cast when viewed in the sun. Usually a dog that carries the gene for red will have this reddish cast to the coat, while the dominant black, or black with the dilution factor, will be the shiny coal black. We will go into this more fully later.

Red, or brown as it is sometimes called, is a color that is hard to describe. The color might best be described as a russet brown, about the color of a Hereford cow. The range of red goes from deepest brown, almost black-brown, to a very washed-out cinammon red. Since the standard is not specific as to which variation of color is desirable, we should prefer a median color, one that is neither very dark nor very light.

Blue is a dark steely blue gray. There are two kinds of blue coats. One is a coat with all the hairs a uniform color. The other has hairs both light and dark gray, giving a roan gray effect. The blues tend to have a lighter silvery head. A blue Doberman can be such a dark blue that it appears black with only the silvery head indicating that it is blue. Again moderation in color is to be encouraged—neither too light nor too dark.

The *Isabella* has been described as a silver beige. It is not the fawn of a Boxer or Great Dane. It is more of the color of russet brown mixed with

Am. & Can. Ch. Brandenhorf's Periwinkle, top winning blue Doberman of all time. By Ch. Felix vom Ahrtal ex Ch. Brandendorf's Sorbet, Periwinkle, Periwinkle has won a Best in Show, 6 Groups and 36 Bests of Breed, and is the sire of 12 champions. Bred, owned and handled by Marilyn Meshirer, pictured guiding him to win under judge James Trullinger. —*Gilbert*

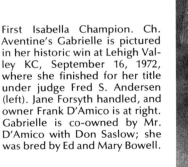

First Isabella Champion. Ch. Aventine's Gabrielle is pictured in her historic win at Lehigh Valley KC, September 16, 1972, where she finished for her title under judge Fred S. Andersen (left). Jane Forsyth handled, and owner Frank D'Amico is at right. Gabrielle is co-owned by Mr. D'Amico with Don Saslow; she was bred by Ed and Mary Bowell.

173

cream. Another description of this color would be light cinnamon. As in the blue the coat may be of one colored hairs, or roaned with light and dark hairs intermixed.

The markings which appear above each eye, in the ears, under the throat and tail, on the chest, legs, and groin are called rust or tan. Rust is the more accurate description of the color. A rich rust color on the black Doberman is the goal of the breeder. However, the markings can become too dark and indistinct. This is called melanism. Melanism causes the markings to become too intermingled with the darker hairs of the coat, and in extreme cases the dog appears to be solid black.

Light yellow or wheat-colored markings are also undesirable. Light markings are usually accompanied by a light brown eye giving the facial expression a hard look.

In red Dobermans the markings are also rich rust, but never so dark as seen in the black. Blues and fawns have their marking colors changed slightly by the same gene which diluted the coat from the black or red to blue or fawn. The markings in these two colors are a deep apricot rust—the darker the better.

Eye color ranges from dark chocolate brown in the black dogs, to medium brown in red dogs, and amber in blues and fawns. The eye color in reds, blues, and fawns will never be quite as dark as the proper eye color for a black dog. Eye color can vary from a very yellow eye in the blacks and reds to a greenish yellow in the blues and fawns. These lighter colors give the face a harsh staring expression and are not desirable.

Coat Color Inheritance

The inheritance of basic coat color (i.e., whether or not a Doberman will be black, red, blue, or fawn) is described by a simple genetic method first introduced by a monk, Gregor Mendel, in 1865. His work on flowers was published in an obscure journal. It was not until many years later that scientists and animal breeders, much less the general public, realized that his work also applied to animal breeding. This accounts for publications as late as 1963 containing the idea that the fawn Doberman and possibly the blue was the result of genetic "weakness" resulting from some sort of inbreeding. Finally, prior to the adoption of the present standard in 1969, it became recognized by most Doberman breeders that coat color inheritance was simple Mendelian inheritance.

The principles upon which the color inheritance is based are these:

1. Each dog has at least two pairs of genes controlling coat color

2. Each parent contributes one half of the genetic makeup of a particular gene pair

3. There are dominant and recessive genes.

High Halo's Calypso, lovely fawn bitch sired by Ch. Marks-Tey's Hanover ex Ch. High Halo's Brooke of Kondo, pictured going Reserve Winner under Major Godsol, the first such win for a fawn in the history of the breed. Calypso was whelped in January, 1965 — had she been born a few years later, there is little doubt that she would have been the breed's first fawn champion. Bred by Mildred Dold, owned by Annlee Konecker and Mrs. Dold, and handled by Keith Walker.

Ch. Housecarl Heather, blue bitch, pictured winning the Group at Wheaton KC 1972 under judge Kenneth Peterson, handled by Howard Herring. Heather, by Ch. Highbriar Bandana ex Dobereich's Duress, is owned by Mr. and Mrs. Robert Silman.—*Petrulis*

175

In other words each parent contributes to each color-determining gene pair, and these contributions make up the so-called *genotype*—that is the genetic character of the dog. If one of a pair of genes is dominant over the other, then it determines the dog's color rather than the other, recessive gene. The term *phenotype* refers to how the genotype is expressed. In simple terms, the genotype tells what the dog's offspring will look like; the phenotype tells what the dog looks like.

The color of a Doberman is determined genetically. First, we will take up the basic black and red inheritance, and later the undiluted (black and red) and diluted (blue and fawn). Finally, we will combine them.

Black is dominant over red. A dog can have the following genotypes and phenotypes:

Genotype	Phenotype
BB	black
Bb	black
bb	red

In this table each letter represents one gene from each parent making up a gene pair. Capital B in a dog's genotype means that the dog will be black because black is dominant. A red dog must be bb because the only way a dog can be red is to have both genes in the pair recessive. Dogs BB and bb are termed *homozygous* because both members of the pair are the same. Dog Bb is termed *heterozygous* meaning the dog is genotypically a mixed pair.

In the tables below are the six possible matings of these three genotypically different dogs. In the tables are given the phenotype (color) and genotype of each parent (one at the top and one on the left side). The genotypes of the puppies are given in the table itself.

(1) black	black			(2) black	black			(3) black	red	
	B	B			B	b			b	b
B	BB	BB		B	BB	Bb		B	Bb	Bb
B	BB	BB		B	BB	Bb		B	Bb	Bb

(4) black	black			(5) black	red			(6) red	red	
	B	b			b	b			b	b
B	BB	Bb		B	Bb	Bb		b	bb	bb
b	Bb	bb		b	bb	bb		b	bb	bb

176

Mating (1) **BB** x **BB** gives all black **BB**
(2) **BB** x **Bb** gives all black ½ **BB**, ½ **Bb**
(3) **BB** x **bb** gives all black **Bb**
(4) **Bb** x **Bb** gives ¼ black **BB**, ½ black **Bb**, ¼ red **bb**
(5) **Bb** x **bb** gives ½ black **Bb**, ½ red **bb**
(6) **bb** x **bb** gives all red **bb**

Notice that in mating (4) black to red ratio is 3:1, and in (5) the ratio is 1:1. The laws of chance tell us that in a given litter one need not get these exact ratios, but on the average these matings will give these ratios.

When we now consider the blues and fawns, the same matings as above can be made except we must substitute blue for the black and fawn for the red.

Let D stand for the dominant normal and d stand for the recessive dilution. We will have these phenotypes and genotypes:

Genotype	Phenotype
DD	black or red
Dd	black or red
dd	blue or fawn

We can go on to develop tables as we did for the matings of the **BB**, **Bb**, **bb** genotypes. Except for the change in letters, the results will be the same.

The complications arise when we combine all four colors. When we do we can get 9 genotypes and 4 phenotypes (the four colors are in the standard). In the table below the genotypes for black and red must have at least one D while the diluted colors (blue and fawn) must have dd because dilution is recessive.

Genotype	Phenotype	DPCA No.
BBDD	black	1
BBDd	black	2
BbDD	black	3
BbDd	black	4
BBdd	blue	5
Bbdd	blue	6
bbDD	red	7
bbDd	red	8
bbdd	fawn	9

On the right in the above table is the DPCA color code number for that particular genotype. The DPCA has published a color chart containing this list as well as phenotype percentages obtained from the 81 possible combinations of

177

matings. Space does not permit making tables for all 81 combinations here. The color chart may be ordered from the Doberman Pinscher Club of America for a small fee. The most complicated possibility will probably serve as the most helpful illustration. Both parents will be black #4, that is they are both heterozygous for red and black and for dilution (BbDd). Remember each parent contributes a (B or b) and a (D or d) to each puppy.

	BD	Bd	bD	bd
BD	BBDD	BBDd	bbDD	BbDd
Bd	BBDd	BBdd	BbDd	Bbdd
bD	BbDD	BbDd	bbDD	bbDd
bd	BbDd	Bbdd	bbDd	bbdd

On the average the mating of 2 black #4 will give:

DPCA No.	Genotype	Phenotype	Number of puppies
1	BBDD	black	1 ⎫
2	BbDD	black	2 ⎪ 12 ⎫ 9
3	BBDd	black	2 ⎬
4	BbDd	black	4 ⎭
5	BBdd	blue	1 ⎫ 3
6	Bbdd	blue	2 ⎭
7	bbDD	red	1 ⎫
8	bbDd	red	2 ⎬ 4 ⎫ 3
9	bbdd	fawn	1 ⎭ ⎭ 1

Notice that the ratio of normal (black and red) to dilute (blue and fawn) also is 12:4 which reduces to 3:1, like the ratio of black to red.

You may want to set up similar tables for your own dogs. If you do we hope the examples given will show you how. If you need more detail see the DPCA chart. One thing is absolutely true. If you breed a blue to a red, YOU WILL NOT GET PURPLE PUPPIES.

12

Doberman Temperament

by Vic Monteleon

T HERE ARE MANY TERMS floating around in the bowl called "dog jargon," and quite a few of them are either ill-defined or generally misunderstood. The term "temperament" is one of these . . . often used, but meaning something slightly different to each individual in the fancy. As such, it has been rather difficult to establish any meaningful dialogue on the subject without the discussion rapidly degenerating into an argument over semantics.

In contemplating the differences between temperament and disposition, I am reminded of a story told to me about two dogs, one a Labrador Retriever, and the other, a Beagle. The Labrador was a retrieving dog without peer. His style was flawless, he was a powerful swimmer, and no job was too difficult for him, single and double retrieves, blind retrieves, all were executed with ease and great desire. He had a single hangup — this tremendous dog hated people! Unless you were one of his chosen few, he'd just as soon bite you as look at you.

The Beagle, on the other hand, was a lover of all mankind. He was outgoing, sunny and optimistic in his dealings with people, and gave every passing stranger more than the benefit of the doubt, greeting each with a cheerful wag of the tail. But this Beagle could fall dead asleep in a field of rabbits! He had no interest whatever in furred game of any kind, and his owner swore that he'd never seen this so-called "scent-hound" ever drop his nose to the ground to follow a trail.

The Lab had a great temperament, but a thoroughly lousy disposition. The Beagle had a very good disposition, but an awful temperament. This anecdote may help to illuminate the definition of temperament and disposition implicitly, but rather than leave the definitions to inference on the part of the reader, let's try to explicitly define them.

One of the versions of Webster's Dictionary defines temperament as "the totality of traits manifested in one's behavior or thinking." The key is in the phrase "*totality of traits,*" for it implies that there are definite components of behavior that, when summed up, define temperament. As such, the term temperament takes on the coloration of an "umbrella term" . . . the all-inclusive term describing behavior.

This is directly analogous to the term *conformation,* which refers to the overall structure of a dog . . . the structure itself consisting of defineable components such as topline, ribspring, forechest, angulation, etc. The various components that contribute to a given breed's conformation are spelled out in that breed's American Kennel Club approved standard. Yet these breed standards don't specify *all* structural components; they focus on the structural or conformational attributes that make a breed a dog. If they didn't, a breed standard might include the following idiotic phraseology: "The Cayoodle shall have four legs, each terminating in a foot, said foot to be moderately proportioned and having four distinct toes."

The same is true for temperament. When discussing a given breed's temperament, we need only focus on those behavioral attributes that make a breed unique, and can afford the luxury of ignoring the behavioral traits common to all canines. With this in mind, let's redefine temperament à la Webster to provide a more usable term:

Breed Temperament: "the totality of traits manifested in a breed's behavior that permit individuals of the breed to be what they were intended to be, and do what they were intended to do."

In short, breed temperament could be thought of as Behavioral Type! Other definitions that are useful in a discussion of temperament are:

Disposition: Definitely a component of temperament, disposition refers to a dog's attitude towards people. Shyness, viciousness, distrustfulness, outgoingness, and aloofness are specific examples.

Character: Used as in "breed character," a prevailing personality trait, or combination of personality and physical traits, so strongly associated with a breed that it almost "trademarks" the breed, — as in Bulldog tenacity, Cocker Spaniel merriness, Afghan aloofness, etc.

Personality: a pattern of behavior of an individual dog as expressed by mental and physical activities and attitudes. Those attitudes, together, that make a dog unique. Two dogs can and often do have the same temperament. No two dogs have the same personality.

Doberman Temperament — The Past

Using this definition, let us identify the specific components of Doberman temperament. A logical starting place is the history of the breed. Most fanciers know that the ancestors of the Doberman include the Rottweiler, the German Pinscher, the Greyhound, and the Manchester Terrier. There is also some speculation that an old black and tan shepherd type dog is in the fabric of the breed — the same smooth-coated dog that is the ancestor of the German Shepherd. With such a heritage, one can reasonably expect to see the following temperamental components:

> *Gameness and Determination*—The desire to stick to it and never give up . . . inherited from the terrier ancestry in the breed.
> *Strong Hunting Drive* — Inherited from the Greyhound, this trait expresses itself in the desire to chase moving game, be it rabbits, deer, or fleeing suspects.
> *Loyalty* — A trait that is legendary in the Rottweiler.
> *Circumspection of Strangers* — Coupled with a one family orientation, this trait is also passed down from the Rottweiler.
> *Intelligence and Trainability* — Inherited from both the old Shepherd type dog and the Rottweiler.
> *Courage and Fearlessness* — from the Terrier and Rottweiler.

We will never know whether these specific traits were chosen by conscious intention of Herr Dobermann or not, but all would agree that such traits are highly desirable in a working dog, supposedly capable of police or protection work. Add to this behavioral makeup, the blending of conformational traits:

> *Speed* — from the Greyhound.
> *Endurance* — from the Rottweiler.
> *Muscle Mass* — from the Terrier and Greyhound.
> *Agility* — from the Shepherd and Terrier.

and you have a dog that is the best of all worlds for work. This is the heritage of the Doberman.

But this is not to say that Dobes today are as described above. Times change, and with it, dogs change also.

When the Dobe emerged as a distinct breed around the turn of the century, the world was basically rural and agrarian. Society was essentially closed. A sharp dog was highly desirable, and all trespassers were fair game. The few people who came visiting, legitimately, gave long notice, and the dog was put away. At all other times, the dog was expected to be tough, incorruptible, and unafraid of "the devil himself."

Such a dog in today's world could be useful as an area guard in fenced yards, and many guard dog services would give their eye teeth for one like it. But society has opened up and has become largely urban. The original Dobe would be as out of place in urban society as a Neanderthal would be on the streets of Manhattan.

Doberman Temperament — The Present

Our breed standard states that a Doberman should be "energetic, watchful, determined, alert, fearless, loyal, and obedient," while being neither shy nor vicious. These are components of temperament. Let's look at each:

Energetic — Does the dog have a medium-to-high activity level, or is he lazy or lethargic?

Watchful — Is the dog visually aware of his environment? Does he purposefully focus on things going on? Does he have "eye," that is, does he fix his gaze in novel situations?

Determined — Does the dog have a "stick to it" attitude about him? Is he game, or does he give up easily?

Alert — This is watchfulness, plus the use of the rest of his senses. Is the dog aware of changes in his environment? Does he use his nose and ears? Does he immediately pick up on strange sights, scents, and noises?

Fearless — Does the dog meet novel or strange situations head on with either an aggressive or investigative response, or does he back away uncertainly? Does the dog have ego?

Loyal — Will the dog choose to be with you when he's got the option to leave with a random stranger? Does he clearly belong to your pack?

Obedient — This is a matter of training; however, the temperament component we're interested in is trainability or teachability. Is the dog willing and eager to learn?

These then, are what the Standard claims the ideal Dobe should possess. However, to fulfill the requirements of a working companion and personal protection dog, he must also possess these additional traits:

Mild Independence — A dog to be used as a protector cannot be a psychological or emotional dependent. He must be able to work on his own, in some cases at a distance from his master. However, overdone, independence can be synonymous with "bull-headedness or hammerheadedness," and we definitely don't want that.

Combativeness — This is more than the fearlessness our standard calls for. It is a willingness, perhaps even a desire, to fight when threatened. A fearless dog is unafraid, but a combative dog will show aggression even when the option to run away is available.

These, then are the temperamental components that make up the ideal. Our Standard also states that a dog should be neither shy nor vicious. Viciousness is easy to define as unjustified aggression. A dog that attempts to bite without provocation is vicious. Shyness is not quite that simple to label.

The Doberman Standard states that both shyness and viciousness are serious faults, and evidence of either is grounds for immediate excusal/dismissal from the breed ring. It further states that "a dog shall be judged fundamentally shy if, refusing to stand for examination, it shrinks away from the judge, it fears an approach from the rear, or it shies at sudden unusual noises to a marked degree." Before the last Doberman Pinscher Club of America revision of the Standard, evidence of shyness or viciousness was sufficient cause for the disqualification of a dog from showing privileges. The American Kennel Club, however, felt that this was harsh — especially in the case of puppies who'd received little in the way of training, socialization, or preparation for the breed ring. The DPCA agreed with this line of thinking and reduced the penalty to a dismissal rather than outright disqualification.

This was an excellent decision, as it recognized that one event did not necessarily indicate a true, stable behavior pattern. The dog should indeed be excused to prevent further trauma to him, or more importantly, the judge. The excusal gives the owner a data point, and allows owner and dog to go home and work out the problem with opportunity to try again at a future show. If the dog's shyness is a fixed pattern of behavior, if the dog is excused again and maybe a third time, the owner will, in all probability, forget showing. But in many instances the pattern has been temporary and there are champions today who shied once, then never showed such behavior again. They became rock steady and would unflinchingly stand for examination.

How could this happen? To explain requires an examination of shyness, as a behavioral phenomenon, in some depth. What is it? What causes it? How does it affect a dog? And what can the owner do about it?

We've already stated the Doberman Standard interpretation of shyness, namely, shying away from the judge, fear of an approach from the rear etc. More broadly speaking, though, shyness is generalized avoidance behavior, which shows up as fear of, and desire to escape from, any novel situation . . . that is, "a sudden change in environment." It might be a sudden movement of a person nearby, a waving towel, the approach of a stranger either from the front or rear on the street, a car backfiring, a child running out from a doorway or any number of things. The classic reaction of a shy dog is to bolt to the end of the leash (if on leash) or, if free, the dog will bolt away to a safe distance, so that the stimulus is out of his particular threat zone.

Perhaps at this point, we should mention a type of behavior that is often mistaken as shyness, but is not. Let's call it "distrustfulness." The trait is characteristic of one man or one family dogs. This one is not bothered by sights or sounds. When challenged by a threatening stranger, this type of dog is courageous and a fearless protector. Yet he'll avoid a non-threatening stranger; he would just as soon not be petted by anyone, and will often get behind his owner to avoid being touched. This type of dog doesn't make friends easily, is very reserved and suspicious of strangers, yet once he accepts someone, it's a complete acceptance. If you are accepted by this type of dog, you will never be forgotten. Because of his disdain, distaste, and avoidance of all but his "chosen few," such a dog is often labeled "shy." However, he most assuredly is not.

The first kind of shyness we observe is a total type of reaction, observable at a very young age, in most cases as young as 6–8 weeks of age. This is a genetic problem and evidences itself in an unstable nervous system. The genetic mechanism that causes this is not known; two beautifully tempered parents can produce it, and the rest of the litter can be perfectly normal. Nothing can be done with this type of shyness; it cannot be reconditioned and such a puppy cannot take to training or make a decent companion. So the only humane thing to do is to put it to sleep.

Another type of shyness is environmentally induced between the ages of 7 and 16 weeks. Work performed by Scott and Fuller at Bar Harbour, Maine, and documented in Clarence Pfaffenberger's *New Knowledge of Dog Behavior* indicates that:

1. There are two critical periods of socialization in a puppy's life, namely 7–12 weeks and 12–16 weeks, in which a puppy requires human socialization and interaction. If they don't get it between 7–12 weeks, but do between 12–16 weeks, they'll minimally adjust to one owner but will fear everyone else.

2. If they get it between 12–16 weeks (when discipline and human leadership is established) the puppies will be friendly, but not very trainable.

3. If they don't get proper socialization during either period, they'll fear all people, including their owner.

Unfortunately, if shyness is due to No. 1 and/or No. 3 above, there's little an owner can do to overcome it. No. 3 is hopeless. No. 1 can be brought under a little control, but will be totally miserable unless we leave him and his owner on an unpopulated desert island. No. 2 is OK if you want a hammerhead, unruly dog who'll forever hate human domination, restraint and discipline.

There is also the "Traumatic Shyness," and it is caused by trauma to the dog. Put a perfectly healthy dog in a kennel run. A bunch of rowdy kids go by and they toss a firecracker into the run. The dog, as a result, can become shy both of loud noises and of children who are loud and rowdy. The dog could also rationally develop a fear of being kenneled. This is an example of traumatic shyness. In any event, it is caused by a real event that "scars" the dog mentally. It can be treated, and the dog can be reconditioned.

Let us now discuss methods of treatment for the above types of shyness:

Genetic Nervous Instability — This problem can't be really cured. This type of puppy really has a neurological genetic disorder, causing extreme sensitivity in all senses, and a runaway anxiety responses. Should be put to sleep.

Distrustfulness —This dog can be taught to hold his ground and tolerate strange people. But he'll never become outgoing. Since a characteristic of such a dog is an almost fanatic loyalty, they are willing to please their owners and are easily trained. Teaching such a dog to sit-stay, and stand for examination usually is all that it takes. Once given the command, the dog can be approached, petted or examined. However, when not under command, it requires intelligent handling. Don't let people try to pet or coax him. Tell them to let the dog approach them, and then, only with slow non-threatening motions, may they pet him. Once past the threshold of acceptance by the dog, once he has chosen to make friends, this dog is normal in every respect — you are no longer a stranger.

Lack of Primary Socialization — This dog could have been normal in all respects, but because of the lack of socialization to people, he'll always be uneasy around them. This dog is probably very attached to other dogs, and feels a lot more comfortable if there's another dog around. If the other dog is outgoing, he may even follow its lead in approaching strangers in your home . . . eventually to the point of accepting them. Success in reconditioning this dog is dependent on how long the dog has been allowed to fix the fear pattern. If you start the treatment at four months of age, chances are good that he'll end up almost normal. Another outgoing dog is a help in this, but if not available, you still have a good shot at helping him. He must be around people, immersed in them, with them ignoring him. In the house, on the street, going about their business, this dog must have a non-threatening opportunity to see humans. He must also get very healthy doses of individual socialization from his owners . . . and obedience training with a lot of praise to build his confidence.

Trauma — The best way to handle traumatic shyness is to recreate the situation, without the trauma, and insure that a pleasurable event occurs at the site of the trauma. The pleasurable event is dependent on what "turns your dog on" . . . you are the best judge of what to use. Repeat until the trauma is erased from the dog's memory. Above all, be patient.

Hopefully the above discussion will have clarified at least part of the subject of shyness, and will cause the recognition that each dog must be treated in accordance with his nature.

Temperament Testing and Observation

In conformation, one would consider the judging process to start at birth, and proceed more or less continuously through the growth of the puppy until adulthood. Only at adulthood can we make final judgment on a dog conformation wise. Anything we see before the dog is mature indicates future potential, not actual fact.

The same is true for temperament. We can only identify final temperamental worth of a dog at adulthood, and all observation prior to that, again indicates potential, not fact. Perhaps the determination of temperament is a bit more difficult because of the very strong influence of environment on a dog's behavior. However, whether or not observed behavior is a result of genetics or environment, the testing and observation of temperament has distinct payoff both to breeders and to dog owners. It allows the identification of problems that may be environmentally caused. It allows a clue as to whether or not a given behavior pattern is genetic, and if provides some insight into what's really going on in a dog's mind.

With this in mind, let's outline a data gathering program for temperament. The following table summarizes a typical program of observation and testing from birth to maturity:

DATA GATHERING PROGRAM

Age	Period	Data
Birth – 1 week	Postnatal/parturition	Observation of vigor, nursing reflex, locator reflex, sucking rank, distress vocalizations.
1–3 weeks	Neonatal	Same as above plus, eyes opening, hearing, co-ordination/walking, all ranked with respect to littermates.
3–4 weeks 4–7 weeks	First transitional primary sociali- zation	Self discovery, discovery and awareness of environment, relationship to littermates and dam . . . other dogs, initial reaction to people, weaning behavior, group puppy tests.
7–12 weeks	Human orientation second transitional	Individual puppy tests, mixed pack behavior, reaction to novelty, initial leashbreaking, housebreaking.
12–16 weeks	Juvenile	Reaction to discipline, preliminary training.
4–18 months	Adolescence	Emerging sex drives, guarding, territorial instincts, ego strengths, obedience training, tracking, DPCA type tests.
Beyond 18 months	Maturity	Adult temperament tests; schutzhund training, emotional stability, activity level, fertility (bitches) attitude towards other dogs.

Before discussing actual puppy tests, let's for a moment consider possible causes of variation in observed puppy behavior of littermates which may be due to other than genetic causes. This is at best an incomplete list of causes.

1. Initial Size — from three to five weeks of age smaller pups are usually bowled over by their larger littermates. This might cause either submissive passivity or strong determination.

186

2. Litter relationships are not identical for each pup since each pup has a different set of littermates.

3. Varying health and hunger of pups. The pup who gets to the "faucet" first and fills up . . . the pup who always manages to suck on the biggest, fullest teats, the pup who's healthy, will hardly ever be stressed and will tend to spend the first few weeks of his life grunting and belching with luxurious abandon.

It might be that the temperament of the dam plays a major role in the formation of emerging puppy personalities. Some mothers, like humans, are highly frivolous with their pups. They just can't seem to take their maternal duties seriously. When the pups fight and one yelps, this particular dam will ignore it. When pups are screaming for her to open the milk bar, she'll have to be coaxed into the whelping box. Some mothers don't like pups at all, and have to be watched closely to prevent injury to the pups. Some are overzealous and too maternal . . . smothering their pups with attention, never letting them develop relationships with each other . . . and some are serious and sensible. This type will let the pups play, but if it gets too rough, she will break it up, lick and reassure the one who was yelping. She'll care for their needs and play/socialize them. She knows her puppies and knows when to be concerned. It's interesting to note that genetics are often blamed for temperaments that are (as pups) remarkably consistent when the same dam is involved. It's a distinct possibility that the dam's behavior in the whelping box is the cause . . . and THAT may be genetic.

Now prior to describing the mechanics of puppy testing . . . there are some things about temperament testing that are misunderstood . . . causing some people to turn-off to the idea without really understanding the facts and fallacies.

There is a tendency to believe that what a dog does on any given test on a given day at a given place reveals the dog's true behavior. This is NOT true! Particularly with adults.

One test or set of tests is not generally conclusive. To get a behavioral baseline for a given dog requires at least two, if nor more, tests. This is one of the reasons why our data gathering program is continuous . . . and should not consist of only one set of tests.

Now the tests themselves. We start puppy testing at five weeks of age. From birth, we've been observing the pups, and noticing differences emerge — some are better eaters, some are noisier, some sleep more, some are more agile, more alert. We've hopefully noted our observations somewhere, so we can see if they correlate with our test results. At five weeks of age, pups will have had their full senses for two weeks, and should have been weaned. Our first set of tests is given to the litter as a group (at five weeks).

The Group Puppy Tests (at 5 weeks)

The Sudden Noise — Have the litter in a small area together, with hard flooring such as tile, linoleum, concrete etc. When the litter is engrossed in some activity, drop a pot or pan on the floor (don't drop right on top of the pups—ten feet away) and note the following: Startle or no startle reaction. Curiosity (investigation or not, avoidance).

Visual Novelty — Again with the litter in a small area, drop a stuffed toy or pull a child's pull toy (not one that makes a noise) into their midst. Observe: Alertness, Watchfulness, Startle, Curiosity, Investigation, Avoidance.

Acoustic Novelty — Hide from the pups and blow a whistle for about six short blasts . . . don't make it very loud. Observe: Investigation, (attempt to locate source) Startle and Recovery, Arrival/Non arrival. This one will need two people, the observer and the blower. During this test, the pups should remain on the same footing throughout.

Footing Threshhold — Call the pups from one room into another over a threshhold that involves a change of footing, *e.g.* from tile to carpeting through a doorway. The footing you are calling the pups to should be one they've never been on before. Observe the following: Which come across . . . which don't. Of those that come, which bowl right in and don't appear to notice change; which notice change and enter with caution; and which need considerable coaxing. Of those that don't cross, which really want to, but can't bring themselves to do it.

These are our group tests. We do them together at five weeks because the pups are too young to be tested alone. They really have only been with each other two weeks (from onset of all senses), and to test them alone would cause separation distress that would probably invalidate results. During the period from 7–8 weeks, we do them all again . . . this time with individual pups.

Individual Puppy Tests (7–8 weeks)

We start by doing the group tests on individual pups to note whether behavior of each pup is different or the same in the absence of littermates. This is important, as some "hangers back" may have gained confidence from the earlier presence of the more aggressive littermates. One may expect some variation on this, due to:

Immature nervous systems maturing, giving the pup more stability. Such a pup will be stronger at 7 weeks than earlier.

Pups with a strong dependence will be very litter attached and do worse on their own. There's probably not much wrong with them, they just need a lot of individual socialization.

Pups low in the initial dominance order will do better away from their dominating littermates.

We also administer a group of tests called the "Sociability Tests" which identify an individual pup's initial social status with respect to people. These are useful tests to determine which pups need more time away from littermates and more socialization, and for matching pups with people on the basis of compatible personalities.

These tests should be given either by a stranger or a household member that doesn't feed the puppies. We measure dominance, submissiveness, and independence with respect to people on these tests.

The Sociability Tests were developed by William E. Campbell and are described in his article "Matching Puppies and People" which appeared in *Modern Veterinary Practice*. There are five tests:

1. *Social attraction* — Immediately on entering test area, put pup down gently in center of area, step away several feet in the opposite direction from which you entered, kneel down and gently clap your hands to attract the pup. How readily the pup comes to you, attitude of tail, etc. indicates the degree of social attraction, confidence or social independence of the pup. Do not call the pup to you. Just clap your hands.

2. *Following* — Starting with pup on ground next to you, walk away from pup in a normal fashion. How readily he follows shows his degree of following attraction. Failure to follow indicates independence. However, before you score a pup with an "i" make sure he SAW you leave. No chatter allowed to get the pup's attention.

3. *Restraint* — Crouch down and gently roll the pup onto its back, holding it with one hand on its chest for 30 seconds. How strongly the pup fights or accepts this restraint shows a measure of social/physical domination or submissiveness.

4. *Social Dominance* — Crouch and gently stroke the pup from top of head downwards along neck and back. Whether or not he accepts this indicates his degree of acceptance of your social dominance.

5. *Elevation Dominance* — Bend over and cradle the pup under his belly, fingers interlaced and palms up, elevating him just off the floor. Hold him there for 30 seconds. This places the tester in full control and the pup in none at all. Measures acceptance of human dominance.

On pages herewith you will find a testing score sheet. Sample responses and associated scores are shown on the score sheet. According to Campbell, two or more "dd's" with "d's" in other sections indicate a dominant/aggressive pup . . . not to be placed in homes with small children. Three or more "d's" will be outgoing and dominant . . . again, not good for small children. Three or more "s's" will probably fit more environments and are best with kids. Two or more "s's" are highly submissive and should only be given to warm, calm, patient people. Two or more "i" responses, especially on test 4, will be difficult to socialize and may be hard to train.

189

Assign each pup a letter (A,B,C,etc.). Circle the code letters scored under each pup's letters in each test section.

SECTION NUMBER AND PUP BEHAVIOR	A	B	C	D	E	F	G	H	I	J	K	L	M	N	O	P
1. SOCIAL ATTRACTION																
Came readily - tail up - jumped - bit at hands	(dd)	dd	dd	dd	dd	dd	dd	dd	dd	dd	dd	dd	dd	dd	dd	dd
Came readily - tail up - pawed at hands	d	d	d	d	d	d	d	d	d	d	d	d	d	d	d	d
Came readily - tail down	s	s	s	s	s	s	s	s	s	s	s	s	s	s	s	s
Came hesitantly - tail down	ss	ss	ss	ss	ss	ss	ss	ss	ss	ss	ss	ss	ss	ss	ss	ss
Did not come at all	-	-	-	-	-	-	-	-	-	-	-	-	-	-	-	-
2. FOLLOWING																
Followed readily-tail up-got underfoot-bit at feet	(dd)	dd	dd	dd	dd	dd	dd	dd	dd	dd	dd	dd	dd	dd	dd	dd
Followed readily-tail up- got underfoot	d	d	d	d	d	d	d	d	d	d	d	d	d	d	d	d
Followed readily - tail down	s	s	s	s	s	s	s	s	s	s	s	s	s	s	s	s
Followed, hesitant - tail down	ss	ss	ss	ss	ss	ss	ss	ss	ss	ss	ss	ss	ss	ss	ss	ss
No follow, or went away	-	-	-	-	-	-	-	-	-	-	-	-	-	-	-	-
3. RESTRAINT DOMINANCE (30 seconds)																
Struggled fiercly - flailed - bit	dd	dd	dd	dd	dd	dd	dd	dd	dd	dd	dd	dd	dd	dd	dd	dd
Struggled fiercly - flailed	(d)	d	d	d	d	d	d	d	d	d	d	d	d	d	d	d
Struggled, then settled	s	s	s	s	s	s	s	s	s	s	s	s	s	s	s	s

4. SOCIAL DOMINANCE (30 seconds)

Jumped - pawed - bit - growled	dd	dd	dd	dd	dd	dd	dd	dd	dd	dd	dd	dd	dd	dd	dd	dd
Jumped - pawed	d	d	d	d	d	d	d	d	d	d	d	d	d	d	d	d
Squirmed - licked at hands	(s)	s	s	s	s	s	s	s	s	s	s	s	s	s	s	s
Rolled over - licked at hands	ss	ss	ss	ss	ss	ss	ss	ss	ss	ss	ss	ss	ss	ss	ss	ss
Went and stayed away	i	i	i	i	i	i	i	i	i	i	i	i	i	i	i	i

5. ELEVATION DOMINANCE (30 seconds)

Struggled fiercly - bit, growled	(dd)	dd	dd	dd	dd	dd	dd	dd	dd	dd	dd	dd	dd	dd	dd	dd
Struggled fiercly	d	d	d	d	d	d	d	d	d	d	d	d	d	d	d	d
Struggled - settled - licked	s	s	s	s	s	s	s	s	s	s	s	s	s	s	s	s
No struggle - licked at hands	ss	ss	ss	ss	ss	ss	ss	ss	ss	ss	ss	ss	ss	ss	ss	ss

TOTALS:

dd's = 3
d's = 1
s's = 1
ss's =
i's =

dd	=	strong dominance
d	=	dominance
s	=	submissiveness
ss	=	strong submissiveness
i	=	independence

Score sheet for testing responses.

191

The next set of tests, also given during the 7–8 week period measure the pups' neurological development, emotional state, ego, perception, and problem solving ability:

Height Test — Place the pup on top of a box about ten inches high. Call the pup to jump off. The box is low enough so he can't hurt himself in jumping. Repeat this test several times in succession and note how quickly he learns and gains confidence with coaxing. Pups lacking confidence will tend to crouch without moving (almost frozen) on top of the box. After such a dog is helped down, does he learn to jump down by himself?

Incline Test — Place the pup on a higher box than the height test (about 15″) with a rough surfaced board (good footing) going from the box to the ground. Does the pup discover the incline or does he jump off? Does he crouch and freeze? Coax the pup down the board. How many repeats before the pup needs no coaxing?

Up the Incline — When the pup has successfully gone down the board a few times, try this one. Place a toy or piece of food on top of the same set-up, or drop a chase rag up the board. Can you get the pup to go up the board onto the box?

Isolation Test — Put pup in his own pen by removing his littermates. How long does it take for pup to recognize his isolation and start to cry? Now reassure pup and place him in a strange new area (like a crate). No distractions in the area . . . it should be quiet. Again, how does the pup react? Is there any exploration? Does the pup distress easily?

The V-Barrier — Hinge two six-foot-long by four-foot-high boards together to form a "V." Place the pup toward the closed end, head forward so he can neither see out nor turn around. Back away and call the pup. To get out, he'll have to back up, then turn around. How long does it take for the pup to figure the problem out? If you have to show him, how many trials before the pup does this on his own? Evidence indicates that the more dependent a pup is, the harder time he has in figuring it out. He wants to get to his owner so badly that his emotions actually get in the way.

Tug-of-War — Entice the pup into a game of tug-of-war by wiggling a rag on the ground, moving it away from the pup. Test his pursuit reflex, his desire to seize his prey, and his tenacity. These are all very necessary qualities in a protection dog.

Pain Threshhold — Take the pup's front paw and gently grasp the webbing between the two toes with your thumb and forefinger. Gradually pull the webbing forward until the pup pulls the foot away. Is the pup sensitive or insensitive? Does he forgive? An extremely pain sensitive pup is not desirable. Neither is an insensitive one.

Fetch Test — This is the famous test that's such an excellent indicator of guide dog potential. This is a teaching test. Put the pup in a corridor and

192

excite him with an object (a rag, a ball etc.). Throw it down the corridor and tell him to "fetch." Does he chase and grab the object? Once he gets it, excitedly call him. Does he return with the object? Does he get it and "kill" it? Does he get it and carry it off to chew on it? Give the pup three tries . . . on a collar and a light line. A few days later try again . . . off the line. Try again a third time after a few more days. If the pup gets it after three "workouts," he's got both human orientation, and trainability plus.

After this series of tests, your pup will probably be sold. However, you can still get meaningful feedback from the new owners as the pups grow.

How do the pups respond to leashbreaking? How do they respond to new surroundings? How easily do the pups housebreak? How do they respond to initial conformation training . . . restraint and stacking. Are they stubborn . . . hammerheaded . . . sensitive . . . willing? How do they take to discipline. Are they resentful, sulky? Forgiving? Do they bounce back?

How do the pups compare to each other . . . and how does this data compare to the pups' behavior on the earlier tests?

Maturity Tests

Upon maturity, we're ready to evaluate the fruits of our labor. There are two ways in which this can be accomplished. One is by using a set of adult temperament tests, such as those designed for the DPCA Register of Merit (ROM) Program. These tests measure a dog's reaction to:

(a) Neutral stranger. (b) Friendly stranger. (c) Sudden noises (hidden clattering and gunshots). (d) Sudden visual stimulus (pop open umbrella). (e) Threatening stranger. (f) Footing changes in terms of either approach (investigation or aggression) or avoidance behavior. The strength of reaction to each stimulus is measured.

Another method of actually determining a dog's temperament is to formally train the dog in Obedience, tracking, and protection work via the emerging Schutzhund sport. Of the two methods, the training process gives the most information, but requires tremendous time and energy on the part of the owner. A test or series of them, give less information but measures working ability indirectly . . . sort of an aptitude test requiring no formal training.

In any event, we as breeders have an obligation to maintain the Doberman as a companion and protector, a dog that lives up to his heritage as a total Doberman, sound both in mind and body. Temperament testing is a means to help achieve this, and should be given serious consideration by all who breed Dobes. A dog of form with no substance must be avoided at all costs.

Ch. Civetta's Black Drongo of Kami UD returning the right scent to his owner, Dr. Arnold Orlander. This black Ch. Tarrado Corry's son is yet another example of how beauty and brains can go together.

Ch. Jimel's Julie CD, red bitch, owned by Mr. and Mrs. Victor Monteleon.—*Bergman*

194

13

The Obedience Doberman

by Bernie Brown

BECAUSE of the complex nature of the Doberman Pinscher, the breed represents perhaps the greatest challenge to the serious Obedience trainer. The Doberman is a myriad of extremes: gentle, stubborn, willing, eager to please, nervous, hard-headed, free-thinking, quick to react, immune to corrections. Every trainer who has ever held a Doberman at the end of the leash can add to these adjectives. The Doberman is truly all things to all trainers.

"The Doberman's mind is the closest that I know of to the mind of a human," says Bob Self, noted trainer, American Kennel Club judge, and owner of a past High Scoring Dog winner at a Doberman Pinscher Club of America Specialty.

"The Doberman reacts so fast that when it makes a mistake, by the time you attempt to make a correction, a second mistake has been made," says Velma Janek, the breed's First Lady of Obedience.

"The Doberman is perhaps the most difficult dog in the world to perfect," says Jack Godsil, one of the country's foremost Obedience trainers. "Teaching a Doberman an Obedience exercise is not difficult. But perfecting the exercise is something else again. With a Dobe, it can truly be a trying experience."

"Training a Doberman can leave you in tears with total frustration," says Elaine Brown, whose male Doberman set an American Kennel Club record for Dobes by achieving his three Obedience degrees in the fastest time. "Despite the frustrations, I dearly love the breed. I will always own a Doberman."

To the Doberman lover, no other dog possesses the mystique, the charisma, the nobility, the mere joy of owning a dog. At the same time, no other dog brings out the fear of dogs faster than a Doberman. No other dog has the reputation of man-killer that the Doberman has. Because of this unwarranted reputation, the training of the Doberman has taken on special significance in the years since World War II.

It was during the war years that the name Doberman became synonymous with viciousness. The Germans achieved great success with the Doberman in guard and attack work and the ranks of America's K-9 Corps, which was begun largely with German Shepherds, soon became filled with Dobermans.

For many servicemen who became trainers, it was their first experience with dogs. And for many their first experience with Dobermans. It was a period of great adjustment for all concerned.

"For most of us in the K-9 Corps, it was a case of getting over the fear of working with Dobermans," said Bill Worley, who was one of the first Yanks to take Dobermans into the South Pacific. This fear of the Doberman lead to the development by Worley of what is known in the Obedience ring as the "swing" finish. Worley defined it as the military finish.

"Most of the Army Dobermans were just plain mean. If you brought the dog around behind you to go to the heel position, the dog usually took a bite out of your rear end," said Worley. "To halt this, we developed a way to bring the dog to the heel position whereby we could keep the dog in front of us and always under control. Thus, the swing, or military finish was born."

After the war, dog clubs began to spring up throughout America. While Doberman fanciers were in the minority, many began to realize that the trainability of the Dobe in work other than police, guard and tracking, was quite high. The training potential of the Doberman was obvious to the experienced trainer.

As with all successful efforts, there had to be pioneers in order to achieve success. Due to the efforts of such pioneers as Willy Necker, Ludwig Gessner, Roland Horton, Glenn Staines, Stanley Donon, Mrs. Robert W. Adamson, Bill Worley, Clarence Alexander, Bob Self, and Hugh Crebs, the Doberman slowly began to become recognized as a highly desirable breed for those who wanted a competition dog for the Obedience ring and also as a family dog.

Among the pioneers, it was Chicagoan William Schaefer who was responsible for starting the North Shore Dog Training Club, the first Obedience training club in the United States. Not long after he established the North Shore Club, Schaefer went to Cleveland to help form a similar club. It was in Cleveland that Clyde Henderson, Frank Grant and Maxwell Riddle became active in clubs and in the development of the Doberman for training purposes. A few years after the formation of the Cleveland training club, Mr. and Mrs. Grant formed the Michigan Doberman Pinscher Club.

After Schaefer formed the North Shore Club, Fred Kahl led a dedicated group of Dobe fanciers who banded together on Chicago's South Side. The result was the South Side Doberman Training Club.

196

While the greatest effort to promote the Doberman breed came after the war years, there were many fanciers of the breed training and showing Dobes in the 1930's. The first Dobermans certified for Companion Dog (C.D.) degrees, on November 14, 1936 were: Rollo v Brickley, owned by Charles LeBoutillier, Jr.; Llisa v Brickley, owned by Mr. and Mrs. Samuel Thomas Brick; Prinz v Konigsee, owned by Frida and Nikolaus Schwaiger; and Shadda v Verstaame, owned by John M. Richardson.

On November 1, 1937, the first Dobermans were certified for Companion Dog Excellent (C.D.X.) degrees. They were: Rollo v Brickley, owned by Charles LeBoutillier, Jr.; Marko v Siegerpark II, owned by Frank H. McClellen; and Zola v Flakenburg, owned by Oscar E. Barlow.

On November 10, 1938, almost two years from the day that he had received his C.D. degree, LeBoutillier and his Dobe became the first dog of his breed to receive a Utility degree (U.D.) and a Tracking (T) degree.

One of the earliest of the Dobe Obedience pioneers was Hugh E. Crebs of Chicago. In 1939 Crebs and his bitch, Princess B. Wilhelmina, were judged top scoring Obedience dog in the Doberman Pinscher Club of America trial.

Crebs' score that year was 198, achieved out of the Utility class. In 1944, Crebs and his bitch came back to win the trial at the national specialty with a score of 199.5, again in Utility. In 1954 Crebs and Creb's Betty Girl won the doberman Pinscher Club of America trial with a 197 out of the Open B class.

Only five Dobermans have received their Championship and Utility Dog Tracking degrees in the history of the American Kennel Club. The five are: Ch. Abbenoir, UDT, owned by Mr. and Mrs. Frank Grover; Ch. Commando's Silver Sandal, UDT, owned by Mel and Virginia Spafford; Ch. Charem's Bimini, UDT, owned by Mr. and Mrs. Leonard Weiss; Ch. Sand-Mark's Joint Venture, UDT, owned by Mel and Viginia Spafford; and Ch. Mymistake, UDT owned by Rose Jacobs.

Ch. Abbenoir, or "Abbey," was the first Doberman owned by the Grovers. She was sent to Willy Necker for her basic Obedience. It was Necker who put a C.D. degree on "Abbey," with three scores of 199.5 out of a possible 200 points. Each of her three Novice scores was good enough to take High in Trial. Necker also showed the dog to her C.D.X. title. At the time, Abbey was beginning to win points in the breed ring from the American-Bred Class. The Grovers took Abbey from Necker after she had won her C.D.X. and they put the U.D. and the T. on her. By the time Abbey had finished her U.D., she had nine points toward her championship. Larry Downey then put the remaining six points to finish her. Abbey waited until she was nearly four weeks in whelp with her only litter before she earned her Tracking title.

Ch. Abbenoir UDT, owned by Mr. and Mrs. Frank Grover.

```
                              Ch. Kurt vd Rheinperle-Rhinegold
                    Ch. Westphalia's Rajah
                              Sgn. Ch. Jessy vd Sonnenhohe
          Ch. Westphalia's Apollo
                              Pericles of Westphalia
                    Ch. Westphalia Ursula
                              Sgn. Ch. Jessy vd Sonnenhohe
CH. ABBENOIR, UDT
                              Ch. Ferry v. Rauhfelsen of Giralda
                    Ch. Mars of Moorpark
                              Casa del Canto's Comanche
          Kushner's Alice
                              Ch. Westphalia's Rajah
                    Stanighy 11 Alfreda
                              Westphalia's Xcella
```

Grover's fondest memory of Abbey is of her sweep at the show at which she won her U.D. title. She was first in Utility, and then Winners' Bitch, Best of Winners, Best of Breed and placed in the Group.

Although Abbey had only one litter, by Readington's Dynamite, UD, it was a dandy. Three of her four puppies lived. They were: Ch. Barrierdobes Abbegail CD, Ch. Barrierdobes Adventurer CDX, and Barrierdobes Adventuress CDX (who died when she was three with five points toward her championship, including a major.)

Ch. Commando's Silver Sandal, or "Sandal," was the second Doberman owned by the Spaffords. Mel Spafford had put a U.D.T. on "Sid," their first Dobe. Spafford saw a picture of Ch. Abbenoir on the cover of *Dog News* and decided that he wanted to own a Champion as well as a U.D.T. Doberman. It was shortly after that that Frank Grover moved to the West Coast. Friends of the Spaffords, the Bob Benders, bred their bitch to an Abbey son. From this litter, Sandal was selected.

Sandal was three times High in Trial on way to her C.D. At about the same time that she obtained her C.D.X., Sandal was given to Harry Sangster, who put nine points on the bitch during one swing of shows through the Western states. Because of a lack of entries, Sandal had a problem winning a major, but did get to finish. Spafford showed Sandal one time in Tracking and received her T. At the age of seven, Sandal contracted an undetermined illness and within a matter of months, she was dead.

Ch. Charem's Bimini, "Bim," the only male among the five Dobes to obtain a championship and a U.D.T., got his C.D. in three shows. He was trained for conformation and Obedience, but was not shown in the Obedience ring until he had earned his championship in July, 1967 at Spartansburg, North Carolina, handled by Bobby Barlow.

Bim was a natural clown, and it took the Weisses six shows to get a C.D.X. Two weeks after Bim obtained his title, the dog received his T. degree. In so doing he became the first male Dobe to win four titles. A year after he obtained his C.D.X., Bim became a U.D. Doberman.

Len Weiss was no novice at handling dogs in the Obedience ring. He started with Boxers in 1946 and apprenticed as a trainer under Blanche Saunders and Ed Schact. In 1952, he moved to Youngstown, Ohio, and founded the Youngstown All-Breed Obedience Training Club. He also was the host of his own television show, "Going to the Dogs." The Weisses moved to New Jersey in 1955, where Len became an instructor for the First Dog Training Club of Northern New Jersey. In 1965 they moved to Florida where Len is now director of training for the Hollywood-Ft. Lauderdale Training Club and the Doberman Pinscher Club of Florida.

Ch. Sand-Mark's Joint Venture, UDT was the only offspring produced by Ch. Commando's Silver Sandal, UDT. Mel Spafford recognized "Venture's" keen sense of smell as a puppy and began tracking her at an early age. As a result, Venture got her T. degree at the age of ten months in her first tracking trial. Spafford then began working the bitch in Novice. A month and one-half later, at the age of less than a year, Venture received her C.D.

Venture's first championship points, a three-point major, were earned from the Bred-by-Exhibitor Class. She was later handled by Larry Worth, who put seven more points on the bitch. Spafford then showed her to finish off her championship. During the time that she was being shown in conformation, Spafford was working Venture in Open and Utility, too, and shortly after receiving her championship, she received her U.D.

Venture was bred twice. The first time she did not conceive. The second time she produced five puppies.

Ch. Mymistake, UDT was trained for Obedience by her owner, Rose Jacobs. She had her Utility degree before she finished her championship. Because Miss Jacobs was a registered nurse and did not have the time to actively campaign her bitch, the two got involved in weekend tracking. Most of their spare time was spent tromping through the fields and woods in fair and foul weather. Whenever her busy schedule permitted, Miss Jacobs showed "Missy" in Obedience trials. The two also performed at various church and school functions.

Obedience trainers have reaped the rewards of the efforts of serious breeders to produce Dobes with outstanding temperaments. Sounder Dobes provide better raw material for the serious trainer. Better raw material provides more opportunity for novice and expert alike to get the feel of a Dobe. The sport of Obedience began to see a greater influx of Dobes. And then in the '50s, an attractive woman from Muncie, Indiana, burst upon the training scene in a splash the likes of which the sport had never seen.

Velma Janek was her name and the training of Dobermans was her game. In fact she, more than any other trainer either before or since, brought the Dobe to the forefront of Obedience.

Since the 1950s, Mrs. Janek has scored more than 35 perfect scores, won two Doberman Pinscher Club of America trials, won the annual World Series of Dogs tournament held in Detroit, and has been the sport's most consistent winner.

"She is the only trainer, man or woman, whose mind works like a Doberman," said Jack Godsil.

Ch. Commando's Silver Sandal UDT,
owned by Mr. and Mrs. Mel Spafford.

Ch. Christie's Barrier

Readington's Dynamite, UD

Dawn's Allure

Ch. Barrierdobe's Adventurer, CDX

Ch. Westphalia's Apollo

Ch. Abbenoir, UDT

Kushner's Alice

CH. COMMANDO'S SILVER SANDAL, UDT

Vernhof's Bontemps

Ch. Commando's Comet

Vigilante's Amice

Commando's Breeze

Ch. Orestes of Westphalia

Wardean's Camille

Ch. Wardean's Benita

Ch. Astor vom Grenzweg
Ch. Borong the Warlock, CD
Ch. Florowill Allure, CDX
Ch. Borong the Warlock's Texan, CD
Ch. won Signumd's Faust
Ch. Faust's Siegerin v Sanmahr, CD
Lady Carl Hesterhoff
CH. CHAREM'S BIMINI, UDT
Ch. Astor vom Grenzweg
Ch. Borong the Warlock, CD
Ch. Florowill Allure, CDX
Charem's Magic Touch v Warlock
Bona of Town and Ranch
Baroness vom Charem
Princess Fanchon

Ch. Prinz v Wanderlust
Ch. Saratoga's Black Pirate
Pepperlane Koro of Westwind
Ch. Flashburn's Hesper v Saratoga CD
Ch Fortunas Maestro
Ch. Jussi v Ahrtal
Ch. Zessica v Ahrtal
CH. MYMISTAKE, UDT
Ch. Dobe-Acres Cinnamon
Noir of Starkanhart
Lu of Starkanhart
Dobe-Lea's Jezebel
Honus v Shields
Ch. Sheba of Three Rivers
Duchess v Urban

Ch. Lakecrest Thunderstorm
Ch. Florian v Ahrtal, CD
Ch. Willa v Ahrtal
Ch. Highbriar Hasty Road
Ch. Jet vd Ravensburg
Ch. Highbriar Blackbird, CD
Highbriar Stormette, CDX
CH. SAND-MARK'S JOINT VENTURE, UDT
Readington's Dynamite, UD
Ch. Barrierdobe's Adventurer, CDX
Ch. Abbenoir, UDT
Ch. Commando's Silver Sandal, UDT
Ch. Commando's Comet
Commando's Breeze
Wardean's Camille

Ch. Charem's Bimini UDT, owned
by Mr. and Mrs. Leonard Weiss.

Ch. Mymistake UDT, owned
by Rose Jacobs.

Ch. Sand-Mark's Joint Venture UDT,
owned by Mel and Virginia Spafford.

203

"There is no doubt about it. Velma Janek is the finest trainer of Dobermans that the sport has ever produced," added Hugh Crebs.

Mrs Janek's first Dobe was Rad's Arlotta Lou of First Lady, purchased from Jack Brown of St. Charles, Missouri. She was a Ch. Dortmund Delly's Colonel Jet daughter and her breeder was Caroline Rademaker. The Janeks called her "Happy." Although she never obtained a 200, Happy averaged more than 198 during the years she was campaigned. In the year 1958 she competed in eleven trials, winning High in Trial at seven. She was either second or third in the other four.

When Happy was four, the Janeks purchased another bitch, Rad's Friendly Jest of Summer. Although "Mellody," never obtained her championship, she did have twelve points. She was shown in both Obedience and conformation. In the early '60s at the Anderson, (Indiana) Kennel Club Show, Mellody went Best of Winners for a three-point-major and scored 199.5 in Open B to win High in Trial.

Many people insisted Mellody, who at the time was less than two years old, was too young to be campaigned so actively.

"That's ridiculous," recalled Mrs Janek. "A dog has all its intelligence by the time it's three months old. To let a dog go to a year before training it doesn't make any sense. That dog in a year has acquired some very bad habits and you've got to go all through the trouble of nagging the dog to break those habits. Why not, as a young puppy, get him used to doing it right from the start?"

After Mellody achieved her U.D., Mrs Janek purchased a poodle, "Pixie," a dog that scored six 200's. One of Mrs Janek's most impressive days in the Obedience ring saw Mellody earn a 200 in Utility under Blanche Saunders and Pixie follow with a 200 in Open B, also under Miss Saunders.

Before she retired from showing, Mellody had 27 perfect scores. One of the dog's most memorable days happened in 1964 in Ft. Wayne, Indiana, at the Northeastern Indiana Kennel Club's Annual All-Breed Show and Obedience Trial. Under Paul Essenwine, Mrs. Janek and Mellody earned a 200 in Open B. The pair then went into the Utility ring and scored another 200, this time under Blanche Saunders. Mellody was shown until the age of eight. She died of cancer two months after her last trial. Pixie followed her in death two months later.

Among Mrs. Janek's many mementos are certificates from the Doberman Pinscher Club of America stating that her dogs have been ranked in the top ten in Obedience over the last eighteen years. And this is without missing a single year!

Perhaps the greatest tribute to her Obedience skills came at a Dobe specialty held in St. Louis in 1962. Mrs Peggy Adamson was doing the breed judging. Mrs. Janek's reputation as a trainer was well-known to Mrs. Adamson, but the breed judge had never seen Mrs. Janek in action.

As Mrs. Janek and her husband were about to leave the show grounds, Mrs. Adamson interrupted the judging in her ring and asked Mrs. Janek if she would put on a demonstration. Mrs. Janek readily agreed and as the breed exhibitors formed a ring within the breed ring, the 5-foot 3-inch First Lady of Obedience put her dogs through an Obedience demonstration. When she finished, Mrs. Adamson led the applause.

Ch. Marks-Tey Blue Velvet, UD a black male owned by Elaine Brown, set an American Kennel Club record for Dobermans by achieving all three of his Obedience degrees in five and one-half months. "Valor" obtained his Obedience titles in ten trials, earning two Dog World awards, before the dog received his championship. In 1974 this dog was ranked as the country's sixth highest-scoring Doberman.

One of the new and most coveted awards in Obedience competition is that of Super Dog, given to the top winner at the annual United States Obedience Classics, co-sponsored by the Illini Obedience Association and Gaines Dog Foods. In 1976, Our Own Dark Secret UD, a 10-year old Doberman bitch owned by Norma J. Currier of Oxford, Michigan, came out of retirement to win this award, scoring an impressive 195.58 in the rugged two-day competition to top 40 other highly-trained dogs. Her prizes included $750 in cash, and a specially engraved sterling silver dumbbell.

The Northern California K-9 Cadence Doberman Drill Team pictured at the Doberman Pinscher Club of America Specialty, 1975. One of their features—dogs going over the high jumps while holding eggs in their mouths!—*Bergman*

Highest Scoring Dog in Trial
Doberman Pinscher Club of America

Year	Dog's Name	Class	Score	Owner
1937	Ducat v d Rheinperle	Open A	249	Frank L. Grant
1938	Duke of Schroth Valley	Novice A	98	Henry G. Schmitt
1939	Princess B. Wilhelmina	Utility	198	H.E. Crebs
1940	King IV, CDX	Utility	199.25	Harry Carson
1941	Tiger of Pontchartrain	Utility	199.7	Willy Necker
1942	No event			
1943	Ch. Danny v Neckerheim	Novice A	96.1	Lester Erhardt
1944	Princess B. Wilhelmina	Utility	199.5	Hugh E. Crebs
1945	No event			
1946	Ines Gozo de Feliz	Novice A	95	Dorothy H. Pagel
1947	Fritz v Darburg	Utility	197.5	Gilbert F. Berger
1948	Ch. Assault v Alec CDX	Open B	199.5	Clarence C. Alexander
1949	Von Ritter	Utility	199	Anthony Wilkas
1950	Ch. Abbenoir UDT	Novice B	199	Mr. & Mrs. Frank Grover
1951	No event			
1952	Teresa v Mac CDX	Utility	199	Mr. and Mrs. Joseph McKann
1953	Beechurst's Ajax the Great	Open B	197	Beechurst Kennels
1954	Creb's Betty Girl	Open B	197	Hugh E. Crebs
1955	Readington's Dynamite UD	Open B	196	Mr. and Mrs. Frank Grover
1956	No event			
1957	Ch. Guiding Eye's Magdolin	Novice A	195	Lewis and Bessie Fowler
	(This dog was also Bessie Fowler's Guide Dog)			
1958	No event			
1959	Titan of Ashworth	Novice A	197	Mr. and Mrs. Luke Reilly
1960	Rad's Friendly Jest of Summer	Open B	199.5	Velma Janek
1961	Diablo of Rosevale	Novice A	189	William F. Pickup
1962	Rad's Friendly Jest of Summer	Open B	199	Velma Janek
1963	Ch. Commando's Silver Sandal	Utility	198.5	Mel & Virginia Spafford
1964	Val Jan's Amber	Open B	197	Robert T. Self
1965	Ch. Commando's Silver Sandal	Utility	198.5	Mel & Virginia Spafford
1966	Ch. Commando's Silver Sandal	Utility	198	Mel & Virginia Spafford
1967	Little Mist v Frederick UDT	Open B	198	Rosalie & Fred Simpson
1968	Ch. Aztec's Bellona CDX	Open A	199.5	Teresa Nail
1969	Countess Misty of Manistee CDX	Open B	197.5	Robert & Patricia Schultz
1970	Ava Danica Hartmann UD	Open B	197	Genevieve C. McMillen
1971	Ronsu's Clipper Blue Jacket	Utility	198	Wayne Boyd
1972	Schauffelein's Dilemma	Open B	200	Leon K. Matthews
1973	April Acres Black Magic	Open A	198	Rickie L. Brooks
1974	April Acres Black Magic	Open B	197½	Rickie L. Brooks
1975	Frederick's Timbrel UD	Open B	197	Rosalie & Linda Simpson

Ch. Marks-Tey Blue Velvet UD in action.

Schutzhund training. Deborah Casey's Doberman shows he is more than willing to protect her if necessary.

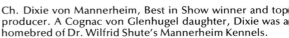

Ch. Dixie von Mannerheim, Best in Show winner and top producer. A Cognac von Glenhugel daughter, Dixie was a homebred of Dr. Wilfrid Shute's Mannerheim Kennels.

Ch. Lowenbrau Aloha Schauffelein, dam of 22 champions from five litters sired by her half brother, Am. & Can. Ch. Schauffelein's Troll Arabesque. Owned by Mr. and Mrs. R. Purdy.

Am. & Can. Ch. Schauffelein's Troll Arabesque, sire of more than 65 champions. Owned by Mr. and Mrs. R. Purdy.

208

14

The Doberman in Canada

by Pat Blenkey

$\mathbf{A}$LTHOUGH it is intended that this chapter should date from the mid-50s, I feel that some mention should be made of the top Dobermans predating this period, which have provided the foundation for the breed in Canada.

During the '40s and '50s the largest concentration of good dogs and the center of conformation showing was in the Windsor, London and Toronto areas of Ontario. The relatively large number of shows in Ontario and the easy access to the Eastern and Central states of the United States, facilitated the breeding of good Canadian bitches to good American sires, and participation of Canadian-breds in AKC shows.

Dr. Wilfrid Shute entered the picture around the late '30s, when his now famous Mannerheim Kennels came into being. He imported a number of American dogs—Ch. Judy of Navigator, Ch. Cognac von Glenhugel (an older brother of Dictator), Am. Ch. Deitrich of Dawn, Am. & Can. Ch. Damasyn the Ember, to mention only a few. Probably his most famous and influential import however, was the great Int. Ch. Defender of Jan-Har, a top winner both here and in the U.S., and the sire of 21 champions.

Among the famous Mannerheim homebreds were the Group winner Ch. Adam (I think from Dr. Shute's first litter), Ch. Dixie (a Cognac daughter) who was both a top producing bitch and Best in Show winner, and Am. & Can. Ch. Renco, also a top winner, who had the distinction of going reserve to the great Dictator at the DPCA specialty in Chicago. Littermates Ch. Flora and Am. Ch. Figaro both won their junior puppy classes at one of the DPCA Specialties, and Figaro was defeated by Defender (the Senior puppy winner) for Best Puppy in Show. Other Group winners were Ch. Goethe and Ch. Presto, owned by Bonnie Moon (Lendvay) of Alberta. Can. & South African Ch. Flame was sent to South Africa, and won consecutive Bests in Show on her first three outings.

Am. & Can. Ch. Sabre von Mannerheim (Ch. Brown's Dion ex Ch. Kaukauna's Gold Braide) proved to be both a Best in Show winner and a very influential sire. He was top winning Doberman in 1964, and it is very interesting to note that the top winners for 1965 — Ch. Kaukauna's Hi-Star, 1966 — Ch. Konigshausen Inspiration, 1967 — Hi-Star again, and 1968 — Ch. Bonnie von Mannerheim Nagidrac, were all sired by him.

In the late '60s, Dr. Shute purchased a Ch. Highbriar Bandana daughter, Ch. Von Usher's Aurora, did quite a bit of winning with her and then bred her to Am. & Can. Ch. Highland Satan's Image, producing the "Z" litter — his last to date.

Mannerheim's latest Best in Show winner is Ch. Schauffelein's Solar Wind (Ch. Schauffeleins Troll Arabesque ex Ch. Lowenbrau Aloha Schauffelein), winner of both the 1971 DPCC specialty under Tess Henseler, and the DPCC award for Puppy of the Year. Incidentally, Solar Wind is the 47th champion for Mannerheim. Although semi-retired from breeding and exhibiting, Dr. Shute still has a great interest in the breed, and is very much in demand as a judge and breed authority.

Mr. Harvey Gratton of Nova Scotia became interested in Dobermans in the late 1930s, and since that time over 100 champions carry the Trollhattan prefix. Not all of these are Dobes however, since his wife breeds Wire-haired Fox Terriers. The show situation on the East Coast has been rather scarce — however, Dobes owned or bred by Mr. Gratton can usually be found in the winners circle across Canada. Looking back over some of the old show results, I see that in 1958, Ch. Grosser Rot v Schauffelein, Ch. Trollhattan's Sabre and Ch. Trollhattan's Astral Isabelle were big winners for his kennel. Ch. Schauffelein's Sleigh Belle and her litter brother Ch. Brigadoon (Ch. Iago v Ahrtal ex Ch. Schauffelein's Silhouette) were both tops in the East Coast shows in 1961 — Brigadoon later siring a total of 11 champions.

Although Mr. Gratton has used the top American sires from time to time (including Ch. Patton's Ponder of Torn and Int. Ch. Brigum of Jan-Har), in the late '60s he purchased Ch. Tarrado's Chaos who, while never offered at public stud, has produced 21 homebred champions. The combination of Chaos and Ch. Warlock Witch v Trollhattan seems to be a very pleasing one, having produced at least four champions, including the Best in Show winner, Ch. Trollhattan's Lana. A Chaos son, Ch. Trollhattan's High Voltage Tye, was a top winner out West, and has recently returned to home grounds. Incidentally, Mr. Gratton had the distinction of awarding Am. & Can. Ch. Srigo's Kimmel (owned by Skead Kennels, Nova Scotia) a Best in Show, thus making him the first blue to win such an award.

Am. & Can. Ch. Defender of Jan-Har, red male, a top winner of the 1950s and sire of 21 champions. Bred by Jane McDonald and owned by Dr. Wilfrid E. Shute.

                                                       Ch. Blank v Domstadt

                                    Ch. Dictator v Glenhugel

                                              Ch. Ossi v Stahlhelm

                    Ch. Sarcen of Reklaw

                                    Ch. Emperor of Marienland

                       Kay of Reklaw

                                    Ch. Nana of Rhinegold

CH. DEFENDER OF JAN-HAR

                                        Ch. Saracen of Reklaw

                       Ch. Brigum of Jan-Har

                       Judy v Burse

                    Ch. Cissi of Jan-Har

                                    Ch. Alcor v Millsdod

                       Kilburn Jiffy

                                  Ch. Kilburn Audacity

Although John Lundberg bred on a very limited scale, five of his Von Gotenberg dogs earned their championships in the U.S.A. and Canada. Sired by Int. Ch. Brigum of Jan-Har ex Am. & Can. Ch. Arista vd Engesburg, they are — Alpha, Axel and Aristo from the first litter, and Brigadeer and Bobo from the second.

In recent years, the name Schauffelein has become very well known. However, every kennel has its beginnings, and in 1947 we find the young Joey Purdy (Wright as she was then) purchasing her first Dobe. Becoming more and more interested in the breed, she then bought a Ch. Goethe von Mannerheim daughter, Ch. Trinka von Edelwessen (who incidentally, was bred by Harvey Gratton, although she did not carry his kennel name). Trinka produced 10 champions, including the Best in Show winner, Ch. Schauffelein's Black Gold owned by Ray Harper, and Ch. Allegro retained by the Purdys. Allegro was bred to Ch. Delegate vd Elbe, and the result was Ch. Steeldust, who became Canada's first blue champion. His litter sister, Ch. Silhouette, bred to Ch. Iago v Ahrtal three times, produced 9 champions including four Best in Show winners. Ch. Humoresque, owned by Jack Anderson of Doron Kennels in Calgary, did a tremendous amount of winning out there, and was the leading Doberman in 1959. The Purdys kept Ch. Bl'kberry Brandy, who went on to become a multiple Best in Show winner and the sire of at least 12 champions.

In 1965 Ch. Schauffelein's Extra Special was born (Specially Fancy bred to her grandsire Ch. Bl'kberry Brandy) and he proved to be a real character — a true free spirit as well as a top show dog. Siring only 3 litters before his sudden and untimely death at the age of 3½, he produced 9 champions. This was a great loss to both the Purdys and the breed in general, since had he lived, I'm sure he would have been a very significant sire. At Arabesque Kennels however, were a litter of Extra Special pups (out of Ch. Midnight Glow of Arabesque) and the Purdys were offered first choice. They took two males — one of them, Schauffelein's Troll Arabesque, went on to become an American and Canadian champion, multiple Best in Show winner, Top Dobe in Canada for 1970, '71 and '72, Specialty winner in 1972, listed in the Top 10 dogs in Canada for three years — but far more important, a top sire and a great influence on the breed, having produced over 65 champion get (with many more pointed) — thus winning the DPCC award for Sire of the Year on three successive occasions. In 1971, Dr. Shute predicted that Troll would undoubtedly become the top producing Doberman sire in Canada, and that he promised to exert the greatest influence of any sire to date. He has more than lived up to this expectation, and his stamp is very evident on Dobermans all across Canada and in the United States. Bred to his half-sister, Ch. Lowenbrau Aloha Schauffelein five times, this combination has produced 22 champions, including five multiple Best in Show winners in this country and two in the U.S.A. — Ch. Vintage Year and Ch. Rendezvous.

Ch. Saracen of Reklaw, a Dictator son and sire of Ch. Defender of Jan-Har.

Am. & Can. Ch. Brigum of Jan-Har, a son of Ch. Saracen of Reklaw and distinguished sire on his own.

Am. & Can. Ch. Defender of Jan-Har and his daughter Ch. Kaukauna's Aldebaran going Best of Breed and Best Opposite under the late Frank Haselman at the Detroit Doberman Specialty in 1957. The handlers are Jane McDonald (Defender's breeder and original owner) and Jack Porter.

213

Vintage Year's show wins are very impressive — multi Best in Show and specialty winner both in the U.S.A. and Canada, Canada's top winning Doberman in 1973 and '74 (also in the top five all breeds) and one of the Top Twenty Dobes in the U.S.A. during 1975. However, he is also showing his worth as a stud dog, having sired at least 35 champions, many of them from Troll daughters.

Schauffelein dogs are also making quite a splash in the Obedience world in this country and the U.S.A. Of particular mention is Salutation, owned by Carol Silverman, who has both her American and Canadian championships, as well as U.D. degrees in each country — and Ch. Signature, owned by Jan Wheeler, who was the top Obedience Doberman in Canada for 1973, '74 and '75.

Norma King (Konighausen) bought her first Doberman from John Lundberg — Am. & Can. Ch. Aristo Von Gotenberg. Being interested in Obedience she trained him, and won her C.D. degree in this country and the U.S.A., racking up a number of fine scores en route, including a perfect 200 in each country! In 1957 she purchased her foundation bitch from Jane Kay — Ch. Kay Hill's Ebonetta (a sister to the famous Ch. Paint the Town Red), and bred to Aristo, Ebonetta produced Ch. Konigshausen the Crusdader, a top winner in British Columbia. The Kings then acquired another Von Gotenberg dog, Ch. Bobo, and bred to Ch. Damasyn the Solitaire, she produced the Best Canadian-Bred in Show winner, Ch. Konigshausen the Buccaneer and the Group winner Ch. Konigshausen Rum Baccardi. Ebonetta was then bred to Ch. Dobe Acres Cinnamon, producing Ch. Destiny and Ch. Dedication. Destiny was the dam of the top Doberman in 1966, Ch. Konigshausen Inspiration (sired by Dr. Shute's Sabre). The Kings also used Ch. Borong the Warlock and Ch. Brown's Dion, and in a very limited breeding program, produced around 14 champions until they decided to retire from dogs in 1965. At this time their friends, Margaret and Bob Johnson (Lowenbrau) had become very interested in Dobes, and were able to lease Ch. Konigshausen Honour (Ch. Dedication ex Sabre) and Ch. Konigshausen Jade (Ch. Destiny ex Ch. Schauffelein's Bl'kberry Brandy) and carry on the line. The first litter for Lowenbrau came from Ch. Honour bred to Ch. Schauffelein's Extra Special and produced three champions, one of which was the great top producing bitch, Ch. Lowenbrau Aloha Schauffelein.

Although the Kaukauna Kennels of Mrs. Bea England has now over 50 champions to its credit, as in many cases, their first Doberman was bought strictly as a pet. Mrs. England had really wanted a red bitch, but on seeing a black that was for sale, just couldn't turn her down. This was Lady Kaukauna. Having made up her mind to breed her dog, Mrs. England decided that only the best was good enough, and selected Dr. Shute's Int. Ch. Defender of Jan-Har. From this first litter came the multi Best in Show and top winning Dober-

Ch. Konigshausen Inspiration, top Canadian Doberman of 1966.

Ch. Kaukauna's Hi-Star, 1963–1970, sired by the Dion son, Ch. Sabre von Mannerheim ex Ch. Kaukauna's Enchantress. Hi-Star, pictured here at 11 months, was bred by Mrs. Bea England.

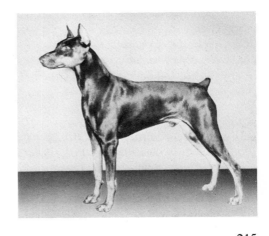

Ch. Kaukauna's Bromeau, brother to Aldebaran. Owned by Mrs. Bea England.

man, Am. & Can. Ch. Kaukauna's Aldebaran. Mrs. England firmly refuses to take the credit for breeding Aldebaran — at that time she was a complete novice and had no knowledge of breeding — but prefers to call her "a gift from the gods." Bred only once, at five years of age, to Top Skipper, Aldebaran produced 5 champions. Mrs. England now reflects that she wished she had had more litters from her, but Aldebaran was being shown most of the time, and indeed was on the road and winning until two weeks before her death. One of the high spots of her American show career was taking Winners over 56 bitches at the New York show.

From the second Defender/Lady Kaukauna breeding, came Ch. Kaukauna's Beau Bromeau, himself the sire of 16 champions. During the years Aldebaran and Bromeau were specialled, they usually ended up winning the breed and best opposite sex to one another. The Defender/Lady Kaukauna breeding was repeated five times, and of Defender's 21 champions, 12 are from her. Dr. Shute and Jack Birkby owned dogs from this breeding — Ch. Gold Braide and Ch. Golden Sceptre, respectively.

In 1965 and 1967, Ch. Kaukauna's Hi-Star became top Doberman in Canada (Ch. Sabre von Mannerheim ex Ch. Kaukauna's Enchantress). Retired from the show ring in 1968, Hi-Star was third top Doberman, defeated each time by a half sister. As previously mentioned, the top winners from 1965–1968 were all by Sabre von Mannerheim, whose dam was Ch. Kaukauna's Gold Braide, a litter sister of Hi-Star's dam. In 1969, Ch. Goldie's Holly of Kaukauna (a Sabre granddaughter) was top winning Doberman bitch, and in 1971 at the DPCC specialty, Tess Henseler awarded Winners Dog to a junior puppy male who became Am. & Can. Ch. Kaukauna's Hi-Star of Jan-Har, owned by Jane MacDonald.

Kay-Jon was registered in 1957. However, Kay Baylis had owned Dobes prior to this. Her first breed winner was Ch. Caesar v Attica, a Ch. Sinbad of Reklaw son. She then purchased Von Gotenberg Bonzella (Brigum ex Arista vd Engelsburg) and bred her to Caesar, producing four champions, including the Group winner, Ch. Kay-Jon's Native Dancer. Also from this litter came Ch. Kay-Jon's Commander, Can. & Am. C.D. In recent years Kay has bred to Ch. Carly of Jerseystone and Ch. Schauffelein's Vintage Year, and in all has a total of 14 homebred champions. In 1975, her Carly daughter, Ch. Kay-Jon's Star's Ebony Mist, was named top winning bitch puppy at the DPCC Annual Awards.

The Bar-Jak Kennels of Jack Birkby and Roger Kennedy came into being in the late 1950s. On reflection Jack feels that his first Dobe must have been mixed with something else. However, his interest was generated, and he purchased a Defender/Lady Kaukauna daughter from Mrs. England, Ch. Kaukauna's Golden Sceptre who, bred to Ch. Sabre von Mannerheim, produced three champions — Ch. Bar-Jak's Cover Girl, Ch. Charming Girl and Ch.

O.T. Ch. Wrath's Apolda Blunderbuss UD, Bda. CD, Top Doberman in Obedience for three consecutive years. Pictured winning the Veterans class at the Doberman Pinscher Club of Canada Specialty, at 9 years of age. Owned by Pat Blenkey.— Weston

Ch. Schauffelein's Solar Wind pictured at 11 months of age winning the 1971 Doberman Pinscher Club of Canada Specialty under judge Tess Henseler, with owner Dr. Wilfrid Shute handling.

217

Caesar — all Group winners. They also owned a litter brother to Gold Braide — Ch. Kaukauna's Fiddler's Folly, who sired 11 champions. Working on the philosophy of going back to line breeding between outcrosses, they have bred around 14 champions — with many more needing only those last couple of points to finish. In recent years they have bred to Schauffelein males, and their Ch. Society Girl bred to Vintage Year, produced three champions. They are also proud of the fact that the 1975 DPCC specialty Winners Bitch (Ch. Windrush Blackberry, owned by Alice Sinclair), is in direct line from their Charming Girl, and their original Golden Sceptre.

Bonnie Lendvay of Alberta (Ravenaire) bought her first Dobe from Dr. Shute — Ch. Presto von Mannerheim, and later acquired Ch. Schauffelein's Solitude. Being very impressed with the Ahrtal dogs, she bought a Felix son, Ch. Dobereich's Defender who, to date has sired 19 champions. Her Ch. Morkinni Windjammer (a Cory son) and his litter brother, Ch. Wildwood, have sired three champions and seven champions respectively (Wildwood has five from one litter). Ravenaire has 22 homebred champions, but Bonnie has either personally owned or handled equally that many to their championships. She is proud of the fact that at least 150 champion Dobermans carry either a Ravenaire sire or dam, and is particularly proud of the fact that the Korella's foundation bitch (Ch. Ravenaire's Quintessa CDX) is from her kennel.

Mizpah Kennels, British Columbia, is owned by Larry House, a well-known breed judge, and among the many fine dogs he has owned or bred is Ch. Schauffelein's Second Coquette, dam of four champions from her only litter to Ch. Mizpah's Sabre v Doran. Sabre was a top winner out West, as was his son Ch. Mizpah's John Benjamin. I have it on good authority that Larry has bred at least 25 champions, and among other top Mizpah winners are Ch. Mizpah's Pamela of Reidcroft, owned by Pam Reid, and Ch. Mizpah's Rising Market, a litter sister to John Benjamin.

Dr. Suzanne Francis did not register her Kurtzhaus name until 1960, on acquiring Ch. Schauffelein's Soliloquy (Iago ex Silhouette). Soliloquy bred to Ch. Storm's Donner, produced the Best in Show winner, Ch. Kurtzhaus Thunder, owned by Shirley de Boer. Veterinary practice interfered with breeding dogs, but but on taking a very early retirement in 1968, she purchased Heldenleben Aira v Kurtzhaus (Ch. Damasyn the Derringer ex Ch. Konigshausen Karma) who has produced 11 champions, including the Winners Bitch at the 1976 Westminster show, Jazz Finale. One of Aria's daughters, Ch. Kurtzhaus Tosca, bred to Vintage Year, has produced five champions.

Suzie is now working on her third generation of champions, and the future seems very bright for her, since Kurtzhaus was the producer of seven champions in 1975.

Our own kennel, Wrath (named incidentally in honor of the top English Doberman, Ch. Tavey's Stormy Wrath) came into being in 1963, although we had been active in Dobes in England prior to this. We bought an Alemap's Checkmate granddaughter, mainly as a pet. Wrath, however, turned out to be a great Obedience worker and chalked up many fine scores. Her highest award however was from the Ontario Obedience Association, when she was named Top Utility Dog (all breeds) for 1967, with an average score in that class of 198½. Bred to a Bl'kberry Brandy son (Ch. Bramalea's Argonaut CD) she produced another Obedience great — O.T. Ch. Wrath's Apolda Blunderbuss UD, Bda. CD (another stolen English name!), who was Canada's top Obedience Doberman for three successive years. Although retired from competition, she was brought out in 1973, just for fun. Entered in only three trials, she wound up second top obedience Doberman for that year! Bred just once, to Ch. Schauffelein's Extra Special, she produced two champions. Her daughter, Ch. Cabanuela CDX, has given us two champions from Troll, including Ch. Wrath's Elegancia CD, named 1971 bitch Puppy of the Year by the DPCC. We incidentally received the award for DPCC Obedience Breeders of the Year at the same time. From a very limited breeding program, we have produced 8 champions from three litters, and 14 dogs carrying our kennel name have Obedience degrees.

Jack Goldberg of Montreal (Thaeburg) was the first Doberman enthusiast to import a Cassio son — this was Ch. Tedel Midas Touch (Cassio ex Ch. Highbriar Valencia). Following this he bought Ahrtal's Cassiduna (Cassio ex Iduna vom Ahrtal) with the intention of establishing a line. However, Cassi never did come through with a live litter, and so Jack bought Ch. Othello II vom Ahrtal, campaigned him, and made him the DPCC Dog of the Year for 1970, and a multi Best in Show and Group winner. Othello has also produced well, having a number of champions to his credit. Am. & Can. Ch. Dobereich's Top of the Line (Ch. Top of the Mark ex Ch. Dobereich's Dawn) was added to the stud force a couple of years ago, and he also is making his mark on the breed.

Pyrmont Dobermans of Thunder Bay, Ontario, is based on German, Dutch and American bloodlines, and the working type Dobe is their aim. The Bersts' first Dobe was Ch. & O.T. Ch. Berst's Palos v Hoytt, Can. & Am. UD, sire of 6 champions out of two litters. In 1965, the Bersts purchased Ch. & O.T. Ch. Cheatah v Sirrahwald UD, Am. CDX., and with Palos formed an Obedience brace team that was the star attraction of many an exhibition. In 1963 Cheatah's litter sister Lisa, joined Pyrmont, giving them three champions from her first litter and four from the second, sired by Am. & Can. Ch. Biggin Hill's Alarich. From this breeding they kept Ch. Pyrmont Cyrus v Alarich, who has given them two Canadian champions and three Indian champions. Indian Ch. Pyrmont Jaguar v Cyrus has made quite a name for himself in that

Ch. Damasyn The Elf and her brother Ch. Damasyn The Ember, pictured in 1953. These red littermates were bred by Helen Kamerer. Elf was owned by Mrs. Kamerer, and Ember by Dr. Wilfrid Shute.

Ch. Rhodan vom Ahrtal, whelped in 1969, black male by Ch. Cassio vom Ahrtal ex Illisa vom Ahrtal (a daughter of the German import, Ch. Lord vom Furstenfeld). Rhodan is sire of 18 champions to date. Bred by Tess Henseler, he is owned by Glenda and Lynell Korella's Defender Kennels in Calgary.

Ch. Ravenaire's Quintessa CDX, dam of 13 champions. By Ch. Tarrado's Banquo ex Ch. Burnheim's Easter Encore, Quintessa is owned by the Defender Kennels of Calgary.

country, completing his Ch. title in three shows and going on to Best in Show twice. His litter sister Jewel, also completed her Indian championship in three straight shows, going best opposite to her brother.

In December 1971, the Bersts imported a red male from Holland, Ch. Graaf Marnix van Neerlandstam CDX. Being very impressed with Marnix they added two more bitches of Dutch bloodlines to improve their stock, Ch. Lone Pine's Artemis and Dutch Imp. Gravin Roeanka van Neerlandstam Since the Bersts began raising Dobes in 1968, they have produced 16 homebred champions and 16 Obedience title holders, several of them grandchildren of their original pair, Palos and Cheatah. Ch. Pyrmont v Rahkstadt, in 1974 was rated second highest Obedience Doberman in Canada, and tied for 9th place Working dog.

Glenda and Lynell Korella of Calgary (Defender Kennels) have come a long way in the comparatively short time they have been breeding Dobes. They bought their first Dobe around 1967, I believe, and he was trained in Obedience. Following this, they obtained Ch. Ravenaire's Quintessa CDX (Ch. Tarrado's Banquo ex Ch. Burnheim's Easter Encore) from Bonnie Lendvay. Quintessa earned her CDX in three straight shows going high in trial each time. When the time came to breed her, the Korellas decided to combine a working holiday with visits to some of the top U.S. Doberman kennels. On visiting Ahrtal they were so taken with a Cassio/Illissa puppy that they just couldn't leave him behind. This was Ch. Rhodan, a Best in Show winner and the sire of 18 champions to date, with many more pointed. Quintessa was bred to Rhodan, and from their offspring the Defender line has basically developed. Quintessa, herself, is the dam of 13 champions to date, with approximately 20 others pointed, so it looks as though she may well finish up as the top producing Doberman bitch of all time. Other homebred bitches that are also producing well are Ch. Lucinda (6 champions), Ch. Gyha (3 champions), Ch. Grenada, owned by Lee Jarcow of British Columbia (4 champions) and Ch. Empress owned by Rick Fehler of Regina, Saskatchewan (3 champions). Probably the biggest winner for Defender Kennels however, is Ch. Naimark (Ch. Du-Rel's Black Power ex Ch. Ravenaire's Quintessa), owned by G. W. Blount. Nairmak has done a tremendous amount of winning out West, and in 1974 was third top Doberman and 9th place Working dog.

Although Fred and Ann Heal of Ottawa (Jagermeister) had owned a Trollhattan Dobe in 1961, they did not seriously get into breeding until 1970, when they purchased a bitch from Joey Purdy from the first Troll/Aloha breeding. This was Ch. Schauffelein's Shady Lady, a Best in Show winner, and Canada's top winning Doberman female of all time, and the foundation of their kennel. Shady was bred back to her father to set type, and then to Ch. Andelane's Indigo Rock producing among other fine champions, their current winner, Can. and Bda. Ch. Jagermeister's Sevencomeleven. From the Shady/

221

Troll breeding they kept Ch. Jagermeister's Renown, also a Best in Show winner and winner of the DPCC award for Dam of the Year on two occasions. Renown also was bred to Indigo Rock, and another Best in Show winner was produced, Ch. Jagermeister's Strawberry Tart, plus several other fine champions.

Ch. Sevencomeleven has had an illustrious show career, starting at the age of 10 months and going undefeated as a puppy — completing his Canadian and Bermuda championships before he was 13 months old. Shown sparingly in 1974, his puppy year, he wound up by winning the famous Show of Shows. This classic dog show is the event of the year and is limited to dogs of any breed who have won a Best in Show in Canada during the current year. The competition is unsurpassed, with the big names in dogdom from all parts of North America in attendance. In 1974 however, Sevencomeleven walked off with the top honors — marking the first time a Doberman has won the prestigious event. In 1975, shown regularly in Central Canada, Sevencomeleven has been a consistent winner — this gained him the top Doberman of the year award from the DPCC and ranked him as the top Working dog in Canada.

In 1967, Pat and Bela Kaposi (Countysquire) bought their Ch. Checkmate's Erik Rudolph daughter — Ch. Moonlight Haven's Viasta. However, their breeding program didn't get started until around 1970, when Viasta was bred to Ch. Gra-Lemor Demetrius vd Victor, producing 5 champions, among them their first blue — Ch. Countrysquire's Delco — and his litter brother, Ch. Deufal, the top winning male puppy for 1972. Since that time they have produced 11 champions, and are one of the very few Doberman kennels in this country producing all four colors.

There are a few other people who deserve some mention here. Harold Butler, now living in the province of Quebec, used to handle for Mrs. England, and piloted Hi-Star through his show career. Harold also co-owned and bred a couple of litters with Dr. Shute — one of these from Bonnie von Mannerheim Nagidrac bred to Ch. Highbriar Minos, produced Ch. Ashuniong's Heidi, who had a very flashy show career. Harold is now a busy all-breed handler, but still finds time for the occasional litter of Dobes, having a number of champions to his credit. His latest is the Best in Show winning blue bitch, Ch. Ashuniong's Nickleodeon.

Gaston Nolin also of Quebec is, I understand, no longer an active Doberman breeder. However, he still has a special interest in the breed. Of special mention are his Ch. Donebelin the Charming Charade who was one of the top winners in 1958, and his stud dog, Ch. Donobelin Ram-Rod stands as sire of at least 8 champions — four of them from Ashuniong breeding.

I must apologize to the Dobe fanciers on the West Coast, but I was unable to get too much information. I have had to rely a great deal on memory (both my own and that of other people) because there are very few records avail-

Ch. Jagermeister's Sevencomeleven winning the Show of Shows 1974. Canada's Top Doberman and Top Working Dog for 1975. Owned by Fred and Ann Heal of Ottawa.

Ch. Jagermeister's Renown, Best in Show winner and twice the Doberman Pinscher Club of Canada's Dam of the Year. Pictured here as a puppy.

223

Ch. Schauffelein's Vintage Year, winner of 20 Bests in Show and sire of over 50 Canadian champions. Two-time winner of the Doberman Pinscher Club of Canada National Specialty. Whelped in October 1970, Vintage Year is by Ch. Schauffelein's Troll Arabesque ex Ch. Lowenbrau Aloha Schauffelein. He was bred and is owned by Joey and Ron Purdy of Ontario, and has been handled by Pamela DeHetre and his owners.

able. Fortunately, I was able to get hold of some Canadian dog magazines from 1957 to 1963, and much of my information came from these.

In closing, I would like to say that due to limited space, it is impossible to mention all the current breeders in this chapter, but I have tried to present an unbiased coverage of the history of the Doberman in this country. If there is any older breeder I have missed — I apologize. I have concentrated mainly on those breeders who have been active for over five years, since it has been said that the measure of a true breeder is he who takes all the bumps and bruises, as well as the high spots, and still comes out dreaming of that perfect Doberman. All too often, especially in view of the current popularity of our breed, we see exhibitors and breeders cropping up and going in great style for a year or so, and then disappearing — never to be seen again. We do have a number of new, young people interested in our breed, who are producing some fine dogs, and who will no doubt, in future years, be contributing to the history of the Doberman in Canada.

15

The Doberman in Europe

by Ingrid Hallberg

GERMANY has been the mother country of many of our pure-bred dogs—the Boxer, the German Shepherd as we know it today, the Schnauzer, the Rottweiler, the Weimaraner, and many more—but one of the most important of all has to be the Doberman Pinscher.

The Germans some time ago dropped the word "Pinscher." A thorough search through many pedigrees revealed that the Pinscher had very little, if anything, to do with the development of the breed. Accordingly, throughout this chapter we will refer to the breed as Doberman.

I should also explain that I will not here go into the history of how the breed started; this is taken care of elsewhere in the book. Our story will begin with the "renaissance" of the breed following World War II—the dogs important to us today.

At end of the Second World War, Germany found her breeding stock virtually depleted. Breeders had to start over again slowly with what was on hand.

The roll of kennels that have been most responsible through this reconstruction period for the Doberman of Germany today includes: "von Germania", August Schneider, Remsheid; "v. Kleinwaldheim", Paul Klein, Leverrusen; "v. Hagenstolz", Walter Mauser, Hagen/Westfalen; "v. Wellborn", Hans Rothmann, Pfungstadt; "v. Romberg", Hanni Reiners, Dortmund; "v. Wurttemberg", G. Tienken, Bremen-Lesum; "v. Furstenfeld", Hermann Palmer, Furstenfeldbruck; and "v. Forell", Ernst Wilking, Villigst, West Germany.

From the immediate postwar era, just a handful of studs can be said to have put their impact on the reconstruction of the breed. They include: Ajax v Simbach, Dieter v Willersee, Frido v Rauhfelsen, Tell v Hinterborn, and most important—Alex v Kleinwaldheim, a name that one finds in the pedigree of al-

World Sieger Ch. Lump v Hagenstolz, 1956. By Alf v Hagenfreund ex Gina v Glockenhof.

Ch. Cito v. Furstenfeld, black son of Ch. Lump v Hagenstolz.

Earl von Forell (Vice-Ch. of the World). By Ch. Bonni v Forell ex Cindy v Forell.

most every top Dobe bred in Germany since his time. Alex may someday be recognized to have played the important part in post World War II Germany that the renowned stud, Lux v Blankenbourg did after World War I.

We pick up our history in the 1956-57 period, when the outstanding males were Prinz v Hugenottendorf and Harry v Sudbezerk, and the outstanding bitch was Carmen v Felsingpass, foundation bitch of the well-known v. Furstenfeld Kennels.

We go on to 1958 with Igon v Wellborn, Gitta v Romberg . . . and start to see names with which we are now very familiar: Dirk v Goldberg, Cita and Cito v Furstenfeld, and Int. twice World Ch. Lump v Hagenstolz, who we find today in so many top pedigrees in West Germany.

Lump von Hagenstolz was twice World Sieger and he merited it in every way—a large handsome male who unfortunately did not live long enough to stamp more get with his beautiful form and character. Lump was sired by Alf von Hagenfreud (also the sire of the beautiful German Siegerin, Hella v. Germania) out of Dina von Klockenhof, another well-known Ch. Astor v Externberg, whose bloodline was carried over to the Alsace Region into France. It was a loss, therefore, when this very prepotent young male passed away suddenly at the age of six, of an undetermined illness.

The von Germania Kennels of August Schneider was one of the finest in postwar Germany, even as it had been in pre-war Germany. The consistent quality that Herr Schneider developed in his breeding program brought the Doberman breed to its height at that time. Particular emphasis was placed on the beautiful long and parallel heads of the Germania line, with a body to go with it (longer than is being produced today). The closest to this type would definitely be the American Doberman. Great elegance and nobility could be noted in many of the offspring of the Germania Kennel, plus an ability to pass these qualities on generation after generation. Unfortunately, with the death of Herr Schneider about 1965 or so, this line has been dying out, except for a strong branch in France. In Germany a new type seems to be cancelling out the type of the Germania Kennel.

One leading kennel that began as very much based on the Germania line (as were so many for a time) was the von Furstenfeld Kennels of Hermann Palmer. Herr Palmer was an independent, with whom you may not have agreed all the time, but certainly had to admire for his determined and devoted passion to the breed. His well-known ''C'' litter was sired by Ch. Lump v Hagenstolz, and after many years of culling, disappointments, etc., Palmer developed his ''trademark.'' He felt, among other things, that through the years, good dark markings had been completely ignored, along with good heads and necks. He set about on a one-man crusade to remedy this, and remedy it he

227

did. His kennel became the best in Germany in this respect, and his dogs were sought after in every city; in fact, his dogs became internationally known for these qualities.

However, the inevitable was to come; one star usually has to yield to a newer star, and one was on the horizon — although in a sense it had been standing in the wings since 1925. The Von Forell Kennel came into its own around the early 1960s with the emergence of its new owner; actually Ernst Wilking had taken over the kennel from his father.

Ernst Wilking was also young (he and Palmer were about the same age), dynamic, and with his own definite ideas of what he thought the Doberman should be. Fortunately for him, he was in position to start putting these ideas into practice.

A member and officer in the Doberman Verein and later President and Chief Judge, he began his rise to fame with the purchase of the very beautiful and outstanding bitch from the Germania Kennels, Cita Germania (her litter brother Cuno was exported to France), whelped in 1962. Cita was really the beginning, on a large international scale, for the v Forell Kennels . . . President Wilking was finally able to voice his long held ideas about the Doberman Standard.

Wilking felt that the Doberman had gotten too far away from the original idea, and that they should go more or less back to the pre-World War II Standard; after all, they had been pretty good then and had been exported all over the world. He also felt that there should be more concentration on breeding deeper chests and a much shorter or cobby and square type; and that the Standard should be fixed at a rigid height of, no more than 70 cm (27 inches) for males, and 66-67 cm (24-25 inches) for females. This he felt made for a much more compact dog. The preference was also for a heavier dog (dogs are very heavy these days, even to being fattened up for the show rings); after all, the Dobe was supposed to be a working breed too!

The most notable success of the v. Forell Kennels, and the one that established Wilking on the international scene, came with his "B" litter. This litter, sired by Vello v Furstenfeld (an outstanding stud who never himself became a champion but who was the sire of many champions and a holder of the Sch. H. III degree) out of Kira v Romberg, produced Ch. Bonni v Forell and his litter brother, Ch. Bryan v Forell (later exported to Sweden). Bonni became the principal stud of the v. Beelen Kennel, of which I will go into detail later.

Three breedings of Cita Germania to three different studs produced five champions and many first place winners. One particularly outstanding mating was that of Cita with Int. Ch. Odin v Forell, a grandson of World Ch. Lump v Hagenstolz and a grandson on his dam's side of Int. Ch. Sch. H. III Dirk v Goldberg. This produced the now well-known top stud of the v. Forell Ken-

Dutch Ch. Bundessieger Winner 1967, Rado von Furstenfeld. Bred by Herman Palmer.

Ch. Odin von Forell, by Bundessieger Falko v Hagenstolz, SchH I, ex Iris v Forell.

Gido von Hagenstern, by Ch. Bonni v Forell ex Ch. Dona Eichenhain. Pictured at 19 months.

229

nel, Ch. Chico v Forell and his litter sister Ch. Cherry v Forell (imported to France). A lesser known brood bitch from the litter is Cindy v Forell. These three champions were all whelped in 1968 and all won the 1970 Bundessieger Show! Quite a formidable feat for one breeder.

Later, Odin was exported to Japan as was another v. Forell Bundessieger of 1964 before him, Ch. Lex v Forell (Ch. Titus Germania ex Vilja Germania).

Among the many breeders, and they are too many to list all in great detail in this chapter, we must not neglect von Felsingpass, who began the work of breeding fine dark markings with their 1953 champion, C. Boris v Felsingpass, and then followed with Carmen v Felsingpass, a foundation brood bitch of v. Furstenfeld Kennels.

We now come to two breeders of recent years, who as coincidence will have it, both began in the same little town of Beelen, West Germany. They are R. Kroner (von Hagenstern) now of Herzbruck, West Germany and Heinz Gerwin (von Beelen).

The v. Hagenstern Kennels came to the fore with the very fine brood bitch and 1970 Bundessiegerin in the Black and Tan class, Dona v. Eichenhain, whelped in 1967 and sired by Ch. Rondo v Forell ex Hella v Forell. Dona has produced several well-known champions: Ch. Edda v Hagenstern, sired by Bonni v Forell, the brown 1972 Bundessieger; Greif v Hagenstern (later imported into England), and Ch Jurgen v Hagenstern, 1972 Bundessieger, also sired by Bonni and exported to Holland. Dona, a very powerful and deep-chested bitch, is a proven producer of champions, an all too rare type of bitch these days. She also, again with Bonni, produced Ch. Ero v Hagenstern, a brown and leading stud who was exported to France to the de Festiano Kennels. Many other dogs from the Hagenstern Kennels have been exported to countries including the United States, Australia, and England, but at this writing they are still young and their qualities are yet to be proved.

The principal stud of the von Beelen Kennels is the 1973 Welt or World Ch. Lex v Beelen who is doing quite well as a sire of champions. He is sired by Ch. Chico v Forell ex Elfie v Hagenstern. He is the sire of the 1975 Bundessieger, French-born Ch. Innez-Lex de Fierre Gueule out of Bundessiegerin, World Ch. Tchiqueta de Festiano.

Other kennels in West Germany have through the years been very consistent in producing fine quality Dobermans. All are not necessarily show quality, for they have concentrated more on their working ability. One such is the "vom Eichenhain" Kennels of Herr J. Bambach. The outstanding bitch, Dona v Eichenhain, mentioned earlier, certainly has the rare quality of being both a champion show dog and a top producing bitch. A fine male from this same kennel was Ino von Eichenhain, sired by Vello v. Furstenfeld ex Hella v Forell. Ino was exported to Norway.

Over the years there have been several other kennels in West Germany that although not as much publicized, are contributing very much to the breed in that country and abroad. Several worthy of mention are: vom Frankenland; vom Niddaltal Kennels, owned by Walter Hensel, now the Head Judge of the Doberman Verein; von Forellenbachle, owned by Gunther Kiss; and in Berlin, the von Buchenhain Kennels.

Another stud from the v. Forell kennels, who has just recently been exported to Japan, has shown promise of passing on his good qualities. He is Ch. Flint v Forell, who sired Ch. Nero v. Hagenstern, leading stud of the Hagenstern Kennels. Flint is by Ch. Chico v. Forell ex Kira vom Romberg.

One of the kennels that has concentrated on breeding Dobermans that excel in Schutzhund work is v. Ellendonc, owned by Fritz Sauermann, himself very active in the Schutzhund ring.

In recent years the Doberman in Germany has been undergoing a change. New ideas, (or are they old?) have been introduced. Suddenly, the longer and more elegant Doberman as we know it, is out of fashion, and strange to say, progeny of the kennels that have contributed so much (such as the v. Germania line) are not considered to be the desirable type. One wonders at the reason for this change; it seems to have started as the purely personal taste of one or two individuals. It is rather like selecting between a weight lifter type and the agile form of a track runner. Both are correct in their respective fields, but it is when we cross over that the problems arise!

The argument Pro is that the Doberman was bred primarily for its guard work ability. The Cons retaliate by asking why then, through the years, were such breeds as the black English Greyhound introduced to add more elegance to the body and longer heads, etc.? And the development of the Doberman in the show ring has also shown that a dog can have elegance and nobility *coupled with* a powerful body; neither element need be exaggerated at the expense of the other.

In all honesty the kennels that have done so much for the Doberman and can still be seen in their many decendants, such as the v. Germania line, and more recently the Furstenfeld and v. Hagenstolz lines, cannot just be ignored and dismissed as not correct with the Standard. This is pure folly and certainly not a credit to the breed, nor a fair reward to many dedicated breeders.

Since the untimely death of Ernst Wilking, and the retirement of past-President Werner Nierman, Hans Wilbishauer has taken over the reins of the Doberman Verein. It will be interesting to see in which direction West Germany will go.

In all the neighboring countries around Germany, practically all Doberman bloodlines were built on the German stock imported before World War II. While they, of course, never achieved the numbers of German dogs or kennels, some fine Dobermans have come from these countries. Many, in fact, have been so to speak, "bringing coals to Newcastle," exporting back to Germany the results of their breeding programs as they improve through the years.

Holland

Holland was one of the first to begin the development of this breed back in pre World War I years. The first Doberman Club in the Netherlands was organized in 1905 under the name of Nederlandshe Dobermann-Pinscher Club. By 1912 the Doberman was well-known in that country. While there were only a few breeders, their breeding was on a level with that in Germany. Only the best stock of Germany was imported, and in addition there were several German breeders living in Holland at that time. Some of the Dutch Dobes of that time were even imported into the United States.

Two famous breeders of that time were Mr. Kloppel under the prefix of "Grammont," and Mr. Shimmelpfeng of "Aus der Hermat". One of the important studs was Ch. Troll v Abbathal, a grandson of Lord v Reid. Then there was the Jaegerhof Kennels with the outstanding Ch. Prinz Moder v Ulm Athan.

One of the best Dutch dogs of th 1930 era was Ch. Prinz Carlo vd Konnigstad, an almost faultless dog and sire of two of the most famous Dutch dogs, Ch. Favoriet vd Konnighof and Ch. Apollo v Ishuetseneck. Prinz Carlo, Prinz Favoriet and Angola v Grammont were all exported to the United States to the famous Swiss-American breeder, F.F.H. Fleitmann of the Westphalia Kennels in New Jersey. Mr. Fleitmann needs no introduction to Doberman fanciers or historians.

The best sire in the 1920s was considered to be Urian v Grammont, and herein lies a story that starts out sad but has a happy ending. As a puppy Urian had a very poor start in an unhappy home, and had been so neglected and starved that he had rickets and remained very small. As an adult he was truly used as a "work" dog by his owner, and had to draw a heavy bread cart every day. Fortunately for Urian, his breeder found him in this state, and bought him back again. All the poor dog had to recommend him was his good head type and good bloodline, but this proved to be quite a lot. For Urian became recognized as the best sire of his day; among his champion offspring, one well-known male Ch. Benno v Rommerhof, who was known for his ideal build, went to the United States.

About this time, a new young breeder began to try her wings. We know her now as Mme. Kniff-Dermout and her well-known kennel is van Neerlandstam. With the advice of the eminent Dr. Kopple, she began with Dora van Englesburg.

Dr. Kopple (Grammont) was not only very knowledgable, but eager to help young and budding breeders get started on a correct breeding program. Mrs.

232

Nord Germania, owned
by Herman Palmer.

Comtesse Charmaine v Franckenhorst, SchH I, sired by BSgr,
DuSgr Chico v Forell ex Amarilda
vd Wachenburg. This bitch was
an important 1973–1974 winner
in Holland.

From the Von Ellendonc Kennels of Sauerman Krefeld—all related!

Cosette, black bitch, early 1960s winner from Switzerland.

Andy von Buckenhain, young Europe Sieger at Berlin show, March 1976. Whelped February 1975, by Bodo v Klippeneck, SchH I, ex Laika v Baskerville, Sch III. Bred by Klaus Buchwald and owned by Joseph Mosl.

Lena D'Estelle de la Mar, seven month-old daughter of Ike de l Clodiniere ex Plana v Fursten feld.

Kniff-Dermout tells a story of this "golden time" of the Doberman in Holland. Mr. Akkeren, of the important Konnigstad Kennels in the Hague, usually would seek Dr. Kopple's advice in regard to breeding. However, one time he did not. Mr. Akkeren was taken with a German import who, although well-built, had a very bad head. This dog was Claus v.d. Spree, who was winning everywhere. Even though Dr. Kopple warned him about the bad head turning up in future generations, Akkeren used him on one of his best brood bitches. Time proved Dr. Kopple right. To the detriment of the good name and reputation of the Konnigstad Kennels, one of these offspring was sent to the United States under the name of Prinz Lustspiel v Konnigstad (meaning Prince Happiness); he was later renamed Prinz Trauerspiel vd Konnigstad (Prince Unhappiness)!

By 1927 there were two Doberman Clubs competing against each other in Holland. This continued until the sad, terrifying days of World War II and the Occupation. At the end of the War there only 13 members of one club left and about 36 of the other, and it was agreed to merge again into one club. New kennels came into importance, and right along with them was the van Neelandstam kennel of Mrs. Kniff-Dermout, who still remembered the old days.

Beginning with the litter brother to the World Ch. Troll vd Eversburg (who came to America), Mrs. Dermout put a championship on Fromm vd Eversburg. She also imported from Germany, Jupp von Naunhof, who had the same parents as German Ch. Igon v Naunhof. And so began a series of Champions for this kennel. Two very well-known champion studs were also imported as puppies, Int. Ch Miko v Furstenfeld and Ch. Rado v Furstenfeld (who was later to go to Japan).

Miko and Rado were two of the best Dobermans to come from the v. Furstenfeld kennels, and left their mark on many fine dogs in Holland. Both were finished to their championship by Mrs. Dermout. One of the many fine descendants of Ch. Rado is his grandson, the National and International Ch. Graaf Questor v Neerlandstam, a big handsome dog, who in the beginning of his show career was kept down because of his size (28¼). His breeder kept showing him despite this so-called fault, and now Questor is even sought after as a stud by well-known German kennels, even though the Germans had been most critical of his size. Questor is by the German Vico vd Brunoberg out of Bdgs. Dutch and Luxembourg Ch. Gravin Faby v Neerlandstam, a daughter of Rado. Faby was a winner in 1968-1969.

Champions from this kennel are numerous; among the better known are Ch. Gravin Nancy v Neerlandstam, sired by American and Canadian Ch. Mar Key of Dobelock ex Dutch and Canadian Ch. Gravin Yorinda v Neerlandstam. Among recent hopefuls coming along is Graaf Polivan v Neerlandstam, who is by Dutch Int. Ch. D.V. Sieger Jurgen von Hagenstern out of Ch. Yorinda. Another fine male was brought from Australia; he is Rama the Rock of Ages, sired by Australian Ch. Elmaro All Fire out of the American import, Ferrings Impish, a Ch. Gra-Lemor Demetrius v.d. Victor daughter. Impish was whelped in England and sent to Australia as a young puppy.

Tasso von Falkenturn, red male, by Allan v Forell Bachle ex Blacky vd Baldenau. Owned by G. Nunge.

Graaf Polivar v Neerlandstam.

Left, Ch. Gravin Nancy v Neerlandstam; *Right,* Ch. Gravin Faby v Neerlandstam. Both bred by Mrs. Vera Kniff-Dermout, Holland.

236

Holland has for many years been the stronghold of well-bred Dobermans. There are not too many kennels, but what there are seem to be breeding quality. One such rather new kennel is Frankenhorst, based on v. Forell bloodlines. Their bitch, Comtesse-Charmaine v. Franckenhorst, Sch.H.I., was a winner in 1973, 1974, and the Luxembourg and Holland winner and German Ch. D.V. Sng. Wurttemberg in 1975. Comtesse was sired by Ch. Chico v. Forell ex Amarilda vd Wachenburg.

As a rule, the trend in Holland seems to be toward the more elegant type of Doberman. So far, they have not followed the drastic change in type that we see in Germany, and as the years pass it will be interesting to follow their progress.

Belgium

Belgium, although a rather small country, is not without its love for the Doberman, and it has a very small group of breeders who though on a small scale, are beginning to show some progress.

There have been several imports, mainly from the v. Furstenfeld kennel. More recently we have seen a male who has been winning in France, Belgium and Holland, from the v. Caeserberg kennels. Vaillant v Caeserberg is truly a type in the present-day German standard, sired by Ch. Flint v Forell out of the kennel's own Saga Caeserberg. Vaillant is very short-loined and high in the shoulders. There have been some very strong pros and cons expressed about this male and it is a question of what type appeals to the public. Other promising dogs from this kennel include Xavier v Caeserberg and Xadia, a litter sister.

For the time being, these smaller countries are more in a position to follow the crowd and take sides as to type, rather than themselves make any great impact on the breed.

Switzerland

The Doberman Verein in Switzerland was founded in 1902 and will be celebrating its seventy-fifth Anniversary in 1977. Mr. Jean Mezieres, a breeder and well-known judge, is current President of the Swiss Doberman Club.

This little country can be considered rather in the middle of the road; no great stars have been produced here, but then again there have been no reports of any great or serious defects or faults in their breeding programs. Several champions have emerged in recent years. Two in particular are: Colette, a bitch who was a winner at the Paris show of 1963, and more recently, Ch. Balbo von der Stolzreute, a fine young male, who has sired some fine litters out of several French bitches.

Italy

Italy has been rather in the background but there seems to have been an awakening in the past five years or so. Again, quite a few imports were made from Germany and again these were from the v. Furstenfeld kennel, a few of which are now champions. Most recently there have been several imports from the well-known de la Morliere kennel of France, sired by the champion stud, Earl v Forell.

Countess de Agostini, whose kennel prefix is dei Piani di Praglia, seems to be the most active breeder at this time. Her kennel has been winning of late with Ch. Quetta de la Morliere and Ch. Droll dei Piani Pragila, out of the bitch Ch. Walkyrie de la Morliere. Both of these champions are sired by Ch. Earl v Forell. Countess de Agostini seems to be beginning to have results with her breeding program and no doubt hers will be a kennel to watch in Italy.

France

The Doberman Club of France, then known as "The Society for the Breeding of the Doberman," was created in 1913 by two enterprising men, Mr. Krai and Mr. Heiss and the first Doberman Speciality was held around 1914, with 34 Dobermans entered. Activity was then interrupted by the first World War, but at the end of hostilities, this same group courageously resumed.

The year 1920 saw the Club become affiliated with the Societè Centralè Canine (the official Cynophilie Français, which is the equivalent of the American Kennel Club.) The group enthusiastically began a marvelous breeding and training program, and made a special effort to import only the best quality breeding stock. There was soon a remarkable improvement and the Doberman became appreciated and admired all over France. Club membership numbered 760. But again a World War interrupted development. Many French Dobermans were destroyed so they could not fall into the hands of the German Army to be used in War Work.

Another new start was made in 1946 under a new president, Mr. Eisele with the aid of Mr. Nuss, a secretary devoted to the breed and the club. These two courageous men, from almost nothing, reorganized the club, and began to again build up the Doberman in France. With the publication of a small newsletter written by Mr. Nuss, and then later by Mr. Wilhelm who was the author of a fine Doberman book in France, communication was established not only between devotees of the breed in France, but also with people in other countries.

In 1967, the dynamic François Striby became National President, a position he still holds to this day. Under his leadership membership has more than doubled, to almost 2,000, and the Doberman Club of France has become one of the most important and influential breed clubs in the Societè Centralè Canine.

238

Nathalie du Vallon des Bonnes Herbes, by Knight de Vierge de Mont. ex Lady v Stolzberg. Bred by Mme. Larzilliere and owned by Mme. Reynaud-Natucci. Pictured at eight years of age.

Quing D'Estelle de la Mar, SchH I, by Cuno Germania ex Nathalie du Vallon des Bonnes Herbes. Pictured at 3 years. Breeder, Annie Reynaud-Natucci, France.

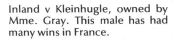

Inland v Kleinhugle, owned by Mme. Gray. This male has had many wins in France.

Junon du Vallon au Sables, owned by M. Borrel, France.

Tchao de la Tretoire, by Olten de la Tretoire ex Betty de la Tretoire. Bred by Mme. Jean Rossel and owned by Mme. Gauteirie, France.

Laetitia Cita de L'Isle en Touraine, nine-months-old bitch, by Ch. Jurgen von Hagenstern ex Undine de L'Isle en Touraine.

Undine de L'Isle en Touraine, by Chico v Forell ex Sprudli de L'Isle en Touraine. Breeder-owner, Mrs. Coulette Foulon.

240

Whereas prior to 1965 just a handful of Dobermans could be seen preparing for their Work degrees, they are now found in clubs all over France not only showing their remarkable ability in this type of training and work, but competing and winning over all other breeds in the National and International Schutzhund Trials.

For the following information on French Dobermans, I am indebted to many fine people but I wish to thank particularly Mme. M. Larzillere. Although extremely busy herself as the President of the DCF section of Provence-Côte d'Azur, she never failed to help, and sought out and contributed many of the details and historical information contained in this chapter. Doberman Club of France and the breed is fortunate to have the selfless devotion of both Mme. Larzillere and President Striby.

The Doberman in France over the past 25 years has become one of the most sought after breeds. His forceful character and outstanding intelligence, combined with a formidable physique make him a splendid companion and ideal for Guard and Police work; and his elegance and beauty has great appeal for the sophisticated French dog show fancier.

A strong emphasis on stability of character, fearlessness and aggressiveness without viciousness, is very much in evidence when one goes through France, attends the shows and especially the Working Clubs. The training of the Doberman in the French version of the German Schutzhund is as important as showing, if not more so. Certainly, if one goes by attendance and the number of these clubs, this would seem to be true.

The history of the Doberman in France corresponds with that of Germany after World War I. However, the number of Dobermans and breeders was not on the same scale as that in Germany; this was to wait until the middle the 1950s and into the 1960s.

From time to time it has been reasoned that the French Beauceron breed, sometimes known as the Berger de Beauce, is in the pedigree of the Doberman. How true this is, has been a question for many years. The only resemblance one sees between the two breeds these days is that the Beauceron is black and tan with the same type markings as the Doberman. The Beauceron seems to lean more towards the Rottweiller; it is a heavier dog (not as heavy as the Rottweiller, but rather in between the Doberman and Rottweiller.) It is primarily native to the Northern part of France, although quite a few are seen in the South. Their main function is as a sheepdog, a herder, but they also work very well in Obedience and attack work. They have cropped ears, a long tail and a much longer coat than the Doberman; and in general, the only resemblance is in the markings.

Because of the German origin of the Doberman, the National Doberman Club of France after World War II decided on a revision of the standard under the direction of various German judges. A conference was held in Strasbourg

Schutzhund training in Europe. *At left,* Quing d'Estelle de la Mar, SchH I, by Cuno Germania ex Nathalie du Vallon du Bonnes Herbes. Bred by Mme. Annie Reynaud-Natucci, and owned by Ingrid Hallberg. *Below,* Sandi du Patoil, owned by M. L. Laget, director of the training club Avignon.

in 1950, which was attended by delegates from France, Germany and Switzerland. In 1959, under the direction of Ernst Wilking, president of the Doberman Club of Germany, a new Standard was proposed and adopted. One important consideration was the question of size; this was fixed at 68–70 cm. (25 to 27 inches) for the male, and 63–66 cm. (24 to 26 inches) for females. In both cases, one inch over the maximum is allowed. Another rule of the standard was the disqualification for missing teeth; it may prevent a dog from winning first place, but a male or female can be given a *"très bonne"* or "very good" and be classed second place and on. However, the French are trying to adhere to this rule in hopes of eliminating missing teeth entirely.

It is interesting to note that in the show rings in France, as those of Germany, a written critique is given to each dog entered in the class. This, obviously, is of great importance, and whether good, bad or indifferent, is of great help to each exhibitor. One knows that the judge has taken the time to really evaluate the animal, and, as we all know — especially in the case of a young dog, this evaluation can change as the dog matures. These critiques, are then usually printed along with the show results in the all-breed magazine for France, *La Vie Canine.*

Training the Guard Dog in France

Great emphasis is put on the Working Doberman, and on earning the French Brevet, which is the French version of the Schutzhund degree, with the exception that in Germany, Tracking is part of the Schutzhund Trial, whereas in France (as in the United States) this is a separate Degree. The French feel that the Doberman, apart from his elegance and beauty is primarily a working dog, and should be trained as such. The French enjoy the sport of training, and Training Club sessions are held each weekend all around the country. At regular intervals, Trials are held under qualified judges.

This training is strenuous and usually a dog is not entered in the classes before twelve to fifteen months. There are cases, and quite recently, of Dobermans winning their first Brevet at the age of twelve or fifteen months; but they are, however, somewhat precocious and no doubt well-developed for their age.

The French Brevet for Chien de Garde et Police consists of several phases of Obedience exercises along with Attack work and, as I mentioned above, the Tracking is a separate class. All the Clubs are affiliated with the Societè Centralè Canine, adhering to their rules and regulations.

Many pros and cons have been expressed, particularly in the United States, as to whether dogs given this type of training are dangerous. I have yet to see a Doberman in Europe, trained in this manner — properly and over a period of enough time, show any change of character due to this type of work. Nine times out of ten a dog trained in this work is better for it; if he is poorly bred or

Ch. Negus du Vandois, by Gogo v Forell ex Linda du Vaudois, owned by Francois Bidault. Chosen outstanding dog of 1970 by the Doberman Club of France for his many show wins and work degrees.

Ilga de L'Isle en Touraine, by Ch. Earl v Forell ex Thetis L'Isle en Touraine. This bitch was bred by Colette Foulon.

Ch. Krac de la Morliere, by Iran de Mercastel ex Cosette v Furstenfeld. Owned by Marcel A. Demangeat.

has a bad character, chances are that it will have been discovered before the age of Guard dog work by the Character Tests a Doberman must go through when he is presented before a judge to receive the grading on his form, character, and general overall appearance, required before a final pedigree is issued to the owners.

I would like to write a bit here about the kind of exercises a Doberman must do to obtain the Brevet. There are the usual Obedience exercises of: Heel on and off leash, with and without a muzzle; a long down in the absence of the handler for three minutes; halt where the dog remains standing on command, and "en avant", where the dog is sent on ahead of his master. The attack work consists of: The handler walks the dog and meets someone to whom he talks; then as he walks away he is attacked from behind, at which time the dog must immediately defend him, and then cease attack on command; again the attack and again a cease attack on command and walking away. *Attack Lancée* is sending the dog out to a distance of about two hundred yards to attack an agggressor, then on command (from the distance) of the handler a cease attack, and return to heel position. There is also a false attack in which the dog is sent out as usual to attack but before reaching the aggressor is commanded to cease and return to heel position without attacking. This can be very useful in cases of emergency, to which your author can attest from experience.

We then have the scaling of walls and barriers at various heights, and the jumping exercises, which are also of various heights. In the more advanced Trials, which are known as the Concours A.B.C., we find more demands put on the dog in regard to seeking out hidden objects, hidden thieves, bringing back articles, guarding of objects — such as personal items, cars and what have you. The dogs can continute to compete in these trials as they begin to accumulate points towards the National Trials and to compete in them for the Work Degree and Championship of France. These Trials are usually very competitive and among all the working breeds, this degree is known as the CACIT which stands for Certificate of Aptitude of International Championship in Working, a most coveted title to win.

The Show Doberman in France

There has been a lot of misconception as to what the initials CACIB represent. They are an acronym for Certificate of Aptitude of International Champion in Beauty, an international title in conformation. The CACIB must be won not only in the country of origin of the dog's birth but in two other countries in Europe, as well as under three different judges. It is not as easy as it may sound, for most of the big shows now have a lot of competition. Large shows, such as the CACIB show of Paris — to name one important International show — usually draw the top winners from all countries.

Simba von Druidenstein. Bred and owned by the vom Druidenstein Kennels of Roger Bousendorffer, France.

Ursa vom Druidenstein, daughter of "Simba", also owned by R. Bousendorffer.

Ramses du Vallon des Bonnes Herbes. By Cuno Germania ex Lady v Stolzberg. Bred by Mme. M. Larzilliere and owned by M. Michelis.

Quriss de Festiano, red bitch, wh. 1967 by Cuno Germania ex Laika de Festiano. Winner of many CACIBs. Bred by Mme. Ramel, and owned by M. Lambelin, Nice, France.

Currently, the colors recognized in Europe for the Doberman are: Black and Rust, Brown and Rust and Blue and Rust. Fawns or Isabellas are not accepted. Eyes are expected in the blacks to be as dark as possible with lighter eyes accepted in the Browns. Another important difference between what is desired in Europe — particularly Germany — and in the United States has to do with markings. In Europe, Black and Rust means just that, a deep red rust color, and not a light tan or straw color such as we have become accustomed to in the United States. The markings on the chest, too, and under the tail, must be small; they must be defined, that is not smoky or running together. Muzzles should be fairly dark. And the most recent requirement I hear is that even the little black dots over several of the toes are now not considered to be desirable, which I must admit I find rather nitpicking. This seems to be so characteristic of the Doberman and his markings, that I don't see how it can be seriously followed.

Tails are as a rule cut much shorter than in the United States, usually at the first joint or less; this can either enhance or many times hide a not too good topline.

There has recently been a revision of the Doberman Club of France, and of its Sections and Delegates. The President General of all France is François Striby, there are now eleven Sections and Delegations, 1. Section of Paris and Ile-d-France. 2. Section de Provence-Côte d'Azure. 3. Section Normandie. 4. Section Rhone-Alpes. 5. Section de Haut-Rhine. 6. Section de Bas-Rhine. 7. Delegate of Sud-Ouest. 8. Delegate of Center-Ouest. 9. Delegate of Midi. 10. Delegate of Nord. and 11. Delegate of Val-de-Loire. Headquarters is at St. Louis, which is near Strasbourg.

My space is limited, but I shall here try to touch on some of the important kennels and individuals who have contributed much to the Doberman breed over the years, especially after World War II.

Among the top kennels of at least thirty years standing is the well-known kennel de la Morliere, situated in the northeastern part of France in Nantes-Orvault. It was founded by Monsieur Marcal A. Demangeat, who is still most active in breeding and who is a well known judge with an international reputation, having judged not only in France, but Germany, Belgium, Italy, and England. He also judged in Chicago some years ago. He has to his credit, in addition to French champions, bred: one Champion of Germany, six vice-Champions of Germany, six Champions of France-Holland-Italy and Luxembourg, one Vice-Champion d'Europe 1975, one Vice-Champion of the World 1973 and most recently one Champion of the World 1975.

Mr. Demangeat has been active in importing some fine stock from Germany and has had particular success with products from v. Forell and Furstenfeld. One of the early champions was Krac de la Morliere, sired by the noted Iran de Mercastel ex Cosette v Furstenfeld. Krac was followed by the German and French Champion Paf de la Morliere by Peer v Forell ex Mouna de la

Porthos de Festiano. By Cuno
Germania ex Katia de Festiano.
Owned by Mme. Amigues,
France.

Igon v Wellborn, German Bldgs.
with 9 CACIBs, imported to
France from Germany by the de
Festiano Kennels.

Int. Ch. Scherzo des Golden. By
Elmo v Furstenfeld ex Ina v Neerlandstam.

Morliere. Paf was tragically killed about a year after winning his German title in 1967. De la Morliere Kennels now has the top winner and top producer, the imported German stud — Earl v Forell. Earl is siring many fine specimens, and time will tell how strong an impact he will have on the Doberman in France.

To go to the South this time for another of the leading kennels, de Festiano. Owner-breeder Mrs. L. Ramel gained her biggest success with the importation (from the renowned German kennel, von Germania) of Cuno Germania, a prepotent stud who carried the best postwar Germany produced. His litter sister was Bdsg. Ch. Cita Germania, foundation bitch of the Von Forell kennels. Cuno's influence was felt throughout Southern France and had much to do with upgrading the quality of the Doberman in general. Naturally all of his get were not of first quality, but on the whole he has had an unusual high average in siring excellent offspring, especially since most of the breedings were a complete outcross. Cuno was retired at the age of ten years, and his place as leading stud in the Festiano kennel has been taken by another German import, this time from another up-and-coming kennel, von Hagenstern. The new stud, Ero v Hagenstern, in his short career, has already shown his prepotence. Ero is of a different type, that is now felt to be more desirable in Germany. Whereas Cuno was a more elegant dog with long head and somewhat longer body, Ero is much heavier, short cobby type. Cuno was black and quite dominant when matched with black bitches. Ero is a deep brown, with very deep chest and closer to 27″ in height; Cuno was almost 29″.

In the south of France, there are a few other kennels that are making a name. In Marseilles, the young breeders and owners of the d'Estelle de la Mar Kennels produced some very fine Dobermans in their first litter, by Cuno Germania out of Nathalie du Vallon des Bonnes Herbes, a fine brood bitch. Two in particular out of this litter were the Swiss Champion Quarina d' Estelle de la Mar, and Quing d'Estelle de la Mar, black and tan winner in the 1969 International show in Marseilles. Quing was subsequently exported to the United States by me, but tragically died less than a year later, before his true worth as a stud could be noticed.

The d'Estelle de la Mar kennels are now producing some fine dogs, and it is hoped that the importation of two German bitches from the Furstenfeld Kennels in Germany, and the first American import into France of Anja av Hagafjord, will be the beginning of a successful and fruitful breeding program for the owners, Jean-Pierre and Annie Reynaud-Natucci.

Another new and up-coming kennel, de Fiere Gueule, only about five years old, is also located in the Southern part of France and is owned by a mother and daughter team, Jacqueline and Claudine Manuel. They own the well-known male, Ch. Oken de Festiano. Mrs. Manuel began her serious breeding program with a German import, the lovely black and rust bitch Ch. Cherry v. Forell (sired by Ch. Odin v Forell ex Ch. Cita v. Germania). Cherry was a fine producer as well as a top winner, and was dam of German and French Champion Vamp-Cita-Cherry de Fiere Gueule, who was brown. The sire was Chico, making this a brother-sister mating, and several other youngsters from this breeding are now showing great promise. Mrs. Manuel likes to concentrate her breeding program on in-breedings and has produced fine offspring based primarily on v. Forell bloodlines.

The South of France is leading in excellent quality Dobermans and among these are the well-known working qualities of the dogs of the Vallons de Bonnes Herbes Kennels of Mme. Larzilliere, President of the Doberman Club of France in the Provence-Midi Section. Mme. Larzilliere has had to curtail her breeding activities, because she is so active as a leader in the club and as a judge. However, the fine male, Ramses du Vallon de Bonnes Herbes, is carrying on the tradition of this kennel. Another champion produced in the South is the beautiful Ch. Visa, recently bred to the handsome Ike de la Clodiniere, who is a son of Ch. Earl v Forell. She is by Simbad du Hallier St. Hubert ex Quriss de Festiano, who is a red Cuno daughter. Quriss herself has won many CACIBs and CACs in competition. Ch. Visa is also working towards her Brevet degree.

Toward the center of France we come to du Vaudois, another kennel of many years standing and reputation. Many fine Dobermans have been bred here, including the 1970 Champion, Negus du Vaudois (sired by GoGo v Forell ex Linda du Vaudois), a handsome male and fine producer. He has been followed by Innsbruck de la Sourganne, sired by Spitfire de la Morliere ex Themis du Vaudois, a good young male who has already won one CAC, three CACIBs and two RCACIBs. Owner Mr. François Bidault has been an officer in the DC of France for many years, along with being a breeder for thirty and also a distinguished judge. His many duties and judging assignments have curtailed his breeding activities somewhat in the past years.

Other kennels to be cited for their contribution to the breed over the years include des Golden, home of World Champion and German winner, Scherzo des Golden, who was sired by Elmo v Furstenfeld out of the Dutch bred bitch, Ina v Neerlandstam. Scherzo was named International Champion and sired some very fine puppies in his too short life. Another young male from this kennel who owner Mr. Lemaiere hopes will carry on for Scherzo, is Joker des Golden, sired by Gido v Forell ex Ina van Nerlandstam.

The De la Tretoire Kennels of Mrs. Jean Rossel has also had success through the years. Mrs. Rossel received the Gold Medal, the Medaille d'Or, at the World Championship of the FCI at Paris in 1974. Her kennel produced the outstanding bitch, Ch. Ogresse de la Tretoire, who was owned by Mrs. Harmand of the Hallier St. Hubert Kennels. Mrs. Rossel then followed with her International Ch. Stark de la Tretoire, sired by Lex de Mercastel ex Quassia de la Tretoire. Stark was a very powerful male who excelled in Schutzhund training and in tracking for which he won many medals. Stark,

Ch. Uriel du Baguier, top winner in conformation and Obedience. By Ch. Ero von Hagenstern ex Risca de Noir Feu. Bred and owned by M. Roman, "Beauregard", France.

Int. Ch. Stark de la Tretoire. By Lex de Mercastel ex Quassia de la Tretoire. Bred and owned by Mrs. Rossel's de la Tretoire Kennels, France.

251

who was whelped in 1969 and prematurely died in 1973, was a very important stud, even though on the scene for just a few short years. A new star on the horizon in this field of Working titles is a young male called Siegfried du Hallier St. Hubert, known as ''Spartacus'', sired by Peer von Forell ex Ogresse de la Tretoire. Obedience winner of 1975, as well as being a show champion. Great things are expected of him as a sire and his offspring are just beginning to appear in the rings. Spartacus can now take his place with three other greats listed in the Societè Centralè Canine: Caro de la Grade d'Alsace, who was owned by former Head Trainer Mr. Emile Schrenk, Imac du Pre Cassar (bitch) owned by Mr. Jean Stolz, and Surf de Clos Larry, well known young male who has appeared on TV and is owned by Mrs. Mathieu.

The kennel Hallier St. Hubert, formerly under Mr. Andre Harmand and now taken over by his wife, has contributed much over the years to the betterment and promotion of the breed in the section of Ile de France and Paris.

There are many other breeders, but it is impossible to list them all. Kennels of many years standing such as the Mercastel Kennels have contributed much down through the years through the outstanding produce of such champions as Iran, Quatty and Rex de Mercastel. On the Western border, between France and Germany in the region of Alsace, we have another noted breeder, Mr. Nunge and his v. Falkenturm Kennels. An outstanding stud of his breeding is Tasso v Falkenturm, winner of many shows. And another top kennel on the French-German border is the vom Druidenstein Kennels, owned by Roger Bousendorffer.

Another up-and-coming kennel is that of De l'Isle en Touraine, owned by Mrs. Jean Foulon. The kennel began with a lovely brood bitch, Sprudli de l'Isle en Touraine, who later was bred to the German Ch. Chico v Forell, producing among many the fine bitch Undine de l'Isle en Touraine, who in turn has produced some fine offspring from her mating to Ch. Jurgen von Hagenstern. Mrs. Foulon has another outstanding bitch, Ilga De l'Isle en Touraine, who was awarded Champion title at the age of twenty months, at the World Champion exposition of 1975. Among her other titles are: 11 CAC, 4 CACIB, and a RCACIB, a very impressive list for a bitch so young. Ilga was sired by Ch. Earl v Forell out of Thetis de l'Isle en Touraine. Among other young aspirants are the young bitch, Janis de l'Isle en Touraine, sired by the German Ch. Lex von Beelen out of Sprudli de l'Isle en Touraine.

In summation, the future of the Doberman in France points to a dramatic upsurge in popularity and a truly impressive advance in overall quality. A few important German bloodlines seem to be responsible for this improvement. They are: the Germania line, concentrated mostly in Southern France, followed by von Forell, and here and there a sprinkling of von Furstenfeld, von Beelen and Hagenstern. Time will tell how much impact the last two will have, as they really are off-shoots of the Germania and Forell lines. France is very strong in her own lines and they seem to be very compatible with the German lines of today. However, as breeding is such a fascinating science, one never knows what the outcome will be. The emphasis now seems to be on developing very deep chests and shorter backs. But these can easily become exaggerated, for the Doberman is still meant to be a galloper, and breeders want to retain the elegance it has taken forty years to breed into the line. Too much concentration on breeding for deep chests and very short loins, while ignoring such other important factors as excessive sloping rears to obtain very high withers, a tendency towards shorter necks, etc., would result in a great disservice to the breed in general.

An important forward step taken by the Doberman Club of France in 1970, was the inauguration of the National Exposition Show. This show is now held every two years, each year in a different section of the country and its purpose (apart from the conformation ring) is the testing, by special tests, of the character of the Dobermans, and recording the gradings in the registration books of the Club. The results are then printed in the national all-breed magazine, *La Vie Canine.*

Certainly no breeding program is without its problems, and where in one sector faults are eliminated, other faults may creep in. But France has come a long way in the breeding of the Doberman, and French bloodlines are in great international demand. It is hoped through intelligence, perseverance, and just good common sense, the Doberman will continue to be the valuable and desired breed it is today in France.

Few sights are more thrilling than the Doberman in motion.

Ch. Tavey's Stormy Wrath. This black bitch, whelped May 1961, won 17 Challenge Certificates and 5 Bests in Show before she was retired in 1965. Sired by Ch. Acclamation of Tavey, she was bred and owned by Mr. J. Curnow, Sussex, England.

Tavey's Westwinds Quintessence, owned by Mrs. Curnow.—*Anne Hewitt*

Phileens Duty Free of Tavey, red male owned by Mrs. J. Curnow. Duty Free is by Ch. Tarrado's Corry ex Kay Hill's Outrigger, who was imported in whelp to England. He is proving to be an excellent sire.

254

16

The Doberman in England

by Mike Bradshaw

Eɴɢʟᴀɴᴅ is unique in geography and the consequent historical influences. As a people we have been ruled by numerous nationalities, we have amassed and lost an empire, we have fought in two world wars, and we have been victorious and defeated by our own victories. But this has everything to do with the breeding of Dobermans in England.

No Doberman bred in England is without the indigenous German influence. No success can be measured without due acknowledgement to the very first imported Dobermans. Make what you will of this short incomplete history, but do so noting my definitions and stated omissions.

Prior to 1950 the English Kennel Club registration of Dobermans was nil. Prior to 1950 the Doberman breed was listed as ''Any other breed or variety not separately classified.'' By 1974 we have registrations in excess of 2,000. What of the twenty-four years between?

In the late 1940s and early 1950s importers and breeders concentrated on using Dobermans of known working characteristics and abilities. Many of them had connections with police forces, security, and the armed services and the Doberman quickly established itself as good as, and in many cases better than, the German Shepherd in working ability.

Why the demise in the Doberman as a working dog? I do not give an answer. But from articles I have read from armed forces handlers, from police handlers, and from those responsible for the training of dogs, certain factors are recognizable. Since the second World War armed forces have been depleted in manpower. Within certain police forces, Chief Constables find that economies can be effected in the police dogs by making selection from the German Shepherds offered to the forces rather than by the breeding and selection of Dobermans. In certain European countries the Doberman is near the top in numerical registration, and in those countries there has been direct control of breeding and selection for type and working qualities. In England German Shepherds are by far the most popular of the registered dogs. Perhaps if the Doberman ever reached the same numerical status it would be offered in the same economical way for its working qualities. Dobermans are entered in working trials here and are proving themselves equal to any other breed.

The 1950s were a period of establishment. Influences from German, Dutch, and Swiss imports were the consolidating basis for breeding. Our early pedigrees contain such names as: Treu v.d. Steifurthohe, out of the 1950 Dutch Sgr. Troll v.d. Eversburg SCH ex Bella v.d. Steifurthohe; Alex Von Rodenaer, out of Dinco v.d. Sudhoek N.H.S.B. 144617 ex Clara v.d. Sudoek N.H.S.B. 131385; Cartergate Alpha of Tavey, an all-German breeding in England from Derb von Brunoberg ex Beka von Brunoberg. Lola of Cartergate was produced from a mating between Arko von Dom Schaffertrifft out of the dam Barbell von Edmundsthall. From Holland came Prinses Anja v.t. Scheepjeskerk CD, UD, Roenka v. Rhederveld, Waldox von Neiderlands Star, Tasso vd Everburg who sired ten out of the eighteen placed exhibits at Crufts Championship show in 1956, Britta vd Heerhof and from Switzerland Bruno v Ehrgarten.

Those who used the working qualities of these early imported Dobermans will probably never again have a dog as outstanding as Mountbroune Joe P.D. Ex. TD Ex., WD Ex., CD Ex., from all German bloodlines but bred in England. Dual Champion Jupiter of Tavey CD Ex. was sired by Bruno of Tavey out of Prinses Anja v.t. Scheepjeskerk CD, UD Ex. In the late 1960s Dollar Premium TD Ex., WD Ex., UD Ex., CD Ex. gained Best in Show award under the specialist breed judge Professor J. Bodingbauer. I include his pedigree to illustrate the combination of Show and Working stock and the influence of those early European imports combining with the imports from America. At this time I know of no better reference for the working Doberman in England than the contribution by Jean Faulks in the book, *The Doberman,* third edition. My references on the working Dobermans are made in the belief that their genetic contribution has been crucial but not sustained in its effect on type.

Ch. Steb's Top Skipper

Ch. Acclamation of Tavey

Orebaugh's Raven of Tavey

Ch. Tumlow Impeccable

Ch. Tavey's Stormy Achievement

Tavey's Stormy Governess

Tamara of Tavey

DOLLAR PREMIUM, TD Ex., WD Ex., UD Ex., CD Ex. (Black male, wh. June 28, 1964)

W/T Ch. Ulf Von Margarethenof

Mountbroune Yukon, TD Ex., UD Ex., CD Ex.

Ch. Reichart Judy

Lacrosse Winning Ride

Mountbroune Joe, PD Ex., TD Ex., CD Ex.

Bowesmoor Helde

Bowesmoor Oona

It is a shared belief that if the Doberman is bred in type to the standard it will have the physical capabilities of working. The reverse is also true in part; if it works well it must be soundly constructed. In all the controversies involving working versus show Dobermans that I have read, the main criterion has been to provoke the written word by emphasising the differences rather than accepting mutual coexistence. Many of the points raised are based on little fact and much prejudice. Those with the requisite abilities persist in selecting and training their dogs and continue to win in the show ring as and when the circumstances allow.

We have an explicit criterion for judging the Doberman's working abilities. The working Doberman gains its award in a logical progression of difficulty, or fails. By the same simple criterion we have to accept that if a Doberman is to be successful in the show ring there must be graded assessment by judges and consequent awards. There is progressive difficulty in competition, and the criterion laid down leads first to award of a Stud Book Number and then can lead to the ultimate title of Show Champion.

Regulations for Entries in the Stud Book (24 February 1972):

1. An entry in the Stud Book shall consist of the registered name of the dog, its sex, color, date of birth, owner, breeder, an extension of its pedigree limited to three generations, or a Stud Book Number within that limit.
2. All dogs must be entered in the Stud Book in the name of the registered owner at the time of qualification.
3. To each dog accepted for entry, a Kennel Club Stud Book Number will be assigned.
4. The following dogs are entitled to free entry into the Kennel Club Stud Book subject to Regulations 1, 2 and 3:
   (a) Dogs winning Championship Certificates, Reserve Best of Sex or First, Second or Third prizes in Open, Limit, or Field Trial Classes where Kennel Club Championship Certificates are competed for when such classes are not subject to any limitations as to weight, color or other description.
   (b) All winners of Prizes, Reserves, Awards of Honor, Diplomas of Merit, or Certificates of Merit at Field Trials held under Kennel Club Field Trials Rules and Regulations.
   (c) Winners of Prizes or qualifying Certificates in T.D. or P.D. Stakes at Championship Working Trials held under Kennel Club Working Trial Rules and Regulations.
   (d) Winners of First, Second or Third prizes in test "c", Open, at Championship Obedience Tests.
   (e) Winners of the Kennel Club Obedience Championships.

My problem was to assess the influence of the Doberman imports on the type of the Doberman in England. Note that I do not refer to the English Doberman. There is no such animal. No Doberman in England can claim this false insularity. Even if several new champions were made up in any one year we can hardly call the influence typical, especially when we place the wins of

257

Amsel's Andante of Marks-Tey, pictured at 7 years. This red bitch was imported from the United States in whelp to Ch. Gra-Lemor Demetrius vd Victor. One red daughter, Ferrings Impish—a top producer in her own right, was sent to Australia. Andante is owned by Robert Walker of Ferring, Sussex, England.

Vanessa's Little Dictator of Tavey, whelped May 1963. Sired by Ch. Checkmate's Chessman. Little Dictator was sold to Mr. and Mrs. Curnow by Pat and Judy Doniere of Toledobes Kennels, USA.

Zeitgeist Red Baize, lovely red bitch, sired by American import Gra-Lemor Freebooter ex Tavey's Stormy Pride. Bred and owned by Mike Bradshaw, pictured with her here.

these dogs against the registrations at the Kennel Club of some 1,500 plus contemporaries. Our new champions are anything but typical. They are extraordinary. That is why they gain their titles, and as judges this factor of being extraordinary is what we seek in the ring. The standard is the ultimate Doberman, that insatiable something for which some have spent a lifetime trying to breed. If an import is to be assessed as affecting the Doberman in England it must have been used for breeding purposes. Because "line breeding" and "inbreeding" are the exception rather than the rule in England, I have used the Kennel Club Stud Books to provide the information of the first generation of American imported offspring, both males and females. The fact that they have been awarded a Stud Book Number and entry into the Kennel Club Stud Book has been my criteria for assessing their conformation in the show ring. Sometimes these award winners have continued with their successes to championship status and may not have reached that status when entered into the Stud Book. The fact that some of those Dobermans listed are not prefixed with the title "Champion" is not an oversight.

Having classified this information, make of it what you will. I will not attempt to do so because my researches have made me aware of all those factors that will mislead you. These factors are many and varied from political influences, the abilities of the judges making the awards, the competition during that year and the competition within that particular class, the genetic influences of the dams or sires and the facts that these compilations are related only to American imports. I was invited to write one chapter not a preface to a history of the Doberman in England.

What I leave with you is a reference for pedigrees of Dobermans in England influenced by American importations.

My daughter tugs at me whilst I write. Reminds me of two quotations. One by the English painter Constable, "We see nothing until we truly understand it." The other: "And the man who dug a field looking for buried treasure. He found none, but having dug the field he sowed and in due season reaped the harvest."

American Imports

Registered in 1952, **Quita of Jerry Run,** whelped December 1950, Blue Bitch sired by Arbleu of Jerry Run ex Oenone of Jerry Run. Bred by Mrs. Rhys Carpenter and owned by Mrs. Y. Willett and L. H. Renwick. This was a brother and sister mating, Quita being a sister to Quickly of Jerry Run.

Registered in 1952, **Lady Gretchen,** whelped October 1947, Bitch sired by West Hill Adonis ex Gretchen. Bred by H. F. Corbrunson and owned by Mrs. F. W. Streck.

Registered in 1952, **Damasyn Sirocco,** whelped June 1948, Red Male sired by Ch. Dictator v Glenhugel ex Damasyn The Song. Bred by Mrs. R. C. Polak and Peggy Adamson.

Registered in 1956, **Am. Ch. Rustic Adagio,** whelped December 1949 and sired by Am. Ch. Kilburn Ideal ex Rustic Radiance. This black bitch was bred by G. F. Kiser and owned by A. Curnow.

Ferrings Mike Victor, black male sired by Ch. Gra-Lemor Demetrius vd Victor ex Amsel's Andante of Marks-Tey. Bred by Robert H. Walker and owned by Mike Bradshaw.

Walkaway's Wildfire (at 20 months). By Walkaway's Ablaze of Marks-Tey ex Marks-Tey Bow Bells, he was bred by Mary Jane Ladd of St. Louis, Missouri, and is owned by Mike Bradshaw, Sutton Coldfield, England.

Ferrings Mike's Burgundy. The red bitch, a product of a brother and sister breeding from the Demetrius ex Andante litter, whelped in English quarantine, is owned by Mike Bradshaw.

Registered in 1956, **Mark Antony of Mokan,** whelped May 1953, male sired by Ch. Torn's Desert Gold ex Sky. Breeder Mrs. S. Meyers and owned by Capt. Woodrow Bunten Huff.

Registered in 1957, **Awol of Doggon Acres,** whelped May 1955, male sired by Dell Russet Encore v. Cameron (Am. Ch.) ex Brenda of Doggone Acres. Bred by Miss A. Stanberry and owned by Lt. Col. Thatcher Harwood.

Registered in 1958, **Prince Faust of Van Ide,** whelped June 1951, this male was bred by Mr. A. S. Rotherberg, his sire was Mr. Patrick O'Toole V. Keeloak ex Lady of Shadow Mountain. He was owned by Capt. and Mrs. A. Anderson.

Registered in 1959, **Orebaugh's Raven of Tavey,** whelped March 1956, black bitch sired by Ch. Rancho Dobe's Primo ex Ch. Orebaugh's Gentian. Bred by Mrs. M. R. Orebaugh and owned by Mrs. J. Curnow.

Registered in 1963, **Highbriar Olympik,** whelped December 1960, black male sired by Ch. Florian Vom Ahrtal CDX ex Ch. Highbriar Blackbird CDX. Bred by Ted Linck and Betsy Thomas and owned by A. Billingham.

Registered in 1964, **Westwinds Quintessence,** whelped December 1962, black bitch sired by Elblac Zaturno ex Westwinds Majoram. Bred by Mrs. V. Hoskins and owned by Mrs. J. Curnow.

Registered in 1965, **Distinctive Daneen,** whelped April 1964, red bitch, sired by Ch. Marks-Tey's Hanover ex Ch. Dodie of Marks-Tey CD. Bred by Robin Longbons and owned by Mrs. J. Curnow and E. Hoxey.

Registered in 1965, **Vanessa's Little Dictator,** whelped May 1963, black male sired by Ch. Checkmate's Chessman ex Ch. Valheim's Vanessa. Bred by E. Edgar and Mrs. B. Gerner and owned by Mrs. J. Curnow.

Registered in 1966, **Heidi of Evenna,** whelped May 1965, bitch sired by Marada's C. Bonea ex Bechtold's Heidi of Terribill. Bred by J. W. Havens and owned by J. F. Azzali.

Registered in 1967, **Inge Aus Munchen,** whelped June 1965, bitch sired by Hondi's Apache ex Wotan's Brunnhilde. Bred by M. H. Collier and owned by A. B. Hogg.

Registered in 1970, **GraLemor Freebooter,** whelped May 1968, red male sired by Ch. Marks-Tey Shawn CD ex GraLemor Eve of Destiny. Bred by Mrs. Grace Moore and owned by Robert H. Walker.

Registered in 1970, **Norbon Red Sabre,** whelped February 1969, red male sired by Ventors Crimson Commando. Bred by Bonnie Rosenberg and owned by Mr. and Mrs. W. Froggatt.

Registered in 1971, **Ch. Beau James of Rustic Gold,** whelped July 1965, black male sired by Aladean of Philcra Lane ex Ch. Rustic Gold. Bred by Buck and Lorraine Jacobs and owned by Connie Jo Taylor.

Registered in 1971, **Taylor's Flamme Warlock,** whelped July 1967, red bitch sired by Ch. Underhill's Roc Von Warlock CD ex Lowell's Contessa Rhea. Owned by Connie Jo Taylor, this bitch was brought into England by her owner, in whelp to Ch. Aztec's Beacon.

Registered in 1972, **Arawak Perfecta,** whelped May 1970, red bitch sired by Ch. Dolph Von Tannenwald ex Arewak Hi-A-Leah CD. Bred by Mr. and Mrs. R. Abel and owned by Mrs. J. Curnow.

Registered in 1973, **Amsel's Andante of Marks-Tey,** whelped May 1969, red bitch sired by Ch. Marks-Tey Shawn CD ex Ch. Hanover's Amsel CD. Bred by Mr. and Mrs. T. Hoekman and owned by Robert H. Walker.

Registered in 1973, **Camiereich Day Trip to Tavey,** whelped April 1971, red bitch sired by Ch. Kay Hill's Takeswon to Nowon ex Ch. Study Halls Smarti of Kay Hill. Bred by Mrs. E. S. and J. L. Reich and owned by Mrs. J. Curnow.

Registered in 1973, **Kay Hills Outrigger,** whelped May 1972, red bitch sired by Ch. Dolph von Tannenwald ex Kay Hills Kat a Maran. Bred by Mrs. Jane Kay and owned by Mrs. E. Edwards.

Registered in 1974, **Walkaways Wildfire,** whelped June 1972, red male sired by Walkaway's Ablaze of Marks-Tey ex Marks-Tey Bow Bells. Bred by Mary Jane Ladd and owned by M. Bradshaw.

Stud Book Entries of First Generation Produced from Dobermans Imported from America.

Progeny of TAVEY'S STORMY ABUNDANCE:

Ch. Carickgreen Confederate ex Ch. Carickgreen Walda Nagasta	Black	1961
Carickgreen Carousel, dog ex Ch. Garickgreen Walda Nagasta	Black	1961
Vivacious of Vreda, bitch ex Arden of Trevellis	Black	1961
Adoration of Dunbrill, bitch ex Utopia of Tavey	Black	1962
Doberean Patience, bitch ex Lorelei of Tavey TD Ex., UD Ex., CD Ex.		
Ch. Tavey's Stormy Leprechaun, bitch ex Utopia of Tavey	Black	1962
Brutus of Tavey, dog ex Birling Rachel	Black	1962
Tavey's Stormy Legion, dog ex Utopia of Tavey	Black	1962
Tavey's Stormy Master, dog ex Utopia of Tavey	Black	1962
Tavey's Stormy Vedette, bitch ex Vervain Roulette	Black	1963
Hans of Tickwillow, dog ex Trudy of Ely	Black	1964
Black Satin of Dirksby, bitch ex Marlene	Black	1961
Tumlow Storm Away, dog ex Baba Black Pepper	Black	1960

Progeny of CH. RUSTIC ADAGIO

Ch. Tavey's Stormy Achievement, dog sired by Ch. Rancho Dobe's Storm	Black	
Tavey's Stormy Adagio, bitch sired by Ch. Rancho Dobe's Storm	Black	1958
Tavey's Stormy Aminda, bitch sired by Ch. Rancho Dobe's Storm	Black	1958
Ch. Tavey's Stormy Abundance, dog sired by Ch. Rancho Dobe's Storm	Black	
Ch. Tavey's Stormy Acadia, sired by Ch. Rancho Dobe's Storm	Black	

Progeny of TAVEY'S STORMY ACHIEVEMENT

Tavey's Stormy Gascon, dog ex Tamara of Tevey	Black	1961
Tumlow Storm Caesar, dog ex Ch. BaBa Black Pepper	Black	1961
Tavey's Storm Objective, dog ex Orebaugh's Raven of Tavey	Black	1962
Triogen Top Form, bitch ex Tamara of Tavey	Black	1962
Ch. Annastock Lance, dog ex Annastock Amberlili of Catharden	Black	1963
Annastock Lizbeth, bitch ex Annastock Amberlili of Catharden	Black	1963
Barrimilne Genghis Khan, dog ex Iris Von Wellborn	Black	1963
Annastock Moonraker, dog ex Annastock Amberlili of Catharden	Black	1964
Tumlow Katrina, bitch ex Tumlow Fantasy	Black	1965
Bronvorny's Explorer, dog ex Triogen Tuff Talk	Black	1966
Harvest of Tavey, dog ex Helena of Cartergate	Black	1966
Ch. Tavey's Stormy Medallion, dog ex Ch. Tavey's Stormy Willow	Black	1967
Ch. Heidiland Trouble Spot, dog ex Triogen Traffic Trouble	Black	1967
Tavey's Stormy Pepita, bitch ex Tavey's Westwind's Quintessence	Black	1968
Berkheya of Brief, dog ex Fantasia of Sonhende	Black	1963
Crest of Barrimilne, dog ex Ch. Xel of Tavey	Black	1960
Caliph of Barrimilne, dog ex Ch. Xel of Tavey	Black	1960
Ch. Auldrigg Corsair, dog ex Fascination of Sonhende	Black	1960
Tavey's Stormy Daughter, bitch ex Tamara of Tavey	Black	1959
Tumlow Storm Cloud, dog ex Ch. BaBa Black Pepper	Black	1960

Progeny of CH. ACCLAMATION OF TAVEY

Tavey's Stormy Nymph, bitch ex Tavey's Stormy Governess	Black	1962
Tumlow Fantasy, bitch ex Tavey's Stormy Governess	Black	1962
Ch. Tavey's Stormy Nugget, dog ex Tavey's Stormy Governess	Black	1963
Ch. Tavey's Stormy Wonder, dog ex Tavey's Stormy Governess	Black	1963
Ch. Tavey's Stormy Willow, bitch ex Tavey's Stormy Governess	Black	1963
Ch. Tavey's Stormy Wrath, bitch ex Tavey's Stormy Governess	Black	1963
Tumlow Imperial, dog ex Tavey's Stormy Governess	Black	1963
Ch. Tumlow Impeccable, dog ex Tavey's Stormy Governess	Black	1963
Tumlow Juno of Conrosa, bitch ex Tavey's Stormy Governess	Black	1964

Dolina Naiad and Dolina Nereid, bitches ex Gypsy of Sonhende	Black	1963
Dolina Othello, dog ex Gypsy of Sonhende	Black	1964
Nevanjos Black Orchid, bitch ex Venture of Vreda	Black	1963
Auldrigg Nevanjos Black Honey, bitch ex Venture of Vreda	Black	1963
Barrimilne the Moonraker, dog ex Canasta of Barrimilne	Black	1964
Barrimilne the Minx, bitch ex Canasta of Barrimilne	Black	1964
Ch. Edencourts Avenger, dog ex Tavey's Stormy Daughter	Black	1964
Tumlow Lolita, bitch ex Tavey's Stormy Governess	Black	1966
Auldrigg Dolina Nerissa, bitch ex Gypsy of Sonhende	Black	1965
Dolina Titania, bitch ex Gypsy of Sonhende	Black	1965
Dolina Basilisk, dog ex Gypsy of Sonhende	Black	1966
Triogen Troublesome Turk, dog ex Triogen Tullaherrin	Black	1964
Achtelock Heidi, bitch ex Tumlow Storm Charmer	Black	1964
Caprice of Tramerfield, bitch ex Astral of Tramerfield	Black	1964
Ch. Triogen Traffic Cop, dog ex Triogen Tennage Sensation	Black	1965
Triogen Traffic Jam, dog ex Triogen Teenage Sensation	Black	1965
Triogen Troublesome Fellow, dog ex Triogen Teenage Sensation	Black	1965
Triogen Traffic Block, bitch ex Triogen Teenage Sensation	Black	1965
Triogen Traffic Trouble, bitch ex Triogen Teenage Sensation	Black	1965
Triogen Tropical Spendour, bitch ex Triogen Teenage Sensation	Black	1965
Triogen Touch 'n' Go, dog ex Triogen Teenage Sensation	Black	1966
Triogen Texas Gunslinger, dog ex Triogen Teenage Sensation	Black	1970
Tinkazan Triogen Texas Ranger, dog ex Triogen Teenage Sensation	Black	1967
Triogen Tuppenny Treat, bitch ex Triogen Teenage Wonder	Black	1966
Ch. Iceberg of Tavey, dog ex Juno of Cartergate	Black	1965
Ch. Oberon of Tavey, dog ex Juno of Cartergate	Black	1966
Ch. Opinion of Tavey, bitch ex Juno of Cartergate	Black	1966
Indigo of Tavey, dog ex Juno of Carterate	Black	1967
Pagan Privateer, dog ex Bracken of Cartergate	Black	1965
Danzig of Royaltain, bitch ex Barrimilne Tiger	Black	1965
Doocloone Donathe, bitch ex Heidiland Debutante of Doocloone	Black	1965
Gurnard Gloomy Sunday, dog ex Gurnard's Hedda	Black	1966
Gurnard Gemma, bitch ex Gurnard's Hedda	Black	1965
Largo of Sturmendorf, bitch ex Tavey's Stormy Vedette	Black	1965
Juno of Sturmendorf, bitch ex Tavey's Stormy Vedette	Black	1966
Caliph of Trevellis, dog ex Ch. Satin of Tavey	Black	1960
Classic of Trevellis, bitch ex Ch. Satin of Tavey	Black	1960
Ch. Cordelia of Trevellis, bitch ex Ch. Satin of Tavey	Black	1959

Progeny of VANESSA'S LITTLE DICTATOR OF TAVEY

Vanessa of Tavey, bitch ex Tavey's Stormy Pia	Black	1968
Siddley Sovereign of Tavey, dog ex Tavey's Stormy Romance	Black	1967
Celeste of Tavey, bitch ex Tavey's Stormy Romance	Black	1968
Caprice of Tavey, bitch ex Tavey's Stormy Romance	Black	1969
Nayrilla Artemis, bitch ex Ch. Opinion of Tavey	Black	1969
Ch. Nayrilla Athene, bitch ex Ch. Opinion of Tavey	Black	1969
Nayrilla Adonis, dog ex Ch. Opinion of Tavey	Black	1969
Nayrilla Appollo, dog ex Ch. Opinion of Tavey	Black	1969
Nayrilla Wild Major, dog ex Ch. Opinion of Tavey	Black	1969
Nayrilla Wild Master, dog ex Ch. Opinion of Tavey	Black	1970
Nayrilla Wild Magician, dog ex Ch. Opinion of Tavey	Black	1968
Rusa of Tavey, bitch ex Tumlow Lolita	Black	1968
Auldrigg Yana of Tavey, bitch ex Ch. Tavey's Stormy Willow	Black	1968
Doberean Eclat of Tavey, bitch ex Tavey's Stormy Jael	Black	1969
Stormy Baron, dog ex Triogen Teenage Wonder	Red	1968
Nuance of Tavey, dog ex Tavey's Distinctive Daneen	Black	1970
Skybanks a Gogo, dog ex Skybank Samba	Red	1974

Progeny of HIGHBRIAR OLYMPIK

Navaho Chieftain, dog ex Barrimilne the Minx	Black	1968

Progeny of ARAWAK PERFECTA

Tavey's Sandra, bitch sired by Ch. Kay Hills Dealers Choice	Red	1974

Progeny of GRA-LEMOR FREEBOOTER

Zeitgeist's Red Baize, bitch ex Tavey's Stormy Pride	Red	1974
Zeitgeist's Red Brocade, bitch ex Tavey's Stormy Pride	Red	1974

Progeny of KAY HILL'S OUTRIGGER

Phileens Air Born sired by Ch. Tarrado's Corry	Red	1974
Phileens Duty Free of Tavey, dog sired by Ch. Tarrado's Corry	Red	1974

Kennel Club Registrations for Dobermans (1951–1974)

Registrations to 1950 inclusive – nil.

Year	Total	Year	Total	Year	Total
1951	94	1959	358	1967	1119
1952	112	1960	385	1968	1528
1953	138	1961	510	1969	1553
1954	135	1962	608	1970	1645
1955	205	1963	567	1971	1566
1956	189	1964	875	1972	1594
1957	241	1965	789	1973	1891
1958	236	1966	1017	1974	2029

An interesting picture showing both the cropped and un-cropped Doberman. Int. Ch. Guntherforst Dux and Rimi's A'Cora, owned by H. and K. Lurud, Norway. Both dogs were sired by the German import, Ch. Tex v Frankenland.

Handler Lilith Edstrom shows how to show an uncropped dog in Sweden when competing with cropped ears. The Doberman is BryanStam's Hanni-Harmonie, by Ch. Bryan v Forell ex Ch. Anja vd Haar.—*Dufwa*

265

At left, Int. Ch. Tavey's Stormy Nurmi, whelped 1964, by Ch. Tavey's Stormy Achievement ex C Tavey's Stormy Wrath. *At right,* Int. Ch. Damoiselle of Tavey, whelped 1967, by Vanessa's Little D tator of Tavey ex Octave of Tavey.

At left, Norwegian Ch. Rimangers Prins; *at right,* Norwegian Ch. Rimangers Mira; littermat whelped April 1967, by Int. Ch. Tavey's Stormy Nurmi ex Norwegian Ch. Tessis Dixi. Owned Thor Osthagen.

17

The Doberman in Scandinavia

NORWAY *by Maida Jonsson*

SWEDEN *by Lilith Edstrom*

FINLAND *by Keijo Alen*

T HE DOBERMAN was introduced to Norway the turn of the century. As early as 1910, a man from Hamburg, Germany, brought three of the breed to a Norwegian police dog show and demonstrated their prowess in police work.

Dobermans were first shown here in 1911, when an import from Denmark was exhibited at the Norwegian Kennel Club show. The critique given by the German judge reads: "The one Doberman did not please me. It is heavy, has no elegance of head, forefeet are flat; outside of that, has a white spot on his chest."

Serious interest in the breed began with the '20s, and the Norwegian Doberman Club was founded in 1922, with twelve members. Obedience classes and competitions were started in 1925. They were conducted under Danish rules—a Danish book on police dog training served as the "bible"—and included an exercise "Protecting the Handler" that was accorded 20 points. It was learned (but not soon enough) that this exercise was all too easy to teach a dog, and where a person had such a dog and did not have full control over it, it could lead (and had already) to serious damage to anyone who the dog assumed was about to harm his handler. This, together with the fact that nervous and aggressive dogs were being used for breeding, was to lead to their being proclaimed dangerous. (The exercise was eliminated from the Obedience program in 1928.)

By 1928, the Norwegian Doberman Club had grown to 71 members. And in the same way that American breeders were inviting German judges and learning from them, the Norwegians in 1929 had Peter Umlauff as guest judge, and learned much from him.

In 1930, as in other countries, there was an economical crisis in Norway and puppy buyers were very few. At the same time, the Justice Department proclaimed all German Shepherds and Dobermans as "dangerous", and went so far as to propose that they should all be destroyed.

The Norwegian Doberman and Norwegian German Shepherd clubs organized active protests, and the Justice Department eased its stand somewhat, proposing instead that all future breedings of these two breeds be forbidden. Fortunately, by this time, most of the nervous and aggressive dogs had passed on, and what was left of the latter had been trained for rescue work, and this helped regain some of the lost popularity. Extensive working dog groups were formed, and there were many field competitions won by Dobermans. "That all future breedings be forbidden" never became a law.

At the end of the 1930s, the Doberman in Norway was a very heavy dog, but had very good temperament and very good working dog qualities.

War came to Norway early in 1940, and a law was imposed by the German occupying forces against any large groupings of dogs—so shows, Obedience and working dog groups became almost nil. During the occupation many good dogs were also "requisitioned" by the occupation forces.

Although after the war there were some dogs imported from Sweden and Denmark, it was not until 1957 that things really began to happen. A son of the German stud Nord Germania, whose dam was Ester Germania and whose grandsire was Alex v Kleinwaldheim, was imported from Finland. In 1959, three litter brothers sired by Peer v Sylvester were imported from Sweden. Peer's grandsire was the great Igon v Naunhof. Peer and his champion son, Anios Dobby, are to be found in many Norwegian pedigrees. In 1962 a Swedish-bred bitch sired by Hasso v Romberg was also imported.

By 1964 it became too evident that there were no really good Norwegian-bred studs. The then President of the Norwegian Doberman Club, Thor Osthagen, imported a Rancho Dobe's Storm grandson, his dam an English born granddaughter of Steb's Top Skipper. This import, Tavey's Stormy Nurmi, later became an International Champion. He was used quite a bit in breeding.

Soon after came another Storm grandson, Tavey's Stormy Picador, imported by Rodi Hubenthal, who later used Picador as his prefix. The dam of this import was Westwinds Quintessence, who had been imported into England from America by Fred Curnow.

I came to Norway in 1965 with a Storm half-brother, Bomarc of Ashworth, sired by Ch. Rancho Dobe's Primo ex Allen's Juliet CD.

In 1967 Mr. Osthagen imported Damoiselle of Tavey, an English-born daughter of the American dog, Vanessa's Little Dictator and she is Little Dictator's first champion of record. Damoiselle also became an International

American and Norwegian Ch. Honor Guard's Vesta, CD Owned by Doberhill Kennels. This red bitch, whelped February 1966, was sired by Ch. Thane v Ahrtal ex Honor Guard's Spring Sonnet.

Norwegian Ch. Ino v Eichenhain, whelped June 1969, by Vello v Furstenfeld ex Hella v Forell. Owner, Jens Kollenberg, von Norden Stamm.

Norwegian Ch. Ali Baba, whelped August 1971, by Baron von Finn Heide ex Stangis Laika.

Ch. Guy's Hilo of Norden Stamm, whelped August 1972, by Ch. Bryan v Forell ex Ch. Gunthersforst Burga.

269

Dewi v Franckenhorst, whelped December 1973 in Holland in a litter of 11 ex Olive of Bamby's Pride, who had been artificially inseminated with live sperm from Ch. Bryan v Forell.

Don-Dayan v Franckenhorst, litter brother to Dewi, the top winning male in Holland in 1975.

Picador Quia, whelped May 1973, by Ch. Bryan v Forell ex Arka vom Rotenfeld.

Int. and Nordic Ch. Kirdette-Kora, winner of 3 Bests in Show, sired by Ch. Bryan v Forell ex Ch. Kippis Girl. Bred by Julietteville Kennels.

270

Champion. Later yet another English import made her appearance — Progress of Tavey, whose sire was Ch. Iceberg of Tavey.

Shortly after, two bitches, litter sisters, Gunthersforst Toska and Terze were imported from Finland. Their sire, Zar von Forell, is a full brother to Chico von Forell in Germany.

In 1971, the American Champion Honor Guard's Vesta, sired by Thane v Ahrtal ex Honor Guard's Spring Sonnet, was imported by the Doberhill Kennels of Erling Aasheim, together with four puppies from the breeding to Ch. Agony Acres Devotee of Zeno. Two other puppies from Vesta's daughter, Ava v Herrenhof (by Ch. Cassio v Ahrtal), and sired by Ch. Biggin Hill's Alaric, were also imported.

Through these imports and their use in breeding, the old style of Doberman was fast disappearing. This could have been achieved much earlier but Norway imposes strict quarantine laws, since there has not been a case of rabies here for over 150 years. Norway suffered greatly during the war, but later the economy became more and more stable, and more money became available for imports. However, the quarantine restrictions remain, which although good for Norway, are a hindrance to importation.

I should mention that I have had four different dogs in quarantine and a fifth is there now. I can in no way complain about the conditions there. The station is ideally situated and everything is immaculate. The keepers are generous with their affections and definitely have a way with the animals. There is space for only 48 dogs and the quarantine period is four months, with leash restriction for two months after that.

The next two imports from Germany were: Tex v Frankenland (Boris v Hagenstolz x Lady v Frankenland), imported by the vom Norden Stamm Kennels of Jens Kollenberg, and Roby v Frankenland (Rado v Furstenfeld ex Lady v Frankenland), imported by Picador Kennels. Both Tex and Roby have been Best in Show winners. Tex bred with Kollenberg's Progress of Tavey produced three champions in one litter, a first in Scandinavia, namely: Chs. Gunthersforst Droll, Dux and Danja. Dux and Danja later became International Champions. Andy vd Veste Otzberg, sired by Rondo v Forrell ex Anka v Eichenhain, was purchased by Doberhill from Sweden, where he had been imported from Germany.

As you can see, Finland and Sweden have been a source of imports for Norway, there being no quarantine internments between these three countries. Denmark also enjoyed that status until a case of rabies was reported and since then, all dogs coming from or having visited that country must be quarantined on their return to either Norway, Sweden or Finland.

Another German import of note was Ino v Eichenhain, sired by Vello v Furstenfeld ex Hella v Forell. This dog was imported by the von Norden Stamm Kennels. Ino bred with Anja v Frankenland produced two champions, Guy's Frida and Fia of Norden Stamm and, bred with Carmen vom Norden Stamm, produced Ch. Jago vom Norden Stamm.

271

In 1972 I imported a black bitch from America, Toledobes Keepsake (sired by Ch. The Sundance Kid, who was by Ch. Damasyn Carly of Jerseystone ex Toledobes Team Mascot, a Ch. Ebonaire's Touchdown daughter). A year later I imported a Carly grandson, Toledobes Abilene v Kahn Tex, and an Andelane's Indigo Rock son, Ebonaire's Bueno, whose dam was Ebonaire's Suzerain. Keepsake became a Norwegian Champion in September of 1973.

Shortly after, Doberhill imported the ''G'' vd Veste Otzberg litter from Germany (Vello v Furstenfeld ex Frigga vd Veste Otzberg) and a year later, yet another litter, the ''H'' litter, this time sired by Chico von Forell.

Doberhill Kennels bred Andy vd Veste Otzberg with Int. and Nordic Champion Zita von Western, which produced three champions in one litter, Zafir, Zora and Zacri. Int. Nordic Ch. Zacco, full brother to Zita, had a daughter, Int. Ch. Edda (Doberhill) in Norway and she, bred to Bomarc of Ashworth, the Rancho Dobe Primo son, produced Int. Ch. Doberhill's Black Chip Off Mark.

The Rancho Dobe lines when bred with German or lines of German descent gave some good results. Int. Ch. Tavey's Stormy Nurmi bred with Tessis Dixie produced two champions in one litter, Rimangers Prins and Rimangers Mira. Stormy Nurmi bred with Tessis Disa produced Ch. Anzac. At one show here, judged by Ernst Wilking of Germany, Anzac was Best of Breed, Rimangers Prins Winners Dog and the young dog, Doberhill's Black Chip Off Mark, second winner.

The two Zeno sons and one daughter, Doberhill Cesar, Cuhio and Chana v Herrenhof, became Norwegian champions. Chana bred to an Andy vd Otzberg ex Zita v Western son, Int. and Nordic Ch. and Working Dog Ch. Zafir, produced three champion males: Doberhill's Black Oscar, Ondo and Olymp. Oscar bred to Chana's little sister Carola, produced Ch. Doberhill's Black Unique Case.

The Picador Kennels imported Reni v Frankenland and litter sired by Boris v Herkules. This ''B'' litter produced Int. Ch. Bjango v Frankenland and Ch. Britta v Frankenland.

In 1968, Bryan v Forell was imported from Germany via Sweden. He became a popular winner and stud and a few breeders felt it worthwhile to import within the same lines. Picador imported Hardes v Forell (Flint v Forell ex Cindy v Forell). Picador later purchased Bryan Stam's Femelle Fee, a daughter of Gido v Hagenstern ex Gravin Grazie (a Bryan daughter), who later became a champion of record.

Ch. Gunthersforst Burga, a Tex v Frankenland daughter (dam was Gunthersforst Jasmin) when bred to Bryan v Forell has produced a six champion litter — Guy's Hasso, Hella, Heidi, Hedda, Hanny and Hilo of Norden Stamm. Hella and Heidi are International Champions. Never before have there been more than three champions in one litter in Norway, so this is quite a record.

Int. Ch. Andy vd Veste Otzberg, by Rondo v Forell ex Anka von Eichenhaim. Owned by Erling Aasheim, Doberhill Kennels.

Norwegian Ch. Doberhill's Black K'Arrow, by Int. Ch. Andy vd Veste Otzberg ex Ch. and Obed. Ch. Doberhill's Black Diva. Whelped March, 1972.

Left, Gogo vd Veste Otzberg and *right,* Ch . Gisella vd Veste Otzberg. These two bitches and their littermates by Vello v Furstenfeld ex Frigga vd Veste Otzberg, were imported from Germany by the Doberhill Kennels of Erling Aasheim.

273

Norwegian Ch. and Obed. Ch. Doberhill's Black Diva. This lovely black bitch was whelped in November 1969, by Ch. Rimangers Prins ex Ira Bella.

Brienco's Bara, whelped July 1972, by Norwegian Ch. Doberhill's Black Encore ex Norwegian Ch. Dobehill's Britta v Herrenhof. Owned by Jackman Kennels, Norway.

Int. Ch. Doberhill's Black Chip Off Mark, whelped March 1968, by Bomarc of Ashworth ex Allen's Juliet CD.

Picador Kennels also imported Peer v Beelen (by Flint v Forell ex Edda v Hagenstern) and Panco v Hagenstern (by Jurgen v Hagenstern ex Anushka Bryansdotter), and both have become Norwegian champions.

I have just imported from France, La Saga des Vergers du Cap Sicie, bred by Michel and Danielle Maury, and it is hoped she will lend credence to my prefix — Sagadobes. She is by Ike de la Clodiniere ex French Champion Visa, a Cuno Germania grand-daughter.

Naturally there have been some imports who have not met requirements, either physically or mentally. However, those who have, have certainly given positive results as has been seen at shows and in the results of judicious breedings. We are going in the right direction.

Ear cropping is not permitted in Scandinavia, and shows here do not separate by color nor by ears. And the good dogs win regardless. The Scandinavian people are very fresh air-minded, be it five degrees below freezing or not. Dobermans are often seen carrying their own packs, keeping pace with their owners on skis. There is also quite a bit of equipage competition in the winter.

Many working dog trials are held in Scandinavia and we also have competition trials held with clubs of other breeds — Boxers, etc. Our show rules are practically the same within the three countries; however, Sweden requires that a dog pass a character test before it can compete for winners.

Presently (1976) there are 590 members of the Norwegian Doberman Club plus fifty family members. In the past year four Dobermans were imported from Japan, eight from Germany, two from Hungary and three from Finland. Three were exported to Sweden, one to Canada, four to Germany and two to Italy.

The Norwegian Kennel Club arranges approximately ten International shows per year, plus approximately ten arranged by breed clubs in which Dobermans can be entered.

The Norwegian Doberman Club arranges two shows per year plus puppy matches. At the main Oslo show the honorary title of Norwegian Winner is given to the winner of each class. The three Scandinavian countries are now arranging a yearly show, alternating between Norway, Sweden and Finland with an honorary title of Nordisk Winner to be given. These titles are not registered.

In 1974, 414 Dobermans were registered in Norway, a 30% increase over the previous year. In 1965, only 144 had been registered. In 1970 there were fifty imports: 25 from Finland; eight from Germany, two from Sweden, four from Holland, and eight from America. Now, six years later, we are able to see some sound results in some of the grandchildren appearing this year. We naturally hope that with judicious breeding, the later imports will transmit their best qualities and, what was true years ago still holds true for the present and future, when Philip Gruenig wrote, "The Doberman was not created; he is still in the process of becoming."

Sweden

The Doberman has been in Sweden for a very long time. As far back as 1902, the breed was recognized by the Swedish Kennel Club, and mentioned in the official stud book the same year under the name German Smooth Haired Rathound. Two of the earliest Dobermans to have come to Sweden were the black male Toy-Baldu v Thuringen, whelped March 16, 1909, and Bendor v Thuringen, whelped February 27, 1909. I have in my possession a three-generation pedigree handwritten by the breeder Otto Goller which shows that Toy-Baldu was a son of Bodo Ronneburg-Thuringen ex Walkure v Thuringen and, through Bodo a grandson of Prinz v Ilm-Athen ex Siegerin Susy v Thuringen. On the reverse side of the pedigree, Mr. Goller has an advertisement for his kennel "von Thuringen" — which states that it was founded in 1898 and was the first and thereby the oldest Doberman kennel. He also named all the dogs that he had bred that had received a Sieger title up to that year, and which bitches and males he had available for breeding. He also included an announcement that the second edition of his book, *Dobermann in Word and Picture,* could be had for a small sum of 1.50 German Marks.

In 1911, the first Dobermans, or German Smooth Haired Rathounds — as they were named, were registered in Sweden — Bendor and Toy-Baldu (previously mentioned), Ellen v Thuringen, whelped February 10, 1910 (Amsdorf v Thuringen ex Katinka v Thuringen), Jorge v Thuringen, whelped April 10, 1909 (Bodo Ronneburg-Thuringen ex Rude v Thuringen), Lonni v Meeresstrand, whelped October 16, 1910 (Graaf Carlow v Friesland ex Senta v Rustringen) and Tosen, whelped May 25, 1910 (Zaren ex Lotten). Bendor (Nero v Wonnergau ex Livia v Thuringen) was shown at the Swedish Kennel Club shows in 1910 and 1911 and received a first in quality grading and was Winners dog each time.

In 1912 the name of the breed was changed to "Dobermann Pinscher" and in that year there were four registrations. All were black and tan.

In 1913, the first Swedish-born Doberman was registered: Zaza af Eckeensio, whelped June 6, 1913 (Bendor ex Zaza v Meeresstrand).

The pioneer for the breed in Sweden was Sven Schonbeck, Bjorkhaga Kennels, with lines going back mostly to Thuringen. He imported a number of dogs from Germany and Denmark and in 1921, this kennel registered not less than 21 males and bitches. It was in this kennel that the "grand old man" of the Swedish Doberman first saw light. He was Ch. Bjorkhaga Daddy Long Legs and his importance to the breed is indisputable. He was a very promising young male who fulfilled all expectations, and won a number of firsts at shows. His greatest and last triumph was at the Kennel Club show in Stockholm in 1928, winning the competition in the stud class with nine of his get. Daddy died at an early age of just eight years.

The next dog of importance for the breed in Sweden was the American import, Prince Rudy v Lankersheim, brought to Sweden in 1937 by the Nackas-

276

Norwegian Ch. Doberhill's Black Oscar, pictured at 11 months. Whelped November 1973, Oscar is by Int. and Nordic Ch. (and Working Dog Ch.) Tiklan Zafir ex Ch. Doberhill Chana Herrenhof.

Danja v Eichenhain, sired by Bsgr. Rondo v Forell ex Hella v Forell.

left, Ebonaire's Bueno, whelped June 1973, black son of Ch. Andelane's Indigo Rock ex Ebonaire's Terrain. At right, Norwegian Ch. Toledobe's Keepsake, whelped August 1971, black daughter of Ch. Sundance Kid ex Toledobe's Team Mascot. These dogs were separately imported from the United tes to Norway by Maida Jonsson.

Swedish Ch. Ziqarette av Norbega, wh. 1949, outstanding dam
owned by Astrid Kjellberg.

Swedish Ch. Gambias Faviola. By
Ch. Asso v Alstertal ex Ch. My
Bianca. Pictured in 1963.

Three champion littermates—Zacco, Zuzanne and Zorro, whelped in 1961, by Ch. Asso v Alstertal ex Sorella. Bred by Linnea Backman.

278

kogen Kennels. Prince Rudy became Working Dog Champion. Although his head lacked nobility, bred with suitable bitches he produced good offspring.

Nackaskogen Kennels then imported Ch. Fleuruis Pojken from Denmark and his most noted get were Ch. Arbin av Ena, Ch. Auricco Anjo My Babu and Auricco Cora. Norway imported Ch. Nackaskogens Lux who had influence on the breed there. A Lux grandson, International and Nordic Ch. Robb, Swedish owned, is the grandsire of the bitch Sorella, registered in 1959. Sorella is the dam of some of the best Dobermans whelped in Sweden during the first half of the 1960s.

The owner of the Norberga Kennels is Astrid Kjellberg. Mrs. Kjellberg still owns Dobermans, but over the past ten years has not been as active a breeder as in the past. She got her first Doberman when she was seven years old (in 1918). The first adult dog purchased was the bitch Mountebanks Suzie in 1937, and the kennel name was registered two years later. In the years following, twelve litters were whelped, approximately seventy puppies. In her opinion, her most successful bitch showwise was Zusanne of Norberga, whose wins included a Best in Show. Breeding wise, she thinks that the litter sister Zigarette was the best. Out of an eight puppy litter (three were culled) the five remaining all became champions, Gunga Din, Guy Din, Lucky Din, Zusanne Din and Indra Din of Norberga. Her most successful stud was the German import Ch. Asso v Alstertal, whelped in 1957 and imported to Sweden in 1960. He was only shown a few times and won six Best of Breeds and six Bests in Group. Asso sired 604 puppies in a total of approximately 64 litters, which is probably the largest number of progeny any stud in the Nordic countries has left behind. He received 19 wins in Stud classes and had about 25 champions to his credit. Asso died in 1967. Mrs. Kjellberg's most successful show dog was the German import, Ch. Alf vd Bauget, whelped 1964 (Barry v. Acherstein ex Elsa vd Ehrenreichen). He won 21 Bests of Breed, 9 Group Firsts, and two Bests in Show — all at all-breed shows. Alf was not used extensively in breeding, but did sire eight litters and has three champions to his credit. He died in 1976 at twelve years of age.

In the beginning of the 1950s Ch. Mara Germania (Ajax Germania ex Ch. Ester Germania) was imported, and she won rather easily since the quality of the Swedish Doberman had declined. She is described as a good bitch but one that would not have drawn much attention in her home country, Germany, nor in Holland or Italy. Other imports at the end of the 1950s who made an impact on the breed were Peer v Sylvester, Adda v Muhleneck and Ch. Hasso v Romberg. Hasso was a Best in Show winner and received a number of certificates and CACIBs and also first in Stud Class. Two of his most beautiful get were the littermates, Ch. Carr and Ch. Carri, still found in many Swedish pedigrees.

During the years 1960–1965, the following dogs deserve mention: littermates Ch. Zuzanne, Ch. Zorro and Ch. Zacco, whelped November 12, 1961. Zorro was the most successful, winning 13 Best of Breed, 7 Groups and 3 Bests in Show. Brother Zacco won the breed 14 times, two Groups and one

Best in Show. The breeder, Linnea Backman, repeated the breeding, and three more champions resulted: Ch. Zita, Ch. Zybil and Ch. Zezar, whelped February 10, 1965. These dogs were sired by Ch. Asso v Alstertal ex the previously mentioned Sorella. Both Zacco and Zita became International and Nordic Champions.

Another dog who made a name for himself in the sixties, especially in field work, was International and Nordic Ch. Ajbis Dorm. During the period 1962–1969 he won messenger dog trials fifty times!

A great many dogs were imported to Sweden during 1960–1966, particularly from Germany and Finland. In addition to Asso and Alf, from Germany came Ditto v Furstenfeld (Lump v Hagenstolz ex Carmen v Felsingpass) unfortunately used very little in breeding, Anka and Blitz v Bohmeial, Gavotte v Niddatal, and others. From England came Barrimilne the Viking (Gin v Forell ex Vilja Germania). From Holland, Graaf Yorick and Gravin Yarla v Neerlands Stam (Graaf Cito v Blue Blood ex Gravin Ursel v Neerlands Stam). From Belgium, Julia v Backenhagen, Nigo v Silberpark (sired by Ch. Kurt v Brementhal) and Ch. Nouveau. And from France came the bitch, Ch. Odiane du Chateau Saint-Laurent. Nigo, Nouveau and Odiane were imported by the Ligras Kennels, owned by Eugenie Duffourd, who registered her kennel name in 1962. Her first Doberman was Ch. Ajbis Cissi, whom she bought in 1961 and bred twice. From the first litter (sired by Ch. Bijou) came Ch. Ligras Djinn Marco, Ligras Stella Marina and Ligras Cassie Girl. Djinn Marco's daughter Ambra was bred to the Finnish import Hans v Finn-Heide (Ch. Cliff of Fayette Corner ex Illusion v Finn-Heide) and one of the puppies, Casanova, was to become one of the most successful Dobermans in the 1970s at shows as well as in sled work. Stella Marina was bred to Nigo, and a daughter Ligras Gurrah Girl had many good puppies including Ch. Sally-Mount, Ch. Silver-Penny, Ch. San-Souci and Mansikka. Cassie Girl was bred to Ch. Nouveau and a daughter, Ch. Kippis-Girl, bred to Ch. Bryan v Forell, produced one of the most equal and successful litters whelped in the Nordic countries — dogs that not only became champions, but have also acquired many Breed, Group, and Best in Show wins at all-breed shows.

Ch. Nouveau took over Asso's mantle as top stud. He was whelped October 20, 1964, and imported in 1966, He won 16 Breeds and became a champion in one month! He also had 18 Stud Class wins, and has nine champions to his credit. Three of the best litters were ex Ligras Kennel's brood bitch, Odiane, and produced Pan, Pirouette, and Ch. Pansy; Tilly, Ch. Thibault and Ligras Djimmy; Darko and Dorinne, the last two becoming Working Dog Champions. Ch. Nouveau died in 1975 at eleven years. He was sired by Ch. Kurt v Brementhal ex Fabi v Holzschutz, their common sire being Valbo Germania. Odiane, soon to be twelve years, is a daughter of Nadine, who is a full sister to Nouveau, so that the Nouveau-Odiane combination was heavy on Valbo Germania. In the years 1962 to 1974, the Ligras Kennels bred 32 litters.

280

Ch. Alf vd Bauget, whelped 1964, German import by Barry v Ackerstein ex Elsa vd Ehrenreichen. Alf was a strong winner for Astrid Kjelberg's Norbega Kennels, Stockholm.

Norwegian Ch. Peer von Beelen whelped February 1973, by Flint v Forell ex Edda v Hagenstern. Imported to Norway by Picador Kennels.

Working Dog Champion Kuosman Feri, 1964.

Ch. Nouveau, wh. 1964, by Ch. Kurt v Brementhal ex Fabi v Holzschutz. Imported from Belgium to Sweden in 1966 by Ligras Kennels, he became top stud of his time.

Ch. Bryan v Forell, wh. 1968, German import sired by Vello v. Furstenfeld ex Kira v Romberg. Best of Breed at Swedish Doberman Club annual shows in 1971, 1972 and 1973, and top stud. Owned by BryanStam Kennels.

Ch. Anja vd Haar, by BSgr, DVSgr Chico v Forell ex Vroni vd Brunoberg.

Ch. Asso v Alstertal, whelped March 1957, by Basko vd Teufelshohle ex Blanka v Haffring. Imported from Germany to Sweden in 1960 by Norbega Kennels, Asso became sire of 604 puppies (in 64 litters)—many of whom became famous champions.

Ch. Odiane du Chateau Saint Laurent (pictured at 18 months), notable dam, imported from France to Sweden by Ligras Kennels.

During the past ten years, 1966–1976, a great number of dogs have been imported, mostly from Germany. One who had great impact on the breed as well as successes at the shows is Ch. Bryan von Forell, whelped April 16, 1968, and imported at four months of age. He was sired by Vello v Fursten-feld ex Kira v Romberg. Bryan is a product of inbreeding on Sieger Lump v Hagenstolt on the paternal side, and on the maternal side of an inbreeding on Sieger Alex v Kleinwaldheim, the latter traced to the fourth generation. He has won many Bests of Breed and the various Nordic titles given at special shows in Norway and Finland, plus Bests of Breed at the Swedish Doberman Club's annual shows in 1971, '72 and '73. He also has scored three Groups and Best in Show wins at all breed shows in Sweden and Norway. In 1972, Bryan was the top winning Doberman in Sweden, and those who placed under him were his get: Ch. Kadrille-Kalmere, Ch. Kirdette-Kora and Ch. Gravin-Grazie.

Even though Bryan has had great success at shows, it is as a stud that he has made his real triumphs. During the years 1971–1975 he has had not less than twenty Stud Group wins in Norway, Sweden and Finland. In the Scandinavi-an countries, five of the dog's get must be shown with each Stud exhibited in the Breeder Groups and Stud Group competition. Bryan won a Stud class in Stockholm over 79 Groups of different breeds, and at that same show won Best Breeder Group over a total of 75 groups of different breeds. In 1972 he sired more top winning get in Sweden than any other stud, regardless of breed. He has also competed in sled-dog trials and was Swedish Winner 1973 on the fifteen kilometer run.

Bryan has sired 17 champions to date, but this number could easily in-crease. The best-known of his get is Anuschka-Bryansdotter, exported to Ger-many and becoming the top winning Doberman of all time in Germany. Quar-antine laws restrict Swedes from showing outside Scandinavia and restrain other countries from even wanting to show here. However, a bitch in Holland, Olive of Bamby's Pride, sired by Ch. Odin v Forell ex Rita v Forell, was artifically inseminated by live sperm taken from Bryan and sent by air to Hol-land. A litter of eleven puppies were born December 16, 1973. The kennel re-sponsible was von Franckenhorst Kennels, owned by Sonja David v Fran-quemont-Freudenberg. Nine of these puppies have been shown with excellent results, the two most successful being Don-Dayan v Franckenhorst, who has won the Breed many times and was Best Dog at the 1975 Bundessieger show and also top winning male in Holland in 1975, and Dewi, his litter sister. Dewi, previously owned by Ernst Wilking, was sold after his death to the President of the German Dobermann Club, Hans Wiblishauser. Dewi also has many breed wins, not only in Germany but also in Belgium and Holland, plus a Best in Show at an all-breed show in Germany.

The owners of Bryan, Lilith Edstrom and Bengt Johansson, BryanStam Kennels, also own the previously mentioned Ch. Gravin-Grazie (Bryan ex Assy v Eichenhain) and Ch. Anja vd Haar (Chico v Forell ex Vroni vd Bruno-burg).

283

Littermates BryanStam's Grafin-Graziedotter and Granito-Grazieson are in Holland and were sired by a Bryan son, Kasmir-Kandy ex Gravin-Grazie. Granito was Europe-Youth winner 1974 and the third top winning Doberman in Holland in 1975. Two litter sisters sired by Bryan ex Anja vd Haar were also sold to Holland. BryanStam's Joanja-Jewel has been second best young bitch in both Germany and Holland and BryanStam's Januschka-Jubilee has been fourth best youth winner at the Europe Winner show 1975. Another litter sister BryanStam's Jasmine-Jezebel was exported to Italy and went third winner her first time out.

Ch. Gravin-Grazie was artificially inseminated with sperm taken from Nero v Hagenstern in Germany. One bitch from this breeding was sold to Yugoslavia, BryanStam's Illissa-Idee and she has been a youth winner at two all-breed shows. Illissa was the only Doberman with uncropped ears.

Other Champions and Breed winners that come from this kennel include: littermates Nordic Ch. BryanStam's Fello-Favorit, BryanStam's Frank-Furt, and Ch. BryanStam's Femelle-Fee (Gido v Hagenstern ex Gravin-Grazie); Ch. BryanStam's Graf-Germane (litter brother to Granito and Grafin); and litter sisters BryanStam's Hanni-Harmonie and BryanStam's Honey-Heart (Bryan v Forell ex Anja vd Haar). Grazie herself is the only Doberman bitch with Breed wins in Finland, Norway and Sweden, and has three champions to her credit. Both Grazie and Anja are also Group winners at all-breed shows.

Another Doberman who has had great triumphs at shows, particularly in Sweden, is International and Nordic Ch. and Swedish Working Dog Ch. Casanova, a brown. He has had 16 Breeds and at all-breed shows has had three Groups and two Best in Show number two. He was whelped October 6, 1968 and sired by Hans v Finn-Heide ex Ambra. Casanova won the Swedish Doberman Club's annual show in 1970, 1974 and 1975. In 1975 he passed seven years and won Veterans class at both Stockholm and Gothenburg in competition with other breeds. He has also been successful as a sled-dog and has been on top of the prize lists at almost all of the competitions. He has competed on thirty kilometers and has won five Working Dog certificates and three CACITs (International Working Dog Certificate), and the title of Working Dog Champion.

He has, however, been used very little at stud and has only one adult litter. Of this litter, Swedish Working Ch. Emil is the best known. However, during 1975 Casanova was bred to five bitches and the first litter was whelped in August, 1975. His owners, Maria Harstedt and Yngve Landergard, have just recently imported the German bitch Cherry v Buchenberg, whose full sister and brother have been successful in Germany.

Another kennel deserving mention is Julietteville, owned by Folke Lotborn. His first bitch was an Asso daughter, Mountainville's Juliette. She was bred to Alf vd Bauget and their daughter Ch. Alle has, together with Bryan, produced many dogs of good quality. One is Swedish Ch. and Swedish Working Dog Ch. Ippon, an extremely successful sled-dog, who was Nordic Win-

Ch. Gravin-Grazie, by Ch. Bryan v Forell ex Assy v Eichenhain, a breed winner in Norway, Sweden and Finland—the only bitch to have won in all three countries. Owner, BryanStam Kennels.

Ch. BryanStam's Graf-Germane, by Kasmir-Kandy ex Ch. Gravin-Grazie. Bred by BryanStam Kennels.

Europa-Jugendsieger 1974, Landesgruppe-Jugendsieger, 1974 —BryanStam's Granito-Grazie-son, a litter brother of Ch. Bryan-Stam's Graf-Germane. Granito is now in Holland.

285

ner in 1974 and 1976 and Swedish Winner 1975 and 1976 on the thirty kilometer run. Ippon is the only Doberman who has won the Nordic title twice. Litter brother Swedish Ch. and Swedish Working Dog Ch. Illord is also an excellent sled-dog. Both have good show records. Julietteville's other brood bitch was Ch. Kippis-Girl who, when bred to Bryan produced International and Nordic Ch. Kirdette-Kora, Nordic Ch. and Swedish Working Dog Ch. Kasco-Bryanson, Ch. Kadrille-Kalmere, Kirsti-Kippisdotter and Kasmir-Kandy. Kirdette-Kora has 15 Breeds, 9 Groups and 3 Bests in Shows, scored in Sweden and Finland.

That the Swedish Doberman today has a very high quality can perhaps be shown best by the great interest from foreign countries, and one can only hope that the breeders never stop being critical, quality-knowledgeable and responsible in their breeding programs.

Finland

The Doberman also has a long history in Finland. In 1910, four dogs—a German Shepherd and three Dobermans—were imported to Helsingfors for the police department. These Dobermans, Zilly v Thuringen, Benneo v Volmethal and Minka v Tautenberg gave the start to the breed here. They and their progeny became well-known for their eminence in police work and the breed became popular.

During the 1930s, Dobermans had the largest entries in the Working Group at the shows. This popularity, however, was not the best thing that could happen because some of these Doberman owners were not interested in working with their dogs, but had just bought them for their beauty. The result was that, even now we hear about hard to handle, aggressive dogs, and people wonder now how anyone of their own free will could ever consider keeping such dogs. Happily, however, there have also always been people who have had full understanding for this glorious, intelligent breed.

An architect by the name of Kaarlo Nivera, of von Unser-Heim Kennels, was one of the pioneers who, during the war, managed to keep his faith in the breed and continued to raise them and to work for the betterment of the breed.

In the same mold was the Pellavakasken Kennels of Lauri Lahtinen, the first president of the Finnish Doberman Club. Turtin and Tessie are also Doberman kennels that have their place in the history of the breed in Finland.

But the years go by and men and dogs go with them. After World War II Gunther Groth was our only professional breeder. His kennel, Gunthersforst is certainly one of the best known in all of Scandinavia.

Reijo Lehto, owner of the von Finn-Heide Kennels, was dead set against the Hagenstolz line in the 1960s. His outstanding brood bitch was Tessis Ira Bella. Lehto's ideas on line breeding and inbreeding possibilities were considered practically revolutionary and he received a lot of opposition because of

Int. and Nordic Ch. and Working Dog Ch. Casanova, red male, whelped 1968, by Hans v Finn-Heide ex Ambra. Casanova is an outstanding conformation dog (winner of the Swedish Doberman Club's annual shows in 1970, 1974 and 1975) and has been very successful as a sled dog. Owned by Maria Harstedt and Yngve Landergard.

Nordic Ch. BryanStam's Fello-Favorit, a conformation and Working Dog Winner. Owned by BryanStam Kennels.

Finnish Ch. Cora v Unser-Heim. Type predominate in years after World War II.

Swedish and Finnish Ch. Thibault, by Ch. Nouveau ex Ch. Odiane du Chateau St. Laurent. Breeder, Eugenie Duffourd's Ligras Kennels.

Niddi vd Schwarzwaldperle, 1938–1951. Became a Finnish champion during World War II.

this. Nonetheless, dogs bearing his kennel name were always in the ribbons in the show ring. Just now we do not know what impact Von Finn-Heide has made on the breed, but it will certainly become a positive part.

Von Hasselhof and Timitra are two popular kennels today. Hasselhof began with a Finn-Heide bitch excelling in substance but, behind this kennel's biggest successes lies the bitch Erle v Eichenhain. Erle with different males gave harmoniously built get, which is evidence that the studs were also good.

The foundation bitch for the Timitra Kennels was Danja v. Eichenhain, who won over highly merited imports to Sweden and Finland. Now the future of Timitra lies on Timitra Terna's shoulders, and she is making the grade with males carrying Danja and Dona v Eichenhain's lines.

Von Birkenrinde continue their breeding programs with a bit of Holland, van Neerlands Stam, combined with Gunthersforst lines.

The Doberman Club of Finland is an organization which, since 1950, has tried to bring together enthusiasts of the breed. The club is a member of the Finnish Kennel Club which supports the Doberman Club's independent work within sports multiple areas.

Gunthersforst Oiri, Best Bitch under judge Ernst Wilking in Oslo, Norway in 1970. The Finnish kennel, Guntherforst, is one of the best-known in Scandinavia.

18

The Doberman in Australia

by H. Peter Luyten

W HEN JOANNA WALKER invited me to outline the breed's history and development in Australia, I was very pleased to formally commit to the record the outstanding debt that we in this country owe to breeders in other countries, particularly America. While American blood does not form the sole basis of our entire breeding stock, much of the quality that we in this country enjoy today stems directly from the stock that has been exported to us over the years by reputable American fanciers and breeders. Without the introduction of these dogs into our initial imported British lines, we would still be suffering an array of the most dismal mediocrity, surely the worst form of failure in dog breeding.

The first Doberman came to this country as the "trophy" of a returning fighting force who captured their specimen on the front lines of the 1914–1918 conflict in Europe. Regretfully this dog failed to survive the then crude quarantine facilities, and he now surveys his captors from a glass case in the Australian National War Museum in Canberra.

We are indebted to a Mr. Pilko of Sydney, New South Wales, for the first show-destined Dobermans to come to this country.

Records reveal that the first Dobermans exhibited at the Sydney Royal Easter Show, the one-time prestige canine event in Australia, were not shown until 1952. The Melbourne Royal Show, for many years now recognized internationally as the premier canine exhibition of the Australian circuit, did not see the first Doberman entered until 1954. The original stock was imported into Australia from the kennels of British foundation breeders who obviously lacked sufficient quality specimens to breed with, let alone export to their colonial brethren across the seas. Hence the development during the first few years seemed painfully slow.

Australian Ch. Rama the Rare Courage—Top Doberman in South Australia, 1974–75. By Marks-Tey Yancey (imp. USA) ex Rama the Rarebit. Bred by Peter and Jennie Luyten; owned by Mr. and Mrs. W. Devodier.

Australian Ch. Rama Rio Senora. Of pure American blood with uncropped ears, by Marks-Tey Yancey ex Ferrings Impish. Bred and owned by Peter and Jennie Luyten. A Best in Show winner.

Australian Ch. Rama the Ramadan (at 13 months). By Ch. Rama the Right'n'Rong (a son of Jemoel's Michael v Warlock) ex Rama the Rich Renown (Marks-Tey Yancey daughter). Bred and owned by Peter and Jennie Luyten.

Rama the Rock of Ages (at 9 months). By Ch. Elmaro All Fire ex Ferrings Impish (imp. U.K.) Bred by Peter and Jennie Luyten, and exported to Holland where he was rated Excellent at his first show.

Early Australian foundation stock imported from the United Kingdom cannot be favorably compared with American or Continental Dobermans of the same era, or even a decade prior. This meant that we started with a sizeable handicap in foundation material—breeders almost completely devoid of any breed knowledge and judges who were already licensed to judge the breed before it arrived. Undoubtedly due to economic factors and the long quarantine periods from any other countries, we relied too heavily on Britain in the initial introductory stage. Dogs coming from the United States or the Continent must first undergo a full year's detention in the British Isles prior to becoming eligible for acceptance here. This is the law of the land, and has so far saved us from suffering the ravages of the dreaded rabies.

In any case the continental breeders who in turn started the Britishers, were no doubt at a low ebb after suffering untold harm in the last war and insufficient time had elapsed to allow for the rebuilding of top stock which has now been so cleverly carried out. Despite this, the basic genetic material acquired during the 1950s has remained true to its heritage and when wisely used, has been able to give a minority of excellent types.

As early as 1959 Dobermans had started to make their presence felt in top class competition, for it was in that year that K.C.C. Champion Carmenita Dianna was awarded Best Exhibit in Group under the English judge, The Earl of Northesk, at the premier dog show, the Melbourne Royal Show. It was also in that same year that the first Doberman organization, The Doberman Club of Victoria, was formed, and it remains active as a social club to the present day. Based in Melbourne, it conducts one annual Parade where championship points are not awarded, and one Championship Show a year.

Ever since that time, the hotbed of Doberman development has remained in Melbourne, and spurred on by keen competition, many imports have been brought to this state. Their offspring have fanned out over the nation and have made it possible to improve our standards.

One early and significant stud force that Australian breeders owe a great deal to was K.C.C. Champion Tavey's Stormy Accolade, an imported son of American Champion Rancho Dobe's Storm born in English quarantine. Mated to the stock of his close relative, R.A.S.K.C. Champion Tavey's Stormy Defender CD, Accolade proved successful in producing some quality bitches. He was really the first "taste" of American bloodlines experienced by Australian breeders.

The first direct import of an American dog was Ebonaire's Bravo. Sent to us by Judy and Edward Weiss, this was the son of the new legendary American Champion Steb's Top Skipper, out of Ebonaire's On Guard. There can be no doubt that this dog has widely influenced many modern Australian bloodlines. He combined very well with a few of Accolade's daughters and produced another first for the breed in this country, Best Exhibit in Show at the prestigious Melbourne Royal. This honor fell to his daughter Australian Champion Koning Brave Lustre, and was won under the late Albert E. Van

Court of the United States, who claimed her to be able to hold her own anywhere in the world at that time. Generous words indeed!

Hot on Bravo's heels, we had the first imported American-bred bitch in Alnwick's Blackberry Wine. She was the daughter of Meistersinger von Ahrtal. This good headed bitch was regretfully never used to full advantage and history cruelly records that she is behind few of the winners of today.

Inspired by the success and quality of the previous American imports, also mindful of the faults already facing Australian breeders, the writer embarked on a search for yet another stud force to advance the Australian standard. We wound up with a Triple International Champion Borong the Warlock son, acquired at the recommendation of the late Henry Frampton. This import from Louise Babcock's American Champion Hi Dave's Korry Kay of Ingraham was Jemoel's Michael Von Warlock, born in 1965, and before his death in 1975 he was to sire over 35 champions of record.

Through the good offices of Bravo daughters and granddaughters, a large number of top winners were produced. Living as we do, in Melbourne, we personally enjoyed the dog's stud capabilities before passing him on to friends in Sydney. He actually stood for a greater number of years in Sydney but never produced as brilliant offspring in that state, doubtlessly due to the fact that he was never appreciated by some breeders there, nor used as wisely. Mike lived an active life for many more years and I feel that his Champion tally has not yet been completed.

Another semi-climax was reached with the importation of the first German-bred male Mohr von Forrell, as with his introduction we saw breeders offered another radical type choice. However, no one, not even the original importer, has seen fit to establish a family from this dog. This is not only a real pity, but dangerous; in the face of so little genetic variation, attention should be paid to all alternatives. Regretfully, breeders in the main were not prepared to gain his virtues at the risk of his shortcomings. Upon reflection this may not have been the wisest path to tread as color of markings and toplines could well have benefited from judicious use of this blood.

In the meantime Sydney siders had finally taken the plunge to "go it alone" in importing an American-bred dog—Elfred's the Gallant Gentleman, son of Champion Elfred's Spark Plug. History harshly records that most Southeastern breeders found little favor in this colossus whose blood is now mainly carried on further north, in Queensland, where he has founded a race of "Amazons."

In the interim, Melbourne saw the importation of the English dog, Tavey's Stormy Perfection. He was sent to Sydney shortly after his arrival and has some twenty champions to his credit.

Another American-bred bitch imported onto Melbourne, Ebonaire's Holiday, would have been instrumental in founding a new and powerful dynasty, had it not been for the hand of fate. She was a American Champion Ebonaire's Entertainer daughter, so that when paired to her paternal uncle "Bravo" she produced two fabulous daughters. Regretfully, one was lost to snake bite after an auspicious start of her show career, while the other had to be spayed to save her life, after she had already been mated to Jemoel's Michael von Warlock. This left nothing from these two "flyers", the equal of which had not been seen. Holiday blood was not entirely lost as she was paired to a Bravo son, upon the death of the imported dog.

To Sydney were then imported the first German-bred bitch, Petra von Forrell, from the famous von Forrell strain (but she was never used knowledgeably), and two more American-breds, a dog and bitch. The dog, Sojoles Bukkles of Marks-Tey, is a son of the noted American Champion Marks-Tey Shawn CD, and is producing recognizable stock. The bitch, the first brown, Damasyn Bo Tandy of Ardon, was regretfully well past her prime upon her arrival. She together with the dog and my own imported Marks-Tey Yancey were unavoidably delayed in England during the rabies outbreak, adding another year and a half to their confinement. She has therefore reportedly produced only one noteworthy puppy, a dog whose influence upon the breed is far too early to judge.

In search of yet another worthwhile stud force, the writer after considerable drama, purchased from Keith and Joanna Walker, Marks-Tey Yancey, a fabulous headed son of American Champion Gra-Lemor Demetrius vd Victor out of Marks-Tey Stacy, who was a full sister to Chs. Marks-Tey Shawn, Sonnet and Shay. This dog has proved most successful in a very short space of time, having thus far produced over 22 Australian Champions of record plus numerous Obedience titleholders, incuding the Best in Trial at the first National Specialty.

Additionally, a Demetrius daughter, Ferring's Impish, whelped in English quarantine, was imported by this writer in order to add to the qualities already brought here by the Marks-Tey blood. This bitch was bred by Robert H. Walker of Ferring, Sussex and her dam is the Shawn daughter, Amsel's Andante of Marks-Tey. Mated to Marks-Tey Yancey she has produced Best in Show stock. Being a brown, and purchased as a puppy, she has so far had three litters and is giving this color a badly-needed shot in the arm.

In order to further bolster the genetic material of Australia, two German-bred bitches of the famous von Hagenstern Kennels are being imported in whelp by a new Melbourne fancier; these will give an additional slant on the scene. The writer, too, has a von Hagenstern bitch with characteristic German breed type, just released from quarantine. Her capabilities will be keenly watched. The writer has also obtained two Dutch-born Van Neerlandstam bitches from the world renowned kennel of Mrs. Knijff-Dermout. These will be used to advantage to blend with Marks-Tey, Warlock and Top Skipper blood already here.

Ch. Tavey's Victor and a bitch, Tavey's Elsinore, both of Kay Hill's ancestry, are two Sydney-based English imports carrying American bloodlines.

Australian Ch. Rama the Rarebit, 1967–1975. Winner of many Bests in Show; Best Exhibit at the DCV Specialty, 1971. By Jemoel's Michael v Warlock ex Vonmutig Vedanta CD; bred and owned by Peter and Jennie Luyten. Her uncropped ears were naturally erect.

Australian Ch. Rama the Rongbit, by Ch. Rama the Right'n'Rong ex Ch. Rama the Rarebit. Bred by Peter and Jennie Luyten, and owned by Miss D. Bell. Best in Show winner.

Australian Ch. Rama the Rudika. By Ch. Rama the Right'n'Rong ex Ch. Rama Rampage. Owned by O. E. Lee; exhibited by her breeders, Peter and Jennie Luyten. A multi Best in Show winner, she is pictured here after winning Best in Group (1,110 entries) at the Melbourne Royal 1972 under Swedish judge Mrs. K. Lindhe.

Rama the Rudella, Best Exhibit at the DCV Specialty 1975. By Marks-Tey Yancey ex Ch. Rama the Rudika. Bred and owned by Peter and Jennie Luyten.

Two other English-bred imports carrying American blood have been recently based in Sydney and all will have their followers.

Before these arrived two English bred imports of the Tavey's kennel accompanied their owner to Australia. The dog Ch. Barage of Tavey was shown by the new owners when he was sold to Sydney and the bitch Yasmin of Tavey produced a new strain whose most notable children are in New Zealand and Western Australia and are in the main, browns.

The latest dog of American breeding was the black Hallmark September Song, sired by American Ch. Highlands Satin's Image. His very recent introduction leaves insufficient time to gauge his contribution to the breed.

There have been others, but while the list above may not be entirely complete, it most certainly represents the main strains that are now in use. Any that are excluded are not so treated intentionally.

The bloodlines of the imports have rightfully read like a "Who's Who" in Dobermans, but let me hasten to add that we are not without our problems, the same that plague breeders in other lands. We are troubled with faults of type, teeth, temperament, color and other common problems. Possibly the greatest failing in our stock is the failure of good head type to dominate, due no doubt to a partial lack of appreciation on the part of the judges and the breeders alike. Also there are few bitches with good head properties, a fault which even the best-headed imports have found impossible to completely eradicate. In our defense I would venture to say that our best Dobermans are very good indeed in general conformation. I repeat . . . our "best". This is due no doubt to the large number of conformation conscious judges that we have here, who while perhaps not completely grasping breed type, pay little respect to any but the best and soundest conformed dogs in the land. It is therefore up to the breeders to be completely singular in their efforts to gain the utmost in breed type.

Before I touch on the best of our homebred dogs, let me briefly discuss some factors which have influenced our destiny. First, the breed has been here for only 25 years and during that time we have seen a coming and going among fanciers and breeders that has left us with very few longtime exponents of the breed. Many breeders or importers have not maintained their interest beyond their initial import or original stock. The result has been that most of the breeding is left in the hands of persons who, while filled with the best of intentions cannot read a pedigree beyond the names on the paper. This shortage of experience is also extended into the ranks of judges and finds us with an almost complete lack of established strains upon which local breeders can rely to gain a certain point or points. Hence there is need for continued imports from established families. But, let me add, not all imports have thus qualified, and some have failed to add lustre to their names.

Dobermans are here exhibited in the Non-Sporting Group, which is the largest Group of all and comprises much of the American Working Group.

Marks-Tey Yancey (imp. USA), whelped May 30, 1969. By Ch. Gra-Lemor Demetrius vd Victor ex Marks-Tey Stacy. Bred by Joanna Walker; owned by Peter and Jennie Luyten.

Ferrings Impish (imp. U.K.), red daughter of Ch. Gra-Lemor Demetrius vd Victor ex Amsel's Andante of Marks-Tey. Dam of many champions including multi Best in Show winners. Bred by Robert H. Walker (England); owned by Peter and Jennie Luyten.

Sojoles Bukkles of Marks-Tey (imp. USA). By Ch. Marks-Tey Shawn CD ex Marienburg's Olivia. Bred by John Gossert and owned by Ebonstorm Kennels, New South Wales. Bukkles and his kennelmate, Damasyn Bo-Tandy, were held up in a quarantine for a year before being allowed to proceed to Australia.

Australian Ch. Barjude Bright Spark, a Best in Show winner. By Ch. Elmaro Incorruptible ex Ch. Rilten Revelation. Bred by Barry Finchbeck and owned by Mrs. Gilbert.

Danes, Boxers, all Poodle varieties, and even Miniature Schnauzers are exhibited against Dobermans. We have had the judgment of mainly English and American judges, with only a smattering of Continentals, but rarely have we had the benefit of their opinions beyond the breed ring. No Rothfuss, Fleitmann or German breed warden has ever passed on their thoughts on our dogs. This does not promote intelligent discussion, which after all is the cradle for intelligent action. Very few specialist judges are available and fewer still are used to advantage because the breed is of insufficient size. Registrations, Australia wide, rarely exceed 3000 annually and entries at normal shows hover around the fifty mark. Specialty shows and international judges generally attract 100-200 entries and Champions compete for the Championship points.

To gain the title of Australian Champion, an exhibit must win one 100 Challenge points under a minimum of four judges who can award a maximum of 25 points at any one show. Points are awarded on the basis of five points for the best of each sex plus one point per dog exhibited. Cropped dogs cannot be shown under our rules, so that is why cropped imports are seen by very few judges and fanciers, whose experience is therefore tied to the local exhibits. However, a few of our top judges travel widely abroad and overseas opinions coming to our shores have in the main been favorable, some too generous.

As in the vast majority of breeds in Australia, Dobermans suffer from a lack of depth of quality through the breed. This feature would surely strike any visiting judges. However, as has been expressed by visiting judges in the past, our Dobermans, that is to say the best of them, compare favorably with those of other countries.

My personal memory of the best of this country's locally bred Dobermans does not seem to want to extend beyond the Melbourne Royal of 1959 when, as stated, a Doberman bitch made Best in Group under an English judge. The following year, our Chairman of the Kennel Control Council (Victoria), Mr. Graham Head, a noted all-breed judge, returned home from his first extended judging tour of the United States and became in my eyes, the first of the local judges no longer limited in his vision to the local dogs. He put up, at the same event, an unknown dog, which was to become the possible first of the elegant brigade.

First lady of the breed in the eyes of many fanciers was Ch. Koning Brave Lustre, who unquestionably distinguished herself by winning Best Exhibit all breeds at the Melbourne Royal Show under Albert E. Van Court of the United States. That was the first time a Doberman had so distinguished itself at one of our classic Royals, and that only ten years after the first Doberman had been shown at Melbourne Royals. Regretfully, she was to be lost to the breed after her pairing to Mohr von Forrell. She underwent a Caesarean section to deliver her three puppies and did not survive. Personally I always considered her little sister, Champion Koning Brave Lady, to be at least her equal. History has proven my judgment not without foundation. She later fortified her claim to fame by winning the vote of Percy Roberts for Best in Show at the Sydney

Ebonaire's Bravo (imp. USA), sire of 45 champions. Pictured at 17 months. By Ch. Steb's Top Skipper ex Ebonaire's En Garde. Bred by Mrs. J. Weiss, and owned by Mr. and Mrs. T. Farmilo and M. McNicholl.

Australian Ch. Koning Brave Lustre, whose win of Best Exhibit in Show all-breeds at the Melbourne Royal was first of that stature for the breed in Australia. By Ebonaire's Bravo ex Elmaro High Comet, Brave Lustre was bred by A. and T. Weaving and owned by Mrs. J. Sender. (We regret that a better picture of this lovely bitch was not available.)

Australian Ch. Koning Brave Lady, a litter sister of Brave Lustre, and like her—a multi-Best in Show winner. Owned by Mrs. J. H. Forrest.

Ch. Tavey's Victor, with American Kay Hill breeding in his ancestry, imported to Australia from England by Mr. and Mrs. N. Archer.

Jemoel's Michael v Warlock (imp. USA) 1965–1975, sire of 36 champions, including many Best in Show winners. By Tri-Int. Ch. Borong the Warlock CD ex Ch. Hi Dave's Korry Kay of Ingraham, Michael was bred by Mrs. L. Babcock, and imported to Australia by Peter Luyten. Later owned by T. and K. St. Lawrence.

Australian Ch. Delderland Black Wonder, Best Exhibit in Show at Queensland Royal show, 1971. A daughter of Jemoel's Michael v Warlock ex Engarde Carmen Sylva. Bred by Mrs. R. Komdur; owned by A. Locke.

Ch. Terpau Donna Anita, No. 2 top winning bitch of all time in Australia. By Jemoel's Michael v Warlock ex Elmaro Santa Juana. Bred by M. Fitzpatrick and owned by O. King.

Royal Show, but alas she had been beaten earlier in the contest. Both these bitches did a great deal of distinguished winning, as did other members of this breeding which was repeated numerous times. Their sire was the first American-bred import, Bravo. When Champion Koning Brave Lady was later paired to Jemeol's Michael von Warlock, out popped Australian Champion Elmaro Sugar and Spice, top winner who went Best Bitch All Breeds Melbourne Royal Show. This tail female line has been wonderfully consistent, as the writer proved when he purchased a sister to Ch. Elmaro High Comet, the dam of Ch. Brave Lustre and Ch. Brave Lady. She was to be Elmaro High Charm CD and using this tail female line, but a totally different tack of the male side, produced in the second generation Australian Champion Rama the Rudika, Best Exhibit in Group at the Melbourne Royal in 1972 over 1,110 group entries — the biggest Group ever won by a Doberman in the southern hemisphere. Rudika has in only one litter produced a Best in Show winner at the 1975 D.C.V. Specialty, Rama the Rudella.

Ch. Elmaro Sugar and Spice in her only litter produced the top male Australian Champion Elmaro All Fire. This is the sort of model consistency that lines can be built upon.

To fully expose the influence of Ebonaire's Bravo on the scene let me relate that in his four or more litters to Champion Stormalure, he produced, I believe, twenty champions. The most outstanding was Chevelier who lives on through his son, All Fire. More of them later. Another consistent bitch winner, still active today is the Bravo daughter, Champion Chaquen Shawnee. Having been kept almost entirely linebred, this line has reached its present status in Champion Lynmar Ballerina.

In Queensland the greatest breed fame was reached when a Bravo daughter was mated to Jemoel's Michael von Warlock and produced Best Exhibit in Show at the Queensland Royal show in 1971; this winner was Champion Delderland Black Wonder. This is yet another example of Melbourne breeding being the start of something big. This sort of exodus from Mecca was repeated when the writer sent a Michael von Warlock daughter to Adelaide where she was combined with a Ebonaire's Holiday son to produce Champion Barjude Bright Spark, winner of the Melbourne Royal Best in Group in 1971 and judged "Top Dog of the Year" under a national dog foods award system.

From another daughter of Jemoel's Michael von Warlock, in fact the only naturally erect-eared Doberman champion in this country, Ch. Rama the Rarebit, have come a number of Best in Show winning Champions. When paired with her brother Champion Rama the Right'n'Rong, she produced Champion Rama the Rongbit, a multiple Best in Show winner for his fourteen year old owner-handler. In mating to Marks-Tey Yancey she has produced the Best in Show winners, Champion Rama the Rare Courage and Champion Rama the Rare Treat, plus Champion Rama the Rare Tart, yet to be tested in the whelping box. From All Fire's first-ever litter she produced multi Best in Show winner Champion Rama the Rare Flicker.

In males the honors are perhaps more spread, partly due to the fact that showing is easier than breeding and that males have a far more extended career. Whichever the reason, a wider variety of bloodlines have shared the limelight.

In Sydney, Champion Vondobe the Maharajar distinguished himself by gaining Best in Show at the Sydney Royal Easter Show in 1969. Unquestionably the greatest Doberman male to reside in the state of New South Wales was the Melbourne-bred son of Bravo, Champion Chaquen Chevalier. Chevalier's richest claim to fame came as a result of the unexpected opportunity to have Champion Sugar and Spice bred to him, after she had been ignored by her sire who was very blase about the girls that beat a path to his door. This chance pairing was admirably suited to produce Ch. Elmaro Sugar and Spice's greatest masterpiece, Ch. Elmaro All Fire.

A dog that I personally considered very typical, despite the fact that we bred him, was Champion Rama the Right'n'Rong, who made his title during only seven outings including Best Exhibit at the prestigious Ladies Kennel Association. He produced the Best in Group winner at the Melbourne Royal 1972 through Champion Rama the Rudika. Since his departure to Fiji his blood, and that of his sire Jemoel's Michael von Warlock, will be carried on through a youngster who made up with three Groups from the classes, Champion Rama the Ramadan.

Ch. Elmaro All Fire will feature heavily in future pedigrees as he has had the greatest possible opportunity and his champion-producing tally is well into double figures. He is combining best with strongly bred Bravo daughters to produce such winners as the noteworthy bitches Ch. Lymara Ballerina and Ch. Enriqueta Prima Coya. To our imported Demetrius daughter, Ferring's Impish, he has produced Champion Rama the Rockabit, a black bitch who won her first Best in Show at a mere eight and a half months. Her brother sent to Holland, was graded "Excellent" at his first show.

South Australia has been dominated by singular males starting with Champion Elmaro Incorruptable, then his son Ch. Barjudge Bright Spark (the only state bred), then Ch. Elmaro All Spirit and now Ch. Rama the Rare Courage. This Marks-Tey Yancey son has had a virtual throttlehold on the male points in South Australia for the last two years, and is a Best in Show winner.

As time passes, out of all this activity we are seeing in Australia a slowly maturing band of fanciers who will eventually accomplish their aims. Experience is being gained by breeders and judges alike. Imports will no doubt continue to flow (though no longer through me), and we will hopefully see the evolution of greater numbers of distinct strains from which breeders can derive wanted qualities. It is also hoped that now, with the advent of National Specialties throughout the nation, we will see a great interchange of ideas to curtail the localization of breeding programs, thereby continuing the improvement of Australian Dobermans toward the international ideal.

Australian Ch. Elmaro Sugar and Spice, record-holder for most Bests in Show won by a bitch in Australia. By Jemoel's Michael v Warlock ex Ch. Koning Brave Lady. Bred by Mrs. J. H. Forrest and owned by Mrs. H. Wetherall.

Australian Ch. Elmaro All Fire, Best in Show winner and outstanding sire. By Ch. Chaquen Chevalier ex Ch. Elmaro Sugar and Spice. Bred by Mrs. J. H. Forrest and owned by Mrs. H. Wetherall.

Australian Ch. Lynmara Ballerina, Best in Show winner. By Ch. Elmaro All Fire ex Ch. Lynmara Up and Coming. Bred and owned by Mr. M. McNicholl.

Australian Ch. Endquetta Prima Coya, Best in Show winner. By Ch. Elmaro All Fire ex Lynmara Pandora. Bred by T. and A. Burke; owned by Mrs. H. Wetherall.

Keizo Sasada of Japan is one of the most dedicated breeders in Asia. He has sent bitches abroad in order to breed them to studs that will give him the traits he needs, and has loaned some of his outstanding studs to breeders in Taiwan and Thailand to help improve the breed in those countries. Mr. Sasada is pictured here with his Japanese Ch. Rosemary of Eastern Castle Sasada (by Ch. Gra-Lemor Demetrius vd Victor ex Belinda's Misbehavin').

Philippines Ch. Jaydel's Kidcat, sired by Phil. Ch. Ralbred's Ramrod ex Phil. Ch. Retrac's Jedra Morgansonne. An important Philippines producer.

Philippines' Doberman, Kristin's Bimbo, sired by Ch. Brown's B-Brian ex Jentry's Moonbeam. The judge is Mr. Keizo Sasada.

304

19

The Doberman in
Southeast Asia

by Roberto A. DeSantos

THE STRONG Chinese cultural dominance in Southeast Asia has brought with it a great love for dogs. The genetic foundation of dogs, however, are strongly influenced by the Western World. The pedigrees of contemporary dogs in Asia reflect the close relationship of some Asian countries with the West. Most Asian countries, however, are controlled by importation and quarantine laws and these sometimes serve to limit the sources for importation.

Attributed to culture, there are peculiarities in preferences to type among many Asian countries. In the case of the Doberman, there is preference for the red and lighter colors due to blacks being symbolic of Death. Next, there is a preference for height, since in most Asian countries anything big is impressive.

With the Asian government's emphasis on security, the need for working breeds was highlighted and emphasized. For selection, however, it was limited to shorthaired breeds since longhaired breeds find extreme difficulty living in the temperate climate. Thus, the Doberman became a well accepted working breed.

There are distinctive traits which are hard to propagate in the Far East due to climatic and environmental conditions. Among these are height and substance. In the past years, there were very few dogs over 25″. Theorists attribute this principally to the sun's effect. They believe that the effects of the sun's rays in the Western World are totally different from what they are in Asia. Others attribute it to improper nutrition and genetic difficulties. With the current upsurge of importation of excellent quality stock, there are improvements visible in overcoming these difficulties. However, total simulation of conditions in the Western World could not be approximated. Even in other livestock and fowl, the necessity to continuously import is inevitable since after two generations, there is a visible reduction in size and quality of stock which make it necessary to revitalize this with new imports. This phenomena makes the aim for height and substance the most crucial challenge to the breeders of today. Asian breeders have to compensate the conditions of the local country with careful genetic programs and proper nutrition.

The countries of Southeast Asia are most conducive for the Doberman since they have vast agricultural land where the breed could be properly exercised. Most countries in Southeast Asia have very little pollution problems. The greatest threat to the Doberman's health is the wide population of mosquitoes, which generally carry heartworm larva. In general, though, through adequate precautionary measures, the Doberman in Asia can live a long and happy life, and even imports face very little difficulty in adjusting to the environment.

Doberman popularity started as early as 1964 in Southeast Asia, when an American champion was imported into the Phillipine Islands by Porfirio Santos. His arrival amazed the dog loving public since American Champion Highbriar American Flag looked entirely different from the contemporary Doberman. It is a pity that there were very few suitable bitches available at that time to be able to preserve his line. Following American Flag's career came two young studs in 1966, namely Honor Guard Satin (a Ch. Borong the Warlock son), and Dragomeer's Blue Rocket (a Damasyn the Gambler son).

The year of 1967 was the prime year for the Doberman here. A top quality stud was imported into the country as a puppy and became the true foundation of the Philippine Doberman of today. Ch. Ralbred's Ramrod (Ch. Damasyn Bo-Taric of Ardon son) is the sire of the most Philippine champions to date, despite the fact that most breedings were outcrosses. His popularity started an emphasis on the Damasyn line, as evidenced in succeeding imports such as Damasyn the Saybrook and Antares Samantha (a Ch. Damasyn Derringer daughter). Later, the Damasyn line evolved into the Checkmate line, capped by American Champion Quinacre's Toreadore and Checkmates Ali Khan, both heavily linebred to Ch. Brown's Dion. In the years that followed, their progenies dominated the show ring.

Damasyn popularity was further complemented with the importation of Turik's Heidi (a Ch. Marks-Tey Shawn CD daughter) who was imported in whelp to Ch. Stacy's Taurus of Marks-Tey. Also several offspring of Ch. Gra-Lemor Demetrius v.d. Victor, such as Kismet's Stutz Bearcat and Redjack's Sparkling Burgundy.

The popularity of the same lines was also evident in other countries in Asia such as Australia and Japan. In the case of Australia, dogs such as Damasyn Bo-Tandy of Ardon, Marks-Tey Yancey and Sojole's Bukkles of Marks-Tey are leaving their mark on the breed. And in Japan, they have Damasyn the Taurus and several of Ch. Damasyn the Troycen's get.

The success of the Doberman in Asia is highly attributable to the dedication of the people that have bred them. Since importing from the Western World to Asia is expensive, only a few were willing to invest in it. Showing and breeding pedigreed dogs is something quite new, less than two decades old in most Asian countries. The height of popularity was evidenced in the 1975 registry of dogs in the Philippines where the Doberman dominated the number of new entries, litter registrations, and the number of imports. It ranked first in population of the Working breeds. That this development took place in less than a decade is rather phenomenal. Once regarded as a treacherous dog, it has now won public approval as a very reliable breed, and is today Southeast Asia's most prestigious dog.

By providing an avenue of communication with breeders of other countries, the Doberman became an effective medium for the promotion of purebred dogs in Asia. With the formation of the Asian Kennel Union, Asian breeders are kept up-to-date on all the latest developments.

The development of the breed in Asia has been brought about in the following fashion: through Ch. Ru-Mar's Morgansonne, there was improvement in hindquarters; with Ch. Checkmate's Nitecap, emphasis was on topline; through Ch. Marks-Tey Shawn CD, came height, substance and head; and now with Ch. Brown's B-Brian and Ch. Gra-Lemor Demetrius v.d. Victor, Asia is hopeful of improving fronts and depth of brisket.

Despite the rapid improvement in the Doberman breed in Southeast Asia, there is still an evident lack of prepotent stock. The Asian countries now speculate on the developments in modern science and transportation which may make it feasible in the near future to artificially inseminate to the stock needed in Asia's programs. This would make Asia's Doberman a continuation, if not the beginning, of a truly remarkable breed.

MALAYSIA AND SINGAPORE

by Jackie Perry

The first importation of Dobermans into the Malay Peninsula (including the then Island of Singapore) was in about 1930, when a few of the European rubber planters brought in dogs from South Africa, which were mainly of German and Dutch bloodlines. As there are no records of registrations with the Kennel Club pre-war it is not known whether in fact these dogs were ever bred from at all, with or without the benefit of a registered pedigree.

The first entry in the post-war register (all records having been destroyed during the Japanese occupation) was for a pair of Dobes brought in from

South Africa. Both of these dogs were of Dutch origin, and it was from these two that the first ever known registered litters of Dobermans were produced.

It was a long spell after this, in fact in 1952, before any more importations were made, and these then were from Germany.

From here on the breed began to catch the eye of the guard dog fanciers and many Dobes were brought in from both England and Germany. Several litters resulted; a few found their way into the show rings by the end of the '40s, but there were really no specimens of outstanding merit.

It took, in fact, until 1960 before the real start of the breed became evident with the importation of the dog Academy of Tavey. This dog was sired by Ch. Steb's Top Skipper out of Orebaugh's Raven of Tavey, who was imported to England in whelp. With Academy came the bitch, Tavey's Stormy Jacinthe. This importation by a rubber planter named Carver started the ball rolling for the subsequent importation of the dog Barrimilne Ghenghis Khan, who was sired by the well-known English Ch. Tavey's Stormy Achievement (a Ch. Rancho Dobe's Storm ex Ch. Rustic Adagio son), and eventually the mating of the Academy progeny to Ghengis Khan himself.

From these lines which were, of course, all from the Tavey breeding plan, many good Dobes began to appear in the ring. Two direct progeny of Ghengis Khan made their titles, Ch. Chocolate Soldier of Bamboo River and Ch. Flashing Gem. The progeny from both these dogs have gone on to prove their worth throughout Malaysia and Singapore and their descendants are still today producing good dogs when mated in the right direction.

Singapore in the 1950s had a large influx of Dobes from Germany. One of these who made his title, was the dog Errol vom Furstenfeld, a really grand dog in his day, but unfortunately not a great producer. Much later, in 1968, a young dog came in from Germany with lots of promise, a son of Int. Ch. Odin von Forell. This dog who subsequently became a Singapore Champion, was Ch. Graf vom Hause Woschech. He was a true Doberman in temperament. Adored people but was a demon with other dogs! Once again, although prolific in reproduction, his progeny have been of little note.

In 1969 several dogs were brought in from the Tavey Kennels. I myself imported two bitches and a dog. The bitches were by Ch. Iceberg of Tavey and Vanessa's Little Dictator of Tavey (Imp. U.S.A.), and the dog by the same sire as the latter. The bloodlines of these three dogs are now well spread through Singapore and Malaysia and did help considerably in lifting the sagging quality of that time. Champions and Best in Show winners were produced from these lines.

In 1969, I founded the Doberman Club of Singapore and things really started to look up. Our entries at shows increased three to four fold and the interest really ran high.

Then in the same year in Malaysia the first ever Doberman to win Best in Show appeared, and she was Malaysian bred. This was a young bitch of fourteen months, Dauphiness of Canistar, bred by Mr. Sit Hin Kin and owned by

Mrs. Jackie Perry of Malaysia with some of her fine Dobermans. From left to right: Ch. Von Klebong's Dark Havoc; Lizmain Spice O'Honey (imported from Australia); Jacade's Miss Mischief (in whelp to Phileens Duty Free of Tavey); and Ch. Von Klebong's Dark Heritage.

Lizmain Spice O'Honey (bred by Lizmain Kennels, Victoria, Australia and owned by Jackie Perry, Malaysia) is pictured at 12 months and three days, after winning Best in Show under the Swedish judge, Mrs. Marie Anne Danielson. Although he had been a very lovely younger puppy, this red male suffered an ugly duckling period and at 7 months was a great disappointment to his owner. Which just goes to prove that the qualities that are there in a 9-weeks-old puppy may leave for a few months, but very often will return as the puppy matures.

Mr. Philip Machado. She was sired by an Australian import of mainly Tavey bloodlines out of a Ghenghis Khan/Academy background. It was very tragic that this bitch died within six months of her triumph, but fortunately not before she left behind her a litter from which emerged a twice Best in Show winner, Ch. Traysan's Flashing Gem II. The sire here was Ch. Flashing Gem who, as previously mentioned, was a Ghenghis Khan son.

While living in Singapore my eyes turned towards Australia and the American bloodlines to be found there. I purchased from Queensland a champion dog of eighteen months, who subsequently became a multi Best in Show winner in Singapore and who really did things for the breed both there and in Malaysia. Being very satisfied with this dog, Australian, Singapore and Malaysian Ch. Delderland Black Regal, I approached his breeder, Mrs. Rita Komduur, to see whether it would be possible to purchase a champion bitch from her, bred along the same lines, which I wanted to breed to the new U.S.A. import of the Ebonstorm Kennels, Sojole's Bukkles of Marks-Tey. I was lucky, and in 1973 I had a beautiful litter from this mating, of which two are now champions and three others have made Best in Show. The dam, Australian Ch. Delderland Black Hera, has indeed been a wonderful bitch having produced to my knowledge, six champions in just two litters, plus many winning progeny here in Malaysia.

There have been several new imports from Australia both into Singapore and Malaysia during 1974 and 1975. Two dogs sired by the lovely Ch. Elmaro All Fire have both done well in the show ring.

On a trip to England last year I purchased a young bitch of strong Tavey breeding, and after much pounding around the shows looking at progeny of winning Dobes, decided to mate her to the Curnow's Phileen's Duty Free of Tavey. I was already very interested in the Corry and Dolph lines carried by this dog, but wanted to be quite sure he was producing what I wanted. I had, in fact, already seen one of his top winning sons in Australia the previous year, Ch. Tavey's Victor, and my trips around the English shows for five weeks proved that he did indeed have what I wanted. So, as I write this, I have eight little lives in a pen just under my window, which I hope will produce in the future some really good stock throughout the country.

In order to really consolidate my lines, I shall in May of 1976, be sending over my bitch Ch. von Klebongs Dark Havoc, to Manila to be bred to the lovely dog Galaxy's Solar Salute whom I saw while judging their Doberman Specialty there in December of 1975. He is sired by Ch. Encore Black Rites ex Ch. Leemac's Coco Puff and eventually by doubling back on these puppies to the Duty Free progeny, I shall gain several lines to Dolph and the vom Ahrtal line. Thus the Doberman should be set for great things in the future in this part of the world.

The Doberman's popularity is universal. Above, 5-week-old puppies of the v. Neerlandstam Kennels, Holland. Below, a Doberman in Russia—1969.

Litter whelped September 1943, by Ch. Demossi of Marienland ex Ann of Royal Dobe. Bred by Mr. and Mrs. Felix Montgomery.

20

Buying and Owning
a Doberman

W<small>E ARE PLEASED</small> that you are considering joining the ranks of
the many happy Doberman owners, and here offer a few tips — not only on
how to select the right puppy, but also (what may be more important in getting
off to a right start) on how to select the right breeder.

If it is at all possible, do go and pick up the puppy yourself, even if it means
a long drive. This will not only enable you to meet the breeder, but you'll also
get a chance to see the dam (and perhaps the sire), and to see the conditions
under which the litter has been raised. Of course, make an appointment, as
breeders are busy people and have many visitors.

When you arrive, take a good look around. Although not everyone has a
fancy kennel with chain-link runs, the facilities can and should be spotlessly
clean. If you find the outside runs and exercise areas dirty and neglected, and
the inside of the kennel and home in the same shape, I would advise you to
look elsewhere, no matter how cute the puppies may be.

To be kept healthy, puppies must be kept clean at all times, and should
have a warm, dry pen with — if they are young puppies — clean papers on the
floor. They should have a bed with clean blankets or rugs. Feed and water
bowls must be clean. Puppies reared in such conditions are far easier to housebreak. Breeders who keep their dogs outside with dog houses, dirty runs, and
food left down to spoil, are to be avoided at all costs. Puppies from such a
kennel will probably be wormy, or worse, and you would be only buying
yourself a pack of trouble.

A concerned breeder will be full of questions about you and the facilities
you have for a Doberman. He is not just being nosy when he asks if you have
a fenced yard, and he may even refuse to sell you a puppy until you have had
time to get a fence up; he does not want to hear in a few weeks that the puppy
has been hit by a car.

Beware the breeder who wants to sell you a puppy at five weeks and before the ears are trimmed. Most likely he is doing this in order to save money by passing on the added expense to you. Also, it can be very upsetting for a novice owner to go through an ear trimming experience with his puppy. This is best left to the expert.

Your puppy should be at least nine weeks old, as by this time he will have had his first permanent shot. He should also be free of worms. He should have a clean shining coat, and his skin should be loose and too big for him. His eyes should be bright, alert and free of matter and he should smell clean.

A normal healthy puppy of nine weeks should weigh an average of 17 pounds for a bitch and 20 pounds for a male. At six weeks, 9 to 12 pounds is a good average. Generally a puppy who weighs much less than this has not had the proper care. We have seen seven-week-old puppies who only weighed 5 pounds!

If you are interested in a show quality puppy, it would be wise to put yourself in the hands of the breeder, and ask him or her to choose a suitable puppy for you. The breeder has had the chance to study the litter since it was whelped, and can spot not only good conformation, but also that little extra something that spells ''show dog''. Request to see the pedigree and have it explained to you, as it is important to learn as much as you can about the puppy's background. To you the pedigree is probably just a bunch of names, but to a good breeder, these names are dogs that he has a mental picture of, and he can tell you something about each one. If possible, see both the sire and dam, inquire about their show records, and ask what they have produced in the past.

If you plan to buy your puppy by mail or long distance telephone, check with other breeders and owners in an effort to determine if the breeder has a really good reputation, what his breeding has done in the past, and if his dogs have good temperaments. Do not be taken in by fancy advertisements and promises that the puppy will grow up to be a Best in Show Dog. A good and honest breeder makes no such claims. He can only tell you that the puppy has no major faults at the time of sale, that the parents are champions or outstanding young dogs, and that the puppy is in top condition when he is shipped to you. He will probably request that you take the puppy to your veterinarian to confirm the puppy's good health. He should also stress the importance of correct feeding habits, and of the equally important training necessary to develop his personality. This training should include taking him out to as many places as possible, so that he can adjust to the stress of everyday life. Then . . . you both hope and pray he will turn out to be a Champion!

If the breeder of your choice does not have any puppies for sale when you inquire, you may have to wait. Or he may be able to recommend someone with a litter out of his breeding. While this recommended person may not be a well-known breeder, he may have an excellent bitch who could be a champion. Frequently, these puppies have received the best of care; more likely than not they were whelped in the owner's kitchen or family room. They are ac-

Just a few hours old—tails and dewclaws will need to be cut at three days.

Ch. Marks-Tey's High Hat at just four and a half weeks of age and already showing the show dog that was to come. Sired by Ch. Ebonaire's Gridiron ex Marks-Tey's Mischief Maker.

315

customed to children and household noises and can be very well-adjusted puppies. Perhaps the breeder who recommended the litter to you planned the breeding, and has helped the owner with advice, and it is possible he or she would be willing to pick the puppy out for you.

Regardless of where your puppy is purchased, you should receive at least a four generation pedigree and the American Kennel Club blue slip for registration, unless the puppy has already been registered by the breeder. In that case, you should receive the registration form correctly signed on the back in order for the puppy to be transfered to your name. Full instructions should be given regarding present and future care and feeding, as well as information on the care of the ears if they are still in tapes.

Above all, a good breeder is there when you need him, and is always willing to help with the various little problems that come up over the years. He will share your joys, and your sorrows too.

As a caution to buyers of purebred dogs, the American Kennel Club advises the following:

When you buy a dog that is represented as being eligible for registration with The American Kennel Club, you are entitled to receive an AKC application form properly filled out by the seller, which — when completed by you and submitted to the AKC with the proper fee — will enable you to effect the registration of the dog. When the application has been processed, you will receive an AKC registration certificate.

Under AKC rules, any person who sells dogs that are represented as being AKC registrable, must maintain records that will make it possible to give full identifying information with every dog delivered, even though AKC papers may not yet be available. *Do not accept a promise of later identification.*

The Rules and Regulations of The American Kennel Club stipulate that whenever someone sells or delivers a dog that is said to be registrable with AKC, the dog must be identified either by putting into the hands of the buyer a properly completed AKC registration application, or by giving the buyer a bill of sale or a written statement, *signed by the seller,* giving the dog's full breeding information as follows:

—Breed, sex and color of the dog
—Date of birth of the dog
—Registered names of the dog's sire and dam
—Name of the breeder

If you encounter any problems in acquiring the necessary registration application forms, it is suggested that you write The American Kennel Club, 51 Madison Avenue, New York, N.Y. 10010, *giving full particulars* and the difficulty will be reviewed. All individuals acquiring a dog represented as being AKC registrable should realize it is their responsibility to obtain complete identification of the dog as described above sufficient to identify in AKC records, or *THEY SHOULD NOT BUY THE DOG.*

316

All puppies are cute—just be sure that the one you buy is also healthy, and that he (or she) comes from a good breeder.

A handsome quartet of puppies sired by Ch. Rancho Dobe's Maestro ex Am. & Mex. Ch. Volte's Cascade of Cognac. Owned by Mr. and Mrs. Donald E. Boelter.

The Joy of Owning a Doberman

There is no doubt that the Doberman is not the dog for everyone and many people who do own them would be far better off with a different breed. It is rather frightening to serious breeders that they are now up to third place in American Kennel Club registrations. Many so-called ''puppy factories'' are offering Doberman puppies at five weeks of age at ridiculous prices. Needless to say, little if any attention is paid to breeding for correct Doberman temperament. It is no wonder that many problems arise with such puppies, and they often end up in animal shelters.

In America we no longer want a dog as sharp as is still required in Germany. Here, most people prefer a dog that can adjust to the easy-going American way of life; a dog that will accept one's friends and not be just a one man dog. This does not mean, however, that we do not want an alert watch dog who will protect us when necessary. There is nothing worse than a shy Doberman and these are often also fear biters. But a Doberman does not have to be a barker and he should most certainly not be high-strung or excitable.

As for all the stories about how Dobermans will turn on their masters, most are hearsay and usually impossible to substantiate. However, we will hear more such stories if the breed gets into the hands of puppy mill operators rather than breeders who care and who breed for correct temperament.

A well-bred Doberman is a highly intelligent animal and as such it needs training and discipline. It also needs plenty of exercise. Dobermans are not well suited to kennel life as they get very bored and then develop all sorts of bad habits such as fence running, side sucking, pad chewing and barking. They are a breed that requires the companionship of man and having something to learn. They need a master who recognizes this and can handle them intelligently.

There is no better family dog and they can be great with children; our own daughter learned to walk by pulling herself up on our first Doberman. However, breeders should be careful not to breed out its watchful alert personality. They must continue to breed for the real working abilities, for a true Doberman can and should be very versatile — a good watch dog and still an affectionate house dog.

There is no reason why he can not get along with other dogs of any breed. We have always kept as many as seven Dobermans in the house and all of them got along just beautifully. I have never kept my dogs apart at any time, except for bitches in season. Very often I bring in dogs that we are showing into our kennels for a few weeks at a time, and they are accepted by the rest of our dogs. It does not take them long to learn who is boss, and they soon fit in as part of the family. The oldest of our dogs is always the one to rule the roost and as that one passes on, the next oldest takes its place. We have even been successful in being able to keep two males together without any problems, but

Ch. Alisaton's Kinderwicke, owned by Joann and Gwen Lynn Satalino, winning Winners Bitch at the 1973 Doberman Pinscher Club of America Specialty from the Bred-by-Exhibitor class. Gwen was only 17 at the time and few of us will forget how Kinder jumped into her arms when she was pronounced winner.

Kinder's son, Ch. Alisaton Damascus (sired by Ch. Gra-Lemor Demetrius vd Victor). This young black male of exciting promise, pictured at just 11 months, is co-owned by his breeders Joan and Gwen Satalino with Peggy Esposito, and handled by young Gwen. Mac finished almost completely from the puppy class, at just past a year old.

I do advise against this. I would only keep a puppy when my older stud dog is at least seven years old. I have yet to have a fight between my males.

Dobermans have a wonderful memory and they never seem to forget someone who has been their friend. Many years ago I sold a young male and did not see this dog from the time he was a year old until he was eight. Kim, as he was called, had been sold to be trained to guard a barber's shop, and when I saw him again I was warned by those who worked in the shop that I could see him but no one could go near him or pet him, except for the owner. I asked that he put on a lead and this was done. I then started to talk to him and held out my hand for him to sniff. At first he went stiff but suddenly his tail started to wag, and before his owner could stop him he was up on me with his paws on my shoulders and licking my face. I then took his lead and led him through the shop to the astonishment of the men working there. Even after all these years, Kim had not forgotten me. I might add that they had not had a single breakin since they purchased Kim from me eight years before.

I expect my own dogs to be good protectors of our home, and of me, and they have proven to me many times that a stranger is ill advised to walk into our home without being invited. One man tried this for, as he told me later on the phone, he did not think show dogs would bite! One of my bitches stood in his way and she warned him, but he did not heed her until she bit him on the leg and backed him out the door. But this same bitch would have made him welcome had I been home and invited him into our home. Our dogs are very friendly with anyone we invite in and make welcome and I have learned to trust their judgment. If they do take a dislike to anyone, I too am very leery of them as they have always been right.

In another instance I had our old Champion Melanie with me at a Specialty. She was then ten years old and had not been shown for many years. She had a wonderful time and really ate up all the attention she got from the many old friends and admirers who greeted her. She is a very friendly and outgoing dog, wonderful with children and full of personality. I took her outside the show building, and from behind me came a greeting of "Well, hello there." Melanie and I turned around ready to greet yet another good friend, but we both immediately realized that here was a complete stranger. What a change of face; up came Melanie's hackles and she stepped in front of me showing all her teeth. It was plain she was thinking, "I don't know you, and you had just better not get too close." So please don't think that just because your Doberman seems to make friends easily and is outgoing, that he or she will not be a guard when the need is there.

You can make a Doberman into just about any kind of dog you wish and it is true that dogs do take on a certain amount of their owner's personality. A highstrung nervous owner can easily make his dog the same way. A well-adjusted person usually has a well-adjusted and happy dog. A Doberman should not be turned into a sissy, nor into a bully. He should be raised as a useful and well-adjusted member of your family.

320

Ch. Andelane's Indigo Rock, black, winner of 24 Bests in Show. Pictured here with his handler, James Berger, Rocky is owned by Robert Bishop of Michigan. He was sired by Ch. Ru-Mar's Morgansonne CD ex Jemoel's Mau v Cassio.

Indigo Rock's lovely daughter, Ch. Bishop's Cassiopeia v Rock, one of the top winners of 1976. Owned by Jean and Fred Meyer, Jr. of Indianapolis, she was obtained from breeder Bob Bishop at the age of 16 months, and won the Group that very day. Like her sire, she is handled by Jim Berger. Her dam is Toledobe's Generation Gap, a Ch. Damasyn Carly of Jerseystone daughter. Cassiopeia already has over a hundred Bests of Breed and is a multi Best in Show winner.

Ch Highland Satin's Image, to date the sire of 44 AKC champions and over 30 Canadian champions. The leading sire for Doberman Pinscher Club of America awards for 1973–1976; leading AKC sire for 1972, second for 1973, again leading sire in 1974, and tied in 1975. Owned by Jim and Lois Addison of Ohio. Image, a black, is pictured being handled by George Rood to Best Puppy in Sweepstakes at the Lake Shore Doberman Specialty (under Owen Blackwood); he went on to Winners under Kenneth McDonald. Image was never specialled, but has more than made his mark as a sire.

Ch. Fanfare's Ringmaster (1966–1976) winning one of his two Bests in Show. A flashy black, he was handled by Monroe Stebbins for owners Patricia Laurans and Terry Lazzaro of Connecticut. Ringer's other wins included 5 Specialty Bests in Show. He stands as sire of 8 champions (and at least two others are close to title).

322

21

Selection of a Stud

THERE ARE many books and articles that go into the technical side of breeding. Rather than add more of this same literature, perhaps it will serve better here to explain what we have done and why in breeding at our own kennels.

It has been said many times that the best investment a would-be breeder can make is a good bitch, and this advice will always hold true. Like a lot of others, I did not take this advice at first, mainly because I did not think I could afford such a bitch. I was lucky that my bitch only had two puppies in her first and only litter; these I sold at a loss when they were seven months old. But this did teach me a valuable lesson and my next bitch was very well-bred and good enough to finish her championship with four majors, owner-handled. This was our lovely red Ch. Damasyn the Waltzing Brook CD.

During the years I owned a pet Doberman, I read everything I could lay my hands on about Dobermans and breeding. I studied pedigrees and kept records of them. Today I have a pedigree, and in many cases a picture, of every champion from 1955 to the present. These are in book form with the pedigree on one side of the page and the picture on the other. I also note sex and color of the dog. In addition to this, I have a large file of pedigrees of non-champion dogs whose pedigrees are also of interest to me.

Before you select a stud for your bitch, you should first study her and her pedigree and try to learn as much as you can about her and her littermates, as well as all the dogs in at least the first four generations of her pedigree. Try to have a mental picture of their faults as well as their strong points and what they have produced or sired. You may have to gamble sometimes to get what you are after, and you will make mistakes, but this does not really matter as long as you learn by those mistakes. In picking a stud, I do watch to see what his get are like out of other bitches; but unless these other bitches are close to the same breeding as your bitch, their offspring is not always a dependable indicator of what you will get from him with your bitch. In fact, I have bred lit-

Marks-Tey Stacy, black bitch, bred by the author and owned by Dorothy McHaney. Stacy is the dam of seven champions, and a full sister to Chs., Shay, Shawn and Sonnet.

```
                                    Ch. Dictator v Glenhugel
                      Ch. Brown's Eric
                                    Ch. Dow's Dame of Kilburn
        Ch. Derek of Marks-Tey
                                    Ch. Damasyn the Solitaire, CDX
                      Ch. Damasyn the Waltzing Brook, CD
                                    Damasyn the Winter Waltz
MARKS-TEY "S" LITTER
                                    Ch. Ebonaire's Gridiron
                      Ch. Marks-Tey's Hanover
                                    Marks-Tey's Mischief Maker
        Ch. Marks-Tey Melanie
                                    Ch. Felix vom Ahrtal
                      Halcyon Impala
                                    Ch. Lauwick Champagne
```

```
                                    Ch. Dortmund Delly's Colonel Jet
                      Ch. Steb's Top Skipper
                                    Damasyn the Easter Bonnet
        Ch. Ebonaire's Gridiron
                                    Damasyn the Captain Sabre
                      Ebonaire's Flashing Star
                                    Damasyn the Flash
MARKS-TEY "H" LITTER
                                    Ch. Brown's Eric
                      Ch. D-Dow's Anchor v Riecke
                                    Ch. Brown's Feegee
        Marks-Tey's Mischief Maker
                                    Ch. Damasyn the Solitaire, CDX
                      Ch. Damasyn the Waltzing Brook, CD
                                    Damasyn the Winter Waltz
```

324

ter sisters to the same stud and gotten different results, one bitch producing far better than her sister. Some studs do, however, seem to throw certain characteristics no matter what bitch is bred to them, so this must be noted and taken into consideration. Like everyone else I have done some breedings that I was not particularly pleased with and that did not give me what I had hoped to get. But even in these cases, they showed me something and brought out some faults that I had been wondering about and this made it easier to try and correct these faults with a different breeding.

After a few litters, I felt a need to improve feet and pasterns in our dogs and with this in mind, I bred my Waltzing Brook daughter, Marks-Tey Mischief Maker to Ch. Ebonaire's Gridiron. At this time he was a young dog and had not sired many puppies, and he was not yet a champion, but his pedigree was excellent and particularly interested me because his dam's sire was Damasyn the Captain Sabre, who was a full brother to my Waltzing Brook. I did not want to do a complete outcross as I hoped to preserve some of the excellent points that Waltzing Brook carried, such as her gorgeous head. Gridiron had the perfect tight cat's feet and iron strong pasterns that I was after, plus a very strong short back. The result was our "H" litter with Chs. Hondo, High Hat and Hanover, plus several others who were also good but did not become champions for one reason or another. Our big disappointment was that there were only two bitches, Holly — who never produced a litter, and Heather — who was the dam of two champions. But the males more than made up for it and each have been the sire of several champions; they gave us much of what I had been after. I got beautiful toplines and tail sets from this breeding and also an improvement in feet, particularly in and through Hanover. I also got rears that were a bit steeper than I wanted, so have since been working to improve this. The real improvement in feet came not so much in this litter but in the next two generations and was particularly noticeable in our "S" litter that contained Champions, Shawn, Shay, Sonnet and also Stacy, who has gorgeous tight feet. They, in turn, are passing this on to their children.

Wishing to bring in a little outside blood without going too far out of our own line, we looked around for a good bitch and we purchased Halcyon Impala, who was a Ch. Felix v Ahrtal daughter out of Ch. Lauwick Champagne (who had Ch. Damasyn the Solitaire CDX on her dam's side.) While this bitch proved to be disappointing as a show bitch, since she hated the show ring, she did — when bred to Hanover — give us our top producing Ch. Marks-Tey Melanie, and her sister Ch. Hanover's Amsel CD. Melanie produced eight champions and Amsel is the dam of four. For her first litter Melanie was bred back into our line and the sire of her litter was our own Ch. Derek of Marks-Tey. This then was the "S" litter. Derek died before this breeding could be repeated but Shawn, who was the only male in the litter, proved to be an excellent sire and passed on his good feet and pasterns and also much improved the angulation of our dogs.

325

All our breeding has been a close concentration of the great Dictator and we have tried to keep the lovely heads and dark eyes that Waltzing Brook got from him. So when we would breed out, it was always with the idea of being able to come back into our line. Breeding to the popular winner of the day without regard for what he can do for your bitch is a big mistake and one far too many people make. I feel it is also wrong to breed only to your own dogs for generation after generation and not to take advantage of what others have also tried to achieve. To line-breed is one thing, but to continue only your own breeding, perhaps to save money on studs or to avoid shipping, is very short-sighted.

I must admit that sometimes I just have a hunch about a certain breeding and this was the case when I bred Melanie to Ch. Gra-Lemor Demetrius vd Victor. I first saw this dog as an eleven-months-old puppy when I judged the Quaker City Futurity and made him my Grand Prize Futurity winner. He had that certain something when he first walked into the ring that forced you to look at him. I could not wait to find out what his breeding was, to see if he would fit into my breeding program. He went on to become a great show dog and a Best in Show winner and the sire of many champions, but at the time I bred Melanie to him, he was not even finished and he had never sired a litter. This breeding gave Melanie three more champions, namely Champions Vixen, Vale and Valika. Out of this litter I kept Vale, who in 1975 won the DPCA award as top producing dam. Vale was bred back into our line and my choice for her was the lovely Derek son, Walkaways Ablaze of Marks-Tey. This red male was not shown due to an injury to his foot. This breeding produced Ch. Marks-Tey Alfie of Rads who finished his championship in four consecutive days with four major wins; it also produced Ch. Marks-Tey Blue Velvet UD and two more outstanding dogs who died young.

Valika was also bred back into our line and our choice for her was Shawn's son Ch. Laur-ik Procyon of Marks-Tey and this breeding produced three champions, namely Spica, Alhena and Regulus. Waltzing Brook has been gone for many years but I can still look at her great grandchildren and see so much of her many beautiful qualities.

I have not said anything so far about temperament but I feel this is every bit as important in the selection of a stud as is conformation. Dogs that have to be tranquilized or given pep pills in order to show well, have no place in our breed. You must breed for sound temperament. After all you have to live with these dogs too. Last, but by no means least, always keep the Standard in mind and try to breed as close to it as you possibly can. This is the guideline for us all and a great deal of thought has gone into its writing.

Winner of the Doberman Pinscher Club of America Award
for Top Producing Dam, 1975—Ch. Marks-Tey Vale (by Ch.
Gra-Lemor Demetrius vd Victor ex Ch. Marks-Tey Melanie). Owned by Joanna Walker and handled by Keith Walker. Vale finished for her title with four majors.

Am. & Can. Ch. Marks-Tey the Maverick, red male, by Ch. Marks-Tey
Alfie of Rads ex Ch. Marks-Tey Yasmine. Co-owned by Joanna Walker
and Stewart Goldsmith. The Maverick is pictured winning the breed under Allen Shi, handled by Keith Walker. He finished his Canadian title
with two Groups and a Best in Show.

Ch. Galaxy's Corry Carina, America's top Working winner of 1974. This beautiful black is a full sister to Ch. Galaxy's Corry Missile Belle and also started her career with a bang—winning a 4-pt. major from the classes in California. She was then sold to Frank and Eleanor D'Amico of New York (who also owned her sire, Ch. Tarrado's Corry) and finished by them. Then, co-owned by Mrs. Cheever Porter with the D'Amicos, and handled by Jane Forsyth, she went on to a record of 24 all-breed Bests in Show, 10 Specialties, and 61 Group Firsts before her retirement to the whelping box.

Am. & Can. Ch. Tranell's Maxwell Smart, owned by Ray Carlisle, owner-publisher of *Top Dobe* magazine. This black male is by Ch. Fanfare's Ringmaster ex Ch. Tranell's Minnalite. Handled by Monroe Stebbins, and later by Jeffrey Lynn Brucker, during his three years as a special (1971–73) Max scored more than a hundred Bests of Breed, some twenty Group Firsts, five Bests in Show in Canada and one in America. During these three years he was always in the Top Five Dobermans in the United States.

22

Grooming Your Doberman

A DOBERMAN is without doubt the easiest of dogs to keep looking well-groomed and — in comparison with other breeds — there is little that must be done to get him ready for the show ring. The most important consideration is that your dog must be in top condition in order to have that gleaming coat and look of vitality; it is, therefore, very important that his diet be a good one.

Here are some of the tools that will help you keep your Doberman looking well-groomed:

A rubber "Premo" brush. These are made in England but are readily available at most pet supply stores in this country. They have teeth about half an inch long, set close together, and they do a super job of getting out the loose dead hair. They are also ideal to use in scrubbing your dog when you have to give him a bath, as they work the soap down deep into his coat.

Curved Scissors. (Do not use pointed scissors.)

Teeth Scaler.

Towels.

Q-Tips for cleaning ears.

Electric clippers (small size is easier to use).

Nail clippers.

Electric Nail Grinder. (We recommend the Dremel Moto Tool with a stone attachment.)

Any type of good quality coat spray such as Mr. Groom, Ring 5 or St. Aubrey.

It is not necessary to bathe your dog often in order to keep him looking his best. You can keep his coat clean by first spraying him with the conditioner and then brushing him with the Premo brush. He will soon learn to enjoy this attention. Finish him off with a wipedown with a towel. If his coat seems a little dirty, rub his coat thoroughly with a damp towel to remove the excess dirt before you spray him. Do not give him a bath the day before a show as this will tend to take the natural oil from his coat and may leave it with a dull look. Many Dobermans have a sensitive skin and will break out in hives from some types of shampoo. I have found that any products that can be used on horses, can also be used on Dobermans without causing any skin problems.

Each week you should do his nails with the electric grinder. This is a *must*. Some people who are too lazy to keep this up find that their dog, come show time, has nails that are far too long and they will then go to the extreme length of having their veterinarian put the dog under anesthetic and cut the nails back to just stubs. There are also those who simply take the clippers and cut the nails back into the quick and apply a blood clotter and then bind up the feet until the bleeding hopefully stops! I consider both of these methods to be extremely cruel and also completely unnecessary. (You would never cut your own nail back into the quick, would you?)

It is quite possible to get nails back into show shape even if they have been neglected, but it does take some time. You simply grind them every three days right back to the quick, but being careful not to draw blood, and in time the quick will recede and your dog will have nice short nails. If the nails are excessively long, I first use the clippers to clip off at least part of the nail before I start to grind them. If you will get your puppy used to the noise of the grinder from the time he is about eight weeks old, he will learn to accept this as a routine part of his grooming. None of them really like it but they can all be taught to accept it. Your dog's nails will at all times be smooth and rounded and will not scratch you or your rugs.

Once a month go over your dog's teeth with a professional dental scaler. Your veterinarian will be glad to show you how to do this correctly but always scale away from the gum line. It is very easy to do and again your dog will learn to put up with it. I make a point of handling my puppies' mouths and rubbing their teeth with a soft paper towel and my nail so they get used to the feel of it. There is no excuse for a dog to have tartar all over his teeth; it makes the mouth smell, the teeth will become decayed and judges do not appreciate opening a dog's mouth and finding dirty neglected teeth.

It is a good idea each week when you do your dog's nails, to also check his ears and clean them with a soft paper towel and your fingers. Then take a Q-Tip and clean all the places you have not been able to reach with the towel. Do not use oil in his ears as this will only make them sore. You can use a little rubbing alcohol if you feel this is necessary to get them clean. On a dog with cropped ears, it is easy to see when this needs to be done; but on drop ears in countries that do not allow ear cropping it is not openly evident, and the ears can become really dirty and even infected if you don't check them often.

Ch. Henlon's Martial Music, red son of Ch. Brown's B-Brian ex New Era The Cinnamon Hexe. "Bacchus" is owned by Warren Henlon and Dee Boyd; Warren (who bred him) has handled him throughout his show career. To date, his spectacular winning includes 6 all-breed Bests in Show, 24 Group Firsts, and 64 Bests of Breed.

Ch. Tedell Indulto v Ri-Jan's, black male whelped July 1972, winner at this printing of 8 Group Firsts, 3 Specialty Bests in Show and 55 Bests of Breed. Breed by Janie Garrick and Kathleen Priest, Indulto is by famous Ch. Tedell Eleventh Hour ex Ch. Ri-Jan's Seneca Love Call, and is himself the sire of Best in Show winner Ch. Tedell Nottingham Palace. He is owned by Theodora S. Linck of Ohio, and handled by George Rood.

331

Grooming for Show

This is all there is to taking care of your Doberman if he is just staying at home. However, if you are going to show him, then he must be trimmed the day before the show. This only takes a short time once you learn how to trim correctly. If you have a grooming table, so much the better, as it is easier to handle a dog who is up off the floor. It is simply a matter of trimming off any long hairs that stick out to spoil the lines of the dog. You first take the curved scissors and cut off his whiskers and eyebrows, also the long hairs under his chin and on the side of his face. You will find your dog has a way of pulling his whiskers in, so be sure to cut them very short as this will give his muzzle a clean look. Next take your electric clippers with a fine blade and clip the hair along the edge of his ears. Next, clean out the hair on the inside of the ear, starting at the top of the ear and going down to the base. You will find it easier if you use your scissors in some places, particularly around the base. This should be cut very short to give a clean look. It is possible to do the ears with just the scissors if your dog is really afraid, but the clipper does do a neater job.

Next, take your clippers and trim the long hair in the loin area. Take off any excess hair on the stomach around the nipples on a bitch and the penis on a dog. Some dogs have quite a bit of hair on the backs of the hind legs, while others have very little; this, too, should be neatly rounded. Some people like to trim the hair on the backs of the pasterns but unless this is very long, it is not really necessary. You can likewise trim off any long hair on the backs of the front legs. If your dog has a cow-lick on the back of his neck, this also should be trimmed down, along with any cow-licks on the side of the dog's neck.

Give your dog a good grooming with the Premo brush, wipe him off with a towel, make sure his eyes are clean and remove any matter in the corner of the eye with a soft tissue, and your Doberman is ready to go in the ring.

Ch. Devil Tree's Black Shaft, whelped 1972, by Ch. Mattappany the Anchor Man ex Moorwood's Wild Thing. Bred by Joe Oniki, owned by George and Sheila West of New York, and handled by Jeffrey Lynn Brucker. Shaft already has an impressive show record of 4 Bests in Show, over 20 Group Firsts, and more than 120 Bests of Breed. He is sire of the 1976 Top Twenty winner Ch. Eric von Alpendobe.

Ch. Eric von Alpendobe, the 1976 Top Twenty winner at Atlanta, Georgia. This black son of Ch. Devil Tree's Black Shaft ex Lujac's Crown Royal, is owned by Jim and Sue O'Brian of Florida and handled by Perry Phillips. Just starting on his serious show career at this writing, he already owns some impressive wins.

Am. & Can. Ch. Liquorish the Ron Rico, young black male, a standout in 1976 with wins of 3 all-breed Bests in Show in the U.S. and one in Canada, along with a Specialty, 10 Group Firsts and 40 BOBs — all within a period of 11 months. Bred and owned by Grace and Jeff Joffe, and handled by Jeff Brucker. Pictured in win at Fort Lauderdale under judge James T. Culp. — *Graham*

Ch. Damsyn the Troycen, red son of Am. & Can. Ch. Damasyn the Tartian ex Damasyn Bo-Tassi of Ardon. Owned by Russ Myer, and handled by Carol Selzle. He is the sire of several champions.

23

Coat and Skin Problems

by Anita and Robert W. Silman

O<small>NE OF THE REASONS</small> that blues and fawns had such an evil reputation among the older breeders is that coat problems and skin problems show up more frequently in these colors than among red and black dogs. Since dogs of any color can have coat and skin problems, there is no particular reason to blame it on the dilution factor. We do not know why the problems show up more frequently among blues and fawns.

Dry scaly skin, and hair loss following a typical pattern may take place because reds and blacks have more hairs per square inch than blues and fawns, so that when hair is lost on black and red dogs, the loss is not as noticeable. A condition which may be the cause of this skin problem is hypothyroidism caused by a decrease in thyroid hormone production. Mild hypothroidism is a common cause of skin and hair abnormalities. A puppy is born with the condition — it has been diagnosed as early as eight weeks of age.

The following symptoms may be present. However, all symptoms need not be present for a dog to have an underactive thyroid gland.

1. Lethargy — sleeps much more than would be expected for the dog's age.
2. Easy fatigue — runs and plays hard for a short while and then is asleep or resting when other puppies or dogs are still playing.
3. Weight gain — eats much less than is normal for age and still stays in good weight or is overweight. Some people would say the dog is an easy keeper.
4. Constipation or diarrhea.
5. Abnormal heat cycles — the cycle is too short, too long, very irregular, or not at all.
6. Infertility — can be total, resulting in a sterile dog or of low fertility resulting in small litters from a bitch or low sperm count in males.

7. Sensitive to heat and cold — will seem to suffer on very hot days and seek out heat outlets during the cold days.
8. Decreased libido — the male shows very little interest in receptive bitches.
9. Dry skin which is cool to the touch — the skin is scaly with large flakes all the time. The belly skin feels cool and slippery to the touch.
10. Secondary staphylococcus infection — this skin infection is characterized by small pustules in various places on the body and head.
11. Hyperpigmentation of the skin — small round dark or light spots are seen usually on the groin or the belly.
12. Hair is dry and brittle and pops out of the skin easily.
13. Beginning hair loss is first seen on the backs of the ears, under the tan of the throat and down the thigh area.
14. The hair loss follows a simple bilateral pattern. The hair is thin over the ribcage, thick down the backbone and shoulders, thin under the neck and on the belly.

A serum cholesterol or a T4 test are used to detect thyroid deficiency. The serum cholesterol test is not specific for thyroid function, but serves a useful purpose because few diseases cause the high cholesterol levels found in many hypothyroid dogs. In about ⅓ of hypothyroid dogs the serum cholesterol is normal. Normal fasting serum cholesterol levels range from 90–280 mg/100 ml with 180 mg/100 ml the average. A few hypothyroid dogs test in the range of 500–700 mg/100 ml.

The T-4 test measures the total serum thyroxine. The normal T-4 is about 80% of the PBI (Protein-Bound Iodine) and ranges from 1.8 to 3.5 mcg per 100 ml. Below these levels indicate hypothyroidism.

Treatment consists of thyroid replacement therapy with either Synthroid or Cytobin. Once replacement therapy is begun, it must be continued for the life of the dog. Within three days of beginning medication, the dog's appetite becomes more normal, and within two weeks the skin scaling has decreased and the hair is less dry. Hair growth takes from 90–120 days to become normal.

Diet is important. A diet high in useable protein and fairly low in fat is recommended. Also the addition of one tablespoon of Brewers yeast, 100IH vit E, plus small amounts of vitamin A for a period of 3 months seems helpful. Your veterinarian will advise you on the best dosages for your dog.

Bathing with Mycodex shampoo is helpful if a secondary staph infection is present. Alpha-Keri rinses may be used on a very dry skin.

At the present time thyroid deficiency is suspected to be inherited. The mode of inheritance is not known, although research is being done. However, thyroid deficiency does not show up in every generation, perhaps suggesting that it is recessive in nature. It does seem to skip a generation. There are many degrees of deficiency from the very mildly afflicted to the very severe.

Your veterinarian is the best person to advise you on the nature and treatment of malfunction of the thyroid.

Ch. Tarrado's Corry, owned by Frank and Eleanor D'Amico of New York. This black dog, by Ch. Felix vom Ahrtal ex Ch. Highbriar Jasmine, is the sire of many champions including the two top winning bitches, Missile Belle and her sister Corina.

Ch. Welwyn Corette, another of Ch. Tarrado Corry's outstanding get. This flashy red, a Group and Specialty winner in 1974 and 1975, and in the Top Twenty both years, was bred by Joan Barrett and is owned by Nancy Pritchard of Massachusetts. Shown for her breeder by Marge Anagnost, and then for her owner by Don Simmons. It is no wonder this bitch has showmanship plus as her dam is the beautiful Ch. Weichardt's A-Go-Go CDX.

Ch. Tarrado's Flair, red son of Ch. Tarrado's Corry ex Ch. Highbriar Piping Rock. Flair was owned by Ed and Shirley McCoy of Pennsylvania.

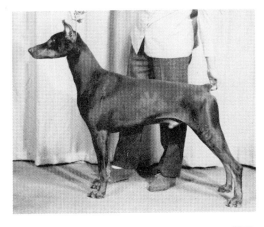

Twelve-week-old puppy showing brace in correct position.

Illustrating the new "Foam Method" for putting up the ears, described in the text on Pages 344-45.

24

Tail Docking and Ear Taping

I DO WISH a little more on tail docking and ear cropping were taught by the veterinary colleges, as so many veterinarians are really in the dark and for the most part must rely on their breeder clients for guidance. I do not intend to give instructions for cropping ears as I firmly believe this is a job for the veterinarian and I suggest that you ask around among breeders of show stock to find out who does the best trims in your area. The same goes for tail docking as Doberman tails are one of the hardest to cut correctly, due to the fact that they are cut shorter than most other breeds.

Tail docking is usually done at three to five days, depending on the condition of the puppies. One sees a great many Dobermans with tails that are far too long; and a few too short, for that matter, and some have very bad scars. We cut our tails not more than a half inch from the underside base of the tail. The skin is then pulled back as much as possible and a second cut is made to remove enough bone to allow plenty of skin to cover the end of the tail. We prefer to have a couple of sutures put in, but this must be done very carefully so that stitch marks do not form. It is quite useless to put anything on the end of the tails after the litter has been returned to the bitch, as she will only lick it off. Any tails that are not just right are corrected at the time we trim the ears.

We trim ears on our puppies at six to seven weeks, again depending on the condition of the litter. At this age they should weigh roughly between nine and twelve pounds. We find it is much easier on the puppies at this age than if you wait until they are nine to twelve weeks of age. When done at this early age, our puppies are ready to eat and play as soon as they come out of the anesthesia and the ears heal much faster when done at this age. It is not unusual for me to be able to get the ears standing by the time the puppy is 12 weeks and long before it starts to teethe. This is half the battle.

There are very few veterinarians who are willing to trim at this early age, so you will have to go along with your veterinarian as to the age at which he is willing to trim ears. Most veterinarians are willing to trim at eight weeks. No matter what the age, the puppy must be in top condition, free of worms and all our puppies receive a shot of distemper serum a few days before they are trimmed. Our own veterinarian likes the early trims as he feels they are easier to cut — the difference between cutting paper and cutting heavy cardboard! I will not go into the trimming itself as every veterinarian has his own ideas on this. We take roughly a third of the length of the ear off depending on the type of trim wanted, taking the head type into consideration.

To get the right length on the ear, we measure the un-cut length of the ear without pulling it taut. We use a swab stick, placing it close to the base of the ear on the dog's skull. We then make our mark on the stick and measure the length of the stick up to this mark. Another mark is made on the stick at roughly a third. The stick is then placed back in position and we make our mark on the inside of the puppy's ear at the length we plan to make our cut. If you cut right at the third mark, you will have rather a short trim so we add a little to this length, depending on the sex and build of that particular puppy. Usually about an extra ¼ to ½ inch is about right. Your vet will learn to judge this for himself. The ear is cut in a straight line from the top of the ear to the base. This line is first marked on the puppy's ear and the base of the ear is cut out to give a neat look when the dog is viewed from the front. Each veterinarian has his own methods, and as stated above, it is best to find the most experienced one and let him take care of the job for you.

Instructions for Taping Ears
(Drawings by John T. Brueggeman)

While the puppy is still under the anesthesia, I tape the ears and this saves my veterinarian a great deal of time when we have a whole litter to do. I apply one and a half inch tape to both sides of the ear, leaving the cut edge completely exposed to the air. The tape is brought up to this edge only and two layers are applied to each side of the ear. If you will spray the first pieces of tape with ether it will make the tape stick better to the ears. I then put on a brace made of half inch tape between the ears, to hold the ears up in the natural position. This brace is placed just halfway up the ears and again is not allowed to cover the cut edge. You are then able to keep the cut edge well

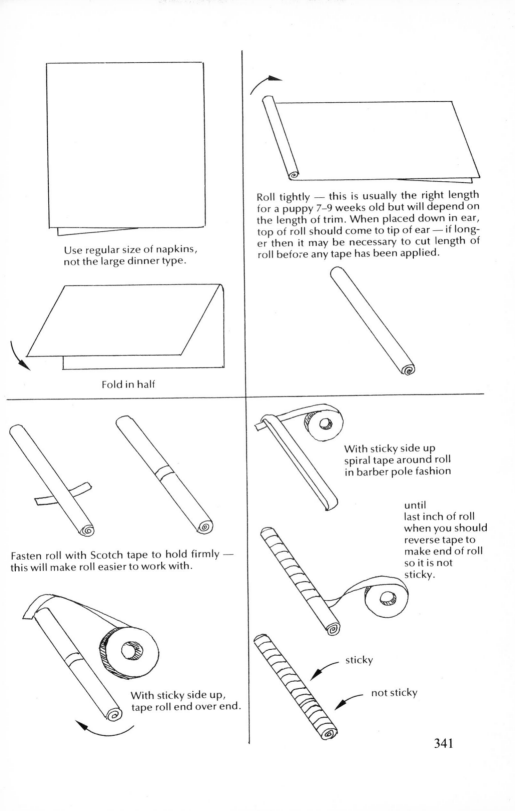

Use regular size of napkins, not the large dinner type.

Fold in half

Roll tightly — this is usually the right length for a puppy 7–9 weeks old but will depend on the length of trim. When placed down in ear, top of roll should come to tip of ear — if longer then it may be necessary to cut length of roll before any tape has been applied.

Fasten roll with Scotch tape to hold firmly — this will make roll easier to work with.

With sticky side up, tape roll end over end.

With sticky side up spiral tape around roll in barber pole fashion

until last inch of roll when you should reverse tape to make end of roll so it is not sticky.

sticky

not sticky

341

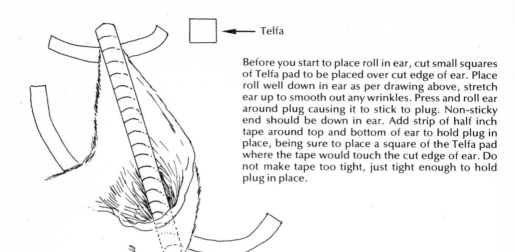

← Telfa

Before you start to place roll in ear, cut small squares of Telfa pad to be placed over cut edge of ear. Place roll well down in ear as per drawing above, stretch ear up to smooth out any wrinkles. Press and roll ear around plug causing it to stick to plug. Non-sticky end should be down in ear. Add strip of half inch tape around top and bottom of ear to hold plug in place, being sure to place a square of the Telfa pad where the tape would touch the cut edge of ear. Do not make tape too tight, just tight enough to hold plug in place.

Above plug properly in place. A brace from one ear to the other is not necessary if ears are taped correctly so they are straight. Be careful not to have ears going over head.

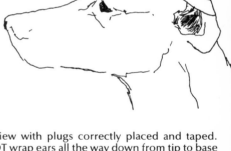

Front view with plugs correctly placed and taped. DO NOT wrap ears all the way down from tip to base — use only the two strips of half inch tape so that as much air as possible can get to the ear.

Do not leave ears rolled for more than five days at a time. If bottom of plug comes out of ear, take ear down as this will cause ear to go over head. Be careful not to tape top of ear too tightly as this can make a bad sore and scar. NEVER leave an ear down for more than one day. If ear falls after being taped, dust with BFI powder and only leave down for rest of day; then re-tape, otherwise you lose much of the ground you have gained. Often only one ear will fall, so with this method it is possible to tape just the one down ear.

greased twice a day, and since it is exposed to the air, the ears will heal far easier. We use Furacin or Panalog to grease the ears and BFI powder is also useful to help dry up the base of the ear particularly. You must keep all scabs picked off, and if there is any indication of puckering, stretch the edge to break the pucker. It is very important that the cut edge be kept free of any puckering or the ears will not stand correctly.

The sutures should stay in just one week and if the ears have been sutured properly with a continuous stitch, there will be only one knot at the very base of each ear. It is quite easy to remove the sutures yourself by clipping the sutures in several places down the ear, and then pulling them out. But be sure you do get every bit out, as left-in pieces of suture can cause scar tissue to form or develop an infection. So, if you have any doubts, let your veterinarian do this for you.

Brace Method of Taping

The above method of taping has been very useful in the case where one ear is up, and the other is almost up but still a little weak. The idea is to let the strong ear hold up the weaker one. You may use one inch tape for this and only enough tape to hold up the ear is necessary. The advantage of this method is that the dog can work his ears and so strengthen them. It does not work well where several puppies are playing together but is ideal if the puppy is on his own or with older dogs. We have found it most successful with puppies whose ears have been up until teething and then drop. Care should be made not to have brace so tight that it pulls ear over head and if you see that this is about to happen, you may cut brace in middle and put in a small extension to brace. In some cases it is a good idea to put brace on the weak ear, just a little higher up than on the good ear.

343

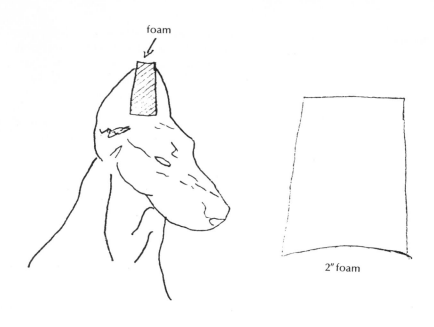

foam

2" foam

The Foam Method

There is another very successful method of putting up the ears as soon as they are trimmed and while the puppy is still asleep. First wash off all blood in the normal way and dry the ears with a hand hair dryer until they are completely dry.

You will need: some two inch thick foam rubber (the softer type used by upholsterers is best); a roll of one inch toupee tape, which can be purchased easily in most men's hair stylists shops as it is used for keeping hair-pieces in place; a roll of half inch cloth tape and a roll of one inch cloth tape. A can of engine starter will help make the cloth tape more sticky and works well for this purpose.

Cut the foam in a slight wedge; the length should be such that when placed on the puppy's head and the ears are stretched up each side, the foam is slightly longer than the ears. Next, shape the widest edge of the wedge so that it is slightly rounded so as to fit the top of the puppy's head (*see sketch*). Now take the toupee tape, which is sticky on both sides and has a backing of paper on one side, and wrap it all the way around the foam, removing the outer paper as you go. The tape goes on the sides, and over the top and bottom of the foam. Now position the foam on top of the puppy's head between the ears so that it sticks to the top of the head and then pull up each ear and stick it to

344

the tape each side of the foam. Be sure the ears are both even, and up straight, so the cut edges are completely straight. Have an assistant hold the ears firmly in place while you take a strip of half inch tape and run it up the inside of one ear, over the top sticking it to the toupee tape and down the inside of the other ear. Next take a strip of one inch tape and run this from the inside of one ear across the front of the foam to the inside of the other ear. This should be about mid-point between the tip of the ears and the top of the puppy's head. Before applying the cloth tape be sure to spray it with the motor starter so it will stick properly. With this method you will find the foam stays nicely in place until the ears are completely healed and the ear will be well stretched with no kinks. When it is time to remove the foam you will find that it comes off quite easily and takes very little hair with it. I have not only found the toupee tape to stick better than the old rubber cement method but it holds up to two weeks before it need be removed. While I prefer to use the one inch tape, it is possible to use half inch quite successfully. Keep cut edge well greased.

I have also found the toupee tape very useful to use under masking tape when putting on a brace as it holds for very much longer.

It must be remembered that you may still have to roll the ears before they are standing for good. No matter what method you use, be sure the ears do not become too sore as you can not expect a puppy to feel like holding up raw and sore ears. The above method is very easy on the puppy and far less bothersome to him (or her) than any method I have seen yet.

I am very much against breeders selling puppies untrimmed, as this is quite an experience for the novice owner to have to go through, and one he or she can well do without. There is only one reason to sell a puppy untrimmed and that is to save money by getting it off the breeder's hands as soon as possible. A responsible breeder wants to make sure that his puppies are not only trimmed correctly but that the most humane methods of after care are employed. Since we trim at an early age, our puppies are often nicely healed by nine weeks and ready to go to a new home and be enjoyed by the owners without all the worry or ordeal of trimming.

Ch. Gambolwood Hellelujah, by Ch. Highland Satin's Image ex Ch. Heller the Gambol CD, bred and owned by Audrey Kibler of Oklahoma. Hellelujah finished to his title at just 13 months of age, owner-handled, with points from the puppy and Bred by Exhibitor classes. He is proving his worth as a sire, and a breeding to Ch. Holli-Berri Florowill produced five champions including Ch. Florowill Patch of Holli.

Ch. Brown's B-Brian, two-time winner of the Doberman Pinscher Club of America Specialty, and three-time winner of the Stud Dog Class at this show. A red male, bred and owned by Eleanor D. Brown of St. Charles, Missouri, Brian was by Ch. Tevrac's Top of the Mark CD ex Ch. Brown's Gigi of Ar-bel. An internationally distinguished sire, Brian died in December 1976, not yet six years old. (Pictured being handled to win of Best of Breed at the 1975 DPCA Specialty by Marj Anagnost, under judge Peggy Adamson.)

25

The Doberman Pinscher Club of America

T HE DOBERMAN PINSCHER CLUB OF AMERICA is a non-profit organization consisting of approximately 1,500 members, from every state plus many members in foreign countries all over the world. There are at present 42 Chapter Clubs located throughout the United States. The DPCA is a member club of the American Kennel Club and as such is the only national Doberman breed club that is recognized and sanctioned by the AKC.

The main objective of the club is to "encourage and promote the breeding of purebred Doberman Pinschers and to do all possible to bring their natural qualities to perfection."

The DPCA holds an Annual Specialty Show each October and this event is held in different parts of the country to give as many people as possible a chance to attend. Along with the Specialty, the club holds its annual election of officers, its Awards Banquet and many educational programs. The whole convention lasts about a week and a great time is had by all. This show has had a huge jump in entries over the years. In 1960 there were 176 dogs shown; in 1975 the entry had climbed to 690 Dobermans!

One of the most exciting events at the Specialty is the Futurity Stakes. To be eligible for this, one must be a DPCA member in good standing. The dam of the litter must be nominated before she whelps and a small fee is required for this (at present this fee is $5). The Futurity Chairman will provide you with the necessary forms for nomination of the bitch and her litter. After the bitch has whelped, each puppy must be nominated before he or she reaches the age of four months. Again a small fee is required. The puppy must then be entered in one of the regular classes or Obedience at the Specialty.

347

The Futurity Stakes have four age divisions which are in months. 6–9, 9–12, 12–15 and 15–18 months. Each age division has four classes; Black Dogs, Any Other Allowed Color Dogs, and the same classes for Bitches. A Winner and a Reserve Winner are selected from each age division and stake prizes are awarded. A Best Futurity Puppy, Best Futurity Junior and then a Grand Prize Futurity Winner are selected. Considerable money is awarded to the owner of the dog, the breeder, and the owner of the sire of the winners.

Other benefits of the DPCA membership are:

a. A free copy of each issue of the *DPCA Pipeline.*
b. Free copies of pertinent information concerning the DPCA and Dobermans, including the Constitution, Breed Standard, color chart and DPCA decals.
c. The opportunity to purchase a listing in the DPCA Breeders Directory. Also a free copy of this Directory.
d. The opportunity to compete in the program of Annual Awards for both conformation and Obedience. These awards are presented at the Awards Banquet held in conjunction with the National Specialty.
e. The opportunity to vote on changes in Standard, the DPCA constitution, judges for the Specialty Show and for Officers and Board of Directors.
f. A special reduced rate on DPCA Educational Materials.

The Educational Materials project was initiated in 1965, to assemble materials of value to the fancy. Before publication they are evaluated by a Review Board of Doberman authorities who have been devoted to the educational aspects of the breed for many years. Each set consists of four to five articles with the exception of the first set which contains eight articles and a cover. Each set is pre-punched to fit a three ring loose leaf binder. There are many interesting articles available on every subject imaginable.

At the 1973 National Specialty and Convention, the DPCA Board of Directors voted to make the Register of Merit (ROM) Study Committee a standing committee of the DPCA. The objective of this committee is to develop the criteria for an award to be given to Dobermans of sound conformation, temperament, and trainability. You can have your Doberman tested by contacting your nearest Chapter Club.

Since committees change from time to time, it is best for anyone wishing information on the DPCA to write The American Kennel Club, 51 Madison Ave. New York, N.Y. 10010, for the name of the current corresponding secretary, who can then put you in touch with the committee that you wish to reach.

Ch. Lujac's Stinger, black bitch, winner of the 1972 Doberman Pinscher Club of America Specialty, and one of the Top Twenty for that year. Bred and owned by Jack and Louise Strutt of Louisville, and always handled by Charlie Cooper, Stinger is pictured scoring a win under judge Theodore Wurmser.

In the 79 shows in which she was shown as a Special (over a period of 18 months), Ch. Housecarl Hope of Diversha won 67 Bests of Breed, 54 Group Firsts and 24 Bests in Show. It is a shame that this great bitch, owned by Mr. and Mrs. Don Coller, never produced a litter. She is pictured here being handled by William T. Kramer to Best in Show at Lubboc, Texas, January 1972, under judge Charles Hamilton.

4 SIBERIAN HUSKY SLED DOGS WON NEW ENGLAND CHAMPIONSHIP TRIAL RACE WITH TEAM LEADER--A *DOBERMAN PINSCHER!*--ALL OWNED BY MR. AND MRS. ALLEN WIGGIN, MOULTONBORO, N.H.

—Reproduced with permission from *Dog Oddities,* copyrighted by the Gaines Dog Research Center.

Four puppies representing the spectrum of Doberman colors, and interestingly they are all from one litter! The pup in front is a black, and the others (from left to right) are blue, red and fawn (Isabella). They are owned by Beverly Capstick's Lutzyn Kennel, Reg.